Daniel E. Bornstein

The Bianchi of 1399

POPULAR DEVOTION IN

LATE MEDIEVAL ITALY

CORNELL UNIVERSITY PRESS

ITHACA AND LONDON

First published 1993 by Cornell University Press.

International Standard Book Number 0-8014-2910-2
Library of Congress Catalog Card Number 93-2311
Printed in the United States of America
Librarians: Library of Congress cataloging information
appears on the last page of the book.

CONTENTS

MAPS

ACKNOWLEDGMENTS

From inception to completion, this book is the product of inter-disciplinary settings. At the University of Chicago, where my research began, the Committee on Social Thought provided a hospitable environment for interdisciplinary inquiries, while the Institute for the Advanced Study of Religion gave me the opportunity to present portions of my work to a group of specialists in the field of religion. At the University of Michigan, an appointment to the Michigan Society of Fellows freed me from many of the normal obligations of teaching and allowed me to spend time on the book. In Florence, the specialized collections and stimulating discussions at Villa I Tatti, the Harvard University Center for Renaissance Studies, encouraged further reflection and facilitated the final revisions. If the end product shows signs of the intellectual excitement and openness to critical inquiry that characterize those institutions, I will be pleased.

A William Rainey Harper Fellowship from the University of Chicago and a Henry J. Haskell Fellowship from the trustees of Oberlin College enabled me to conduct research in Italy for two years, during which I laid the groundwork for this study. Fellowships from the National Endowment for the Humanities and from Villa I Tatti permitted me to return for a year of further research and writing. The History Department of Texas A&M University helped defray the costs of preparing the maps, which were drawn by the Cartographics Laboratory of Texas A&M. To all of these institutions I extend my heartfelt thanks for their generous support.

ix

The archivists and librarians in Arezzo, Assisi, Bologna, Chicago, Cortona, Florence, Lucca, Milan, Orvieto, Paris, Perugia, Pisa, Prato, Rimini, Siena, Venice, and elsewhere, who made the riches of their collections available with unfailing alacrity and courtesy, are too numerous to thank individually here. So too are the many friends, colleagues, teachers, and students who have listened patiently and critically to my thoughts on late medieval religious life and generously contributed their knowledge and insight. Several, however, deserve special mention and thanks. In the early stages of this project, I benefited from Victor Turner's wisdom in matters of ritual, pilgrimage, and symbolic action. Upon Professor Turner's sudden death, Donald Weinstein kindly took his place and gave a draft of the manuscript a discerning and judicious reading. Throughout many years Paul Wheatley embodied to perfection the educated lay reader: he continually urged me to provide more background and ask larger questions. Eric Cochrane and Julius Kirshner, on the other hand, were the consummate professionals: they scrutinized my sources, challenged my interpretations, and pressed me to articulate a precise conceptual framework. Diane Owen Hughes, Richard Kieckhefer, John Marino, and Bernard McGinn also read various drafts and offered helpful comments. My Italian friends and colleagues, and in particular Anna Benvenuti Papi, Roberto Bizzocchi, Laura Gaffuri, Bruno Gialluca, Antonio Rigon, Roberto Rusconi, and Francesco Santi, have made heroic efforts to keep me informed of current Italian scholarly publications, which often do not receive the attention and distribution they deserve.

An earlier version of a portion of Chapter 3 appeared in my article "The Shrine of Santa Maria a Cigoli: Female Visionaries and Clerical Promoters," *Mélanges de l'Ecole Française de Rome, Moyen Age–Temps Modernes*, 98 (1986): 219–228. Part of Chapter 5 was included in "Giovanni Dominici, the Bianchi, and Venice: Symbolic Action and Interpretive Grids," *Journal of Medieval and Renaissance Studies*, 23 (1993): 143–171.

Finally, and most of all, I must thank my wife, Margery Schneider, who has done so much to sustain me and this project throughout the years of research and writing. Her patience allowed me to pursue my study of the Bianchi wherever it led, and her impatience finally spurred me to bring it to an end. Her alert intelligence and broad knowledge of medieval literature improved the text in innumerable ways, as her wit and affection improved my life. It is to her that I dedicate this book.

D. E. B.

THE BIANCHI OF 1399

INTRODUCTION

In the summer of 1399 a great movement of popular devotion spread through northern and central Italy, from the Alps to Rome. In cities, towns, and countryside, men, women, and children donned white robes and undertook nine days of pious processions. These processions generally took the Bianchi—so called because of their white robes—on a circuit of the neighboring towns, but occasionally processions within city walls or in the immediate environs of a city made possible the participation of those who were unable or unwilling to leave home for these devotions. During their nine days of processions, the Bianchi engaged in a variety of devotional practices: they visited churches and heard mass, listened to sermons, recited prayers, sang hymns, observed dietary restrictions, and called for "pace e misericordia," peace and mercy.

These orderly but enthusiastic processions of white-robed devotees made a profound impression on those who witnessed them, whether they were moved to join in or remained simple observers. The reactions of witnesses were recorded in diaries and chronicles, letters and notarial acts, lyrics, prayers, and accounts of miracles; and the responses of governing groups can be found in the minutes of town councils, in legislative decrees, and administrative directives. This rich and varied documentation, however, has not been fully exploited by historians. Indeed, at the time I began my research only two studies of the Bianchi movement had been published. Giampaolo Tognetti had traced the spread of the movement through the cities of northern and central Italy, but his long and careful article was based

almost exclusively on published narrative sources and was more de-
scriptive than analytical.[1] Arsenio Frugoni had sketched a charac-
teristically incisive interpretation of the Bianchi, but his essay was
based on a limited sample of the available sources.[2] I believed that it
would be possible to expand and correct Tognetti's description by
searching through the rich documentary collections in Italian archives, and to add substance and nuance to Frugoni's interpretation
by exploring the sources more extensively and intensively.

In addition to these articles devoted principally to the movement of
the Bianchi, other works have referred to it in passing. In these cases,
however, the Bianchi are simply cited as an instance in support of
some general thesis about late medieval and Renaissance Italy. These
mentions, moreover, are so wildly contradictory that it is hard to believe that they refer to the same thing. David Herlihy used the Bianchi as an example of the new, this-worldly orientation of what he
called "civic Christianity"; Norman Cohn mentioned them as another
of the apocalyptic movements of flagellants which sprang up in the
fourteenth century.[3] While Frugoni deemed their movement a pleasant devotional outing, a sort of pious picnic or light amusement, Benjamin Kedar thought that the clamorous success of the Bianchi in
Genoa was further proof of the heightened, almost hysterical inten-
sity of religious life after the Black Death of 1348.[4] For Eugenio Garin,
the Bianchi represented the last great lay movement of collective salvation of the Middle Ages; for Andrea Battistoni, they offered an example of the new concern for individual salvation mediated by the
sacramental intervention of the clergy.[5] These contradictory and con-

---

[1] Giampaolo Tognetti, "Sul moto dei bianchi nel 1399," *Bullettino dell'Istituto
Storico Italiano per il Medio Evo e archivio muratoriano*, 78 (1967): 205–343.

[2] Arsenio Frugoni, "La devozione dei Bianchi del 1399," in *L'attesa dell'età nuova
nella spiritualità della fine del medioevo*, Convegni del Centro di Studi sulla Spiritualità Medievale, 3 (Todi: Accademia Tudertina, 1962), pp. 232–248, now reprinted
in his *Incontri nel Medio Evo* (Bologna: Il Mulino, 1979), pp. 203–214. See also Frugoni's *intervento* in *Il movimento dei Disciplinati nel settimo centenario dal suo inizio*
(Perugia: Deputazione di Storia Patria per l'Umbria, 1962), pp. 392–393.

[3] David Herlihy, *Medieval and Renaissance Pistoia* (New Haven: Yale University
Press, 1967), pp. 250–254; Norman Cohn, *The Pursuit of the Millennium: Revolutionary Millenarians and Mystical Anarchists of the Middle Ages*, rev. ed. (New York: Oxford University Press, 1970), p. 145.

[4] Frugoni, "La devozione dei Bianchi"; Benjamin Z. Kedar, *Merchants in Crisis:
Genoese and Venetian Men of Affairs and the Fourteenth-Century Depression* (New Haven: Yale University Press, 1976), pp. 113–117.

[5] Eugenio Garin, *La cultura del Rinascimento* (Bari: Laterza, 1967), p. 114; Andrea Battistoni, review of *Il movimento dei Disciplinati*, in *Studi medievali*, ser. 3, 5 (1964): 206–207.

fusing interpretations seem to result in large part from two methodological failings: their proponents either generalize on the basis of a small, usually local sample of the available documentation, or they wrench the Bianchi out of their own time, classifying them as late epigones of medieval religious movements or as early forerunners of Counter-Reformation spirituality. The way out of this labyrinth of conflicting interpretations, then, has been to examine all the available documentation and to use it to set the Bianchi firmly in their historical context—or rather their historical contexts, for as political structures, economic conditions, social order, and cultural traditions varied (within certain limits) from place to place in Italy, so too did reactions to the Bianchi.

I have accordingly used the full range of available sources to describe the origins of the movement of the Bianchi and define the reasons for its inception and success (Chapter 2), to trace the course of the movement as it spread through Italy, with special attention to local and regional variations within the general pattern (Chapter 3), to examine the spirituality of the movement (Chapter 4), and to analyze the relations between this popular movement and the secular and ecclesiastical authorities (Chapter 5). Obviously, certain sources are better suited than others to these various ends. I have relied primarily on chronicles in tracing the progress of the movement, on lyrics and accounts of miracles in exploring its spirituality, and on government archives in studying the official response to it.

Placing the Bianchi within their religious context has proved more challenging. To be sure, the religious life of medieval and early modern Europe has been the subject of an immense number of works. But when I compared what I found in those works with what I had learned about the Bianchi, I became increasingly convinced that several of the major assumptions that have guided much recent work on the religious history of this period are fundamentally flawed.[6]

Studies of "popular religion," for instance, have generally depended on class distinctions. Their authors assume that the beliefs of the elite are not those of the common people and turn away from the traditional historical focus on the elite to practice what Bernard Cohn has called proctological history, history "from the bottom up": "the study of the masses, the inarticulate, the deprived, the dispossessed,

---

[6] For a trenchant survey of recent scholarship on medieval religious history, see John Van Engen, "The Christian Middle Ages as an Historiographical Problem," *American Historical Review*, 91 (1986): 519–552.

the exploited."[7] This is the approach taken by Carlo Ginzburg, who in *The Cheese and the Worms* turns his considerable talents to excavating and explicating the religious beliefs of one sixteenth-century miller. But despite the sophistication of Ginzburg's analysis and the eloquence of his presentation, it is not at all clear that the peculiar beliefs of Menocchio the miller should be deemed "popular religion." After decades of bending the ears of everyone in his village, Menocchio had managed to convert only one person to his unorthodox way of thinking—and that one person was generally considered to be dimwitted.[8] Why should the beliefs of this single individual, rather than those of all the rest of the villagers, be held to constitute "popular religion"?

The answer, for Ginzburg and those who share his approach, is that class distinctions entail class conflict and, in the sphere of religion, that conflict takes shape as the struggle between orthodoxy and heterodoxy. Orthodoxy is considered to be a form of social control that the ecclesiastical powers, in collusion with the secular authorities, try to impose on "the people"; heterodoxy is the ideological expression of popular dissent and social unrest. Thus Ginzburg is able to find "popular religion" not in the beliefs of the orthodox majority, but in those of the lone heretic. Few scholars, however, have been equally willing to take the beliefs of a lone heretic as representing popular religion, and so they have focused their attention on periods when heresy was relatively widespread. Gioacchino Volpe and other Italian historians have examined the heretical movements of medieval Italy, while Delio Cantimori and his students have studied the heresies of the sixteenth century.[9] But since, as Volpe notes, all the popular religious initiatives outside or opposed to the Roman Church and its hierarchy and ritual, so flourishing in the twelfth and thirteenth centuries, had practically vanished by the fourteenth and fifteenth centuries, so too scholarly interest thins out for the later

---

[7] Bernard S. Cohn, "History and Anthropology: The State of Play," *Comparative Studies in Society and History*, 22 (1980): 214.

[8] Carlo Ginzburg, *The Cheese and the Worms: The Cosmos of a Sixteenth-Century Miller*, trans. John Tedeschi and Anne Tedeschi (New York: Penguin, 1982), pp. 80–81.

[9] Gioacchino Volpe, *Movimenti religiosi e sette ereticali nella società medievale italiana, secoli XI–XIV* (1922; rpt. Florence: Sansoni, 1977); Delio Cantimori, *Eretici italiani del Cinquecento* (Florence: Sansoni, 1939). See also the works of Raffaello Morghen, Arsenio Frugoni, Raoul Manselli, Cinzio Violante, and Giovanni Miccoli for the Middle Ages, and of Carlo Ginzburg, Adriano Prosperi, and Antonio Rotondò for the sixteenth century.

period.[10] The number of studies devoted to the religious history of the fourteenth and fifteenth centuries is small by comparison with the preceding and succeeding periods.

Historians who have preferred to speak of "lay religiosity," "lay spirituality," and "lay piety" seem at least to have a clear sense of demographics: in examining the religiosity of the laity, they are treating the religion of the bulk of the populace. But the term "lay religiosity" implies a marked contrast with that portion that was not lay: the clergy. This usage assumes that lay piety differed from clerical piety, that lay religion was distinct in mood and in doctrine from clerical religion; it implies that a great gulf divided the clergy from the laity.[11] Yet there is evidence to suggest that in the later Middle Ages these two groups were distinct juridically, but not socially, economically, or culturally. Parish priests were usually drawn from the same social milieu as their parishioners; they certainly lived in everyday contact with them. It was not until after the canons and decrees of the Council of Trent had taken effect that the parish priest was clearly set apart, in training and in behavior, from his parishioners.[12]

It is easy to see why these concepts of "popular religion" or "lay piety" have taken such firm hold of the scholarly community. Protestant anti-Catholicism, Catholic anticlericalism, and modern agnostic skepticism have all contributed to a scholarly tradition that sees "lay" or "popular" religiosity as distinct from, and often in violent opposition to, the institutional structures and formal teachings of the Catholic church. In the case of Italy, this general attitude was exacerbated by the peculiar circumstances of the Risorgimento, when the kingdom of Italy was unified in the face of the political and military opposition of the papacy. One institutional result of this conflict was the exclusion of theology and related subjects from Italian state universities after 1873; an emotional result has been the profound conviction in some quarters that the Catholic church is—and always has been—the implacable foe of all that was lay, secular, and progressive.[13]

---

[10] Volpe, *Movimenti religiosi*, pp. 205–206.

[11] On this Manichean model of religious history, see André Vauchez, *Les laïcs au Moyen Age: Pratiques et expériences religieuses* (Paris: Cerf, 1987), pp. 7–11.

[12] Jean Delumeau, *Le Catholicisme entre Luther et Voltaire* (Paris: P.U.F., 1971), pp. 57–60, 227–234.

[13] Eric Cochrane, "New Light on Post-Tridentine Italy: A Note on Recent Counter-Reformation Scholarship," *Catholic Historical Review*, 56 (1970–1971): 295; Denys Hay, *The Church in Italy in the Fifteenth Century* (Cambridge: Cambridge University Press, 1977), pp. 3–6.

This presumed gap between popular and elite religion, however, or between lay and clerical piety, did not fit with what I had learned about the movement of the Bianchi. The sources indicated that rich and poor, learned and unlettered, laity, mendicants, and priests all participated on an equal basis in the Bianchi devotions; and the ideas expressed in the Bianchi songs were perfectly consonant with those found in theological writings, even if they were formulated in different terms. This blurring of commonly accepted categories forced me to rethink scholarly assumptions about the nature of late medieval religious life and to devise a more persuasive interpretation.

The understanding of ecclesiastical institutions, devotional practices, and religious movements which emerged from my reflections, and which I present in Chapter 1, stresses the interpenetration of popular and elite religion and the interaction of lay and clerical religiosity. Changes in liturgical practice, the proliferation and transformation of lay confraternities, and the response to popular preachers all disclose a high culture that was substantially open to low culture, and in which the circulation of religious ideas and cultural models among different cultural groups was anything but unidirectional.[14] This picture of the religious culture of late medieval Italy, like the highly speculative account of that culture's long-term evolution which I present in Chapter 6, has, I hope, a value independent of the Bianchi movement. But the Bianchi of 1399 were not independent of their religious culture. On the contrary, the Bianchi derived their organizational structure and devotional practices from the cultural forms available to them, and so cannot be understood apart from the institutions and behaviors described in my opening chapter.

This book thus has a dual purpose. Its core is a detailed monographic study of the Bianchi of 1399 which, in its exploitation of a range of sources and employment of a variety of interpretive tools, aspires to be a model treatment of a popular religious movement. It deals with the genesis of the Bianchi movement, its scope and nature, and its connections with other devotional movements, ecclesiastical and civic politics, social tensions, the bubonic plague, and the development of lay confraternities, among other questions. I hope that my examination of the Bianchi will inspire similar studies of other movements, such as the Alleluia of 1233 and the flagellants

---

[14] For an application of this approach to the widely shared fascination with monsters, prodigies, and portents, see Ottavia Niccoli, *Prophecy and People in Renaissance Italy*, trans. Lydia G. Cochrane (Princeton: Princeton University Press, 1990).

of 1260 in Italy, the flagellants in northern France and the Rhineland in 1349, and the many others that could be cited for France, Germany, the Low Countries, and the Iberian peninsula.

The insights gained from this detailed analysis of the Bianchi movement are then brought to bear on the current debates over the nature of "lay piety," "popular religion," and the history of late medieval Christianity. I tend to agree with the approach of such scholars as Richard Kieckhefer and André Vauchez, who would hold that the principal distinctions to be made are in the social context of pious belief and practice rather than in the beliefs themselves. And the example of the Bianchi tends to support those who, like Bernd Moeller, have argued that this period is "one of the most churchly-minded and devout periods of the Middle Ages."[15] In contrast to the great popular heresies of the High Middle Ages, the Bianchi represent something that might be called popular orthodoxy: a sincere and spontaneous rallying to the approved beliefs and traditional practices of the church.

If orthodoxy was truly popular, if the church commanded the ready assent of the Italian populace, it was because people found that their religion met personal and collective needs. Religious teachings helped people make sense of happenstance and ascribe significance to otherwise meaningless events. Religious ceremonies helped them articulate their fears and joys and cope with their losses. Religious injunctions sustained public and private morality, encouraged charity and neighborliness, and bound clusters of people into communities. The Bianchi, in particular, voiced and responded to an urgently felt need for social pacification. Their origin legend, their actions, their songs, and their miracles all concur in placing peace at the forefront of their concerns. Nor should it surprise us that their yearning for social peace should be expressed in religious terms. In their minds as in their characteristic cry, peace was inseparable from, and dependent on, mercy. Troubled at finding themselves snarled in conflict with those who ought to have been most dear to them, they linked this social wound with the consciousness of sin that estranged them from the God to whom they were devoted. Peace—with God and with neighbor—was the miracle the Bianchi desperately desired.

---

[15] Bernd Moeller, "Piety in Germany around 1500," in *The Reformation in Medieval Perspective*, ed. Steven E. Ozment (Chicago: Quadrangle, 1971), p. 60. See also p. 64, where Moeller asserts that one of the prerequisites for Luther's success was "the extreme intensification of medieval churchly devotion."

THE RELIGIOUS CULTURE

OF LATE MEDIEVAL ITALY

"I don't know what the canonical faith may be, but I believe I am a
baptized Christian."
> —Alberto of Siena, a character in a story by Franco Sacchetti,
> stuttering in fear on being summoned before the inquisitor

On April 4, 1445, Luca da Panzano recorded, with some satisfaction, the institutional resolution of his adolescent daughter's protracted religious crisis. The girl's spiritual aspirations had burst into
the open the year before, when young Lena, not yet twelve years
old, had been invited to stay with one of her father's friends, a re-
spectable widow, in San Gimignano. There Lena and several other
proper young ladies had joined a group of flagellants known as the
Bianchi, a group apparently unconnected with the great devotional
movement of the Bianchi of 1399. Lena and her friends put on white
robes and beat themselves with whips, along with several hundred
other men and women. Some time after this episode—the lapse of
time is unspecified, but it does not appear to have been long—Lena
went one day to the Benedictine convent of San Girolamo in San
Gimignano and refused to leave. When her mind remained un-
changed after a probationary stay of six months in this cloistered
community, her father traveled the fifty kilometers from Florence to
San Gimignano and there confirmed an agreement with his daughter

Epigraph: Franco Sacchetti, *Il Trecentonovelle*, ed. Emilio Facciolo (Turin:
Einaudi, 1970), p. 31.

8

and with the nuns by which Lena would become a permanent member of the large and well-to-do convent of San Girolamo.[1]

The motives and outcome of Lena's choice of a life of chastity—and even the extent to which it was an expression of piety, rather than confusion and fear sparked by the onset of puberty, the prospect of marriage, and the risks of childbearing—must remain obscure. But even as refracted through the elliptical phrases of her father's memoir, Lena's crisis shows how the most intimate religious experience was defined by devotional practices, collective movements, and ecclesiastical institutions. Lena was drawn first to the Bianchi, a loosely structured group of flagellants identified only by their colorless robes. This group seems to have been at least intermittently active for several months in the area of San Gimignano, but there is no hint that it had a formal structure or regular membership, like a devotional confraternity. Instead, participants—members would be too strong a term—joined the Bianchi to share in the collective penitential act of flagellation, which by this time had been a common feature of lay devotional life for nearly two centuries; and whenever the impulse that had led them to join was exhausted, they left. It is hard to imagine this group surviving for very long without a hard institutional shell to sustain and preserve it; as it was, its unstable enthusiasm offered no socially acceptable abode for a young woman of good family. That she found in the most traditional institution of female religious life, the Benedictine convent. San Girolamo's convent walls inside the city walls doubly protected her virginity; its ample patrimony ensured a decent existence; its ordered devotions and stable organization promised a comforting routine and companionable security. At the age of twelve, she had passed through the collective movement of the Bianchi, in which lay men and women gath-

---

[1] Archivio di Stato di Firenze, Carte Strozziane, II, 9: "Ricordi di Luca da Panzano," fol. 119r, as quoted in Anthony Molho, "*Tamquam vere mortua*: Le professioni religiose femminili nella Firenze del tardo Medioevo," *Società e storia*, 12 (1989): 20, n. 29. On Luca da Panzano, see Carlo Carnesecchi, "Un fiorentino del secolo XV e le sue ricordanze domestiche," *Archivio storico italiano*, ser. 5, 4 (1889): 145–173; the passage concerning Lena appears on p. 160. Carnesecchi notes that Lena died a little over four years after entering the convent of San Girolamo, on July 26, 1449. For a brief history of San Girolamo, see Luigi Pecori, *Storia di San Gimignano* (Florence: Tipografia Galileiana, 1853), pp. 424–431. According to the 1428 Catasto, or property tax, among all monasteries and convents, the patrimony of San Girolamo (£1,669 s.12 d.8) was surpassed only by that of Monteoliveto (£1,797 s.2 d.10): Enrico Fiumi, *Storia economica e sociale di San Gimignano* (Florence: Olschki, 1961), p. 187.

ered to perform the penitential act of flagellation, and into the ecclesiastical institution which was to be her home for the rest of her short life.

Ecclesiastical institutions, devotional practices, collective movements: these are the warp and weft and moving shuttle that wove the rich fabric of late medieval religious culture. To understand the place of the Bianchi—not the barely perceptible flagellants of 1445 in San Gimignano, but the great movement of 1399—and to construe their meaning in the religious culture of their time, we must consider how institutions perpetuate customs, how customs are absorbed and transformed by movements, how movements give rise to institutions. And in all of these areas, we must stress the reciprocal influence of lay and clerical religiosity, for both laity and clergy contributed actively to the elaboration of the religious culture which enfolded both.

Ecclesiastical Institutions and Sacramental Practice

The essential framework for religious life was provided by a complex web of ecclesiastical institutions. In theory, all Christendom was apportioned into parishes and dioceses, and these territorial groupings of the faithful were ministered to by the secular clergy.[2] Monks and nuns were similarly rooted in place, but cut off by convent walls from the entanglements of the care of souls; their work for the Christian community was done from within these fortresses of prayer, where they maintained a life of personal chastity and communal worship. The mendicant friars, in contrast, wandered over the face of Europe, supporting the ordinary work of the parish clergy with their extraordinary skill in preaching and commitment to combating heresy. In practice, however, the secular, monastic, and mendicant

---

[2] Gabriel Le Bras, *Institutions ecclésiastiques de la Chrétienté médiévale*, vol. 12 of *Histoire de l'Eglise depuis les origines jusqu'à nos jours*, ed. Augustin Fliche and Victor Martin (Paris: Bloud & Gay, 1959–1964); *Vescovi e diocesi in Italia nel Medioevo (sec. XI-XIII)*, Atti del II Convegno di Storia della Chiesa in Italia (Roma, 5–9 settembre 1961) (Rome: Herder, 1964); *Pievi e parrocchie in Italia nel basso Medioevo (sec. XIII-XV)*, Atti del VI Convegno di Storia della Chiesa in Italia (Firenze, 21–25 settembre 1981) (Rome: Herder, 1984); *Vescovi e diocesi in Italia dal XIV alla metà del XVI secolo*, Atti del VII Convegno di Storia della Chiesa in Italia (Brescia, 21–25 settembre 1987), ed. Giuseppina De Sandre Gasparini, Antonio Rigon, Francesco Trolese, and Gian Maria Varanini (Rome: Herder, 1990).

clergy did not mesh into a smoothly-running machine for guiding the faithful and administering the sacraments: there were too many rivalries and confusions, overlapping jurisdictions and competing claims. The great monastic estates included patronage rights over innumerable parish churches, and so the monks were inevitably, and not necessarily reluctantly, pulled away from their round of prayers and embroiled in the appointment and supervision of parish clergy; some of them even served as parish priests.[3] Parish clergy resented the intrusion of mendicant preachers, who were often implicitly or explicitly critical of the secular clergy and in any case allowed parishioners to evade the control of their resident priest by confessing their sins instead to a visiting friar. Friars and monks competed for the reverence, and the donations, of the laity, often by denigrating their rivals' distinctive way of life—or by praising their ideals, and then reproaching them for failure to live up to them.

These unseemly squabbles cannot obscure the fact that the Catholic church was a dominating presence in late medieval society, one with few rivals in landed wealth, political power, intellectual eminence, moral prestige, or cultural influence.[4] In Tuscany, for example, ecclesiastical institutions owned approximately a quarter of all wealth, and their land holdings were particularly conspicuous in the prized areas close to Florence and Prato.[5] Exercise of church office was one way in which ruling families secured their power; control over appointment to church office was a primary means by which Florence and other great cities extended their control over subject territories, and by which the Medici tightened their grasp on Florence.[6] Control over the

[3] For a model study of one rural parish that was subject to the Benedictine monastery of Santa Giustina di Padova, see Giuseppina De Sandre Gasparini, *Contadini, chiesa, confraternita in un paese veneto di bonifica: Villa del Bosco nel Quattrocento*, Fonti e ricerche di storia ecclesiastica padovana, 10 (Padua: Istituto per la Storia Ecclesiastica Padovana, 1979). For a while, the parish priest was a monk, who proved incapable of managing the care of souls; his successor, a member of the secular clergy, turned out to be notably competent at his job. See pp. 99–124.

[4] See now the overview by Roberto Bizzocchi, "Clero e Chiesa nella società italiana alla fine del Medio Evo," in *Clero e società nell'Italia moderna*, ed. Mario Rosa (Rome and Bari: Laterza, 1992), pp. 3–44.

[5] David Herlihy and Christiane Klapisch-Zuber, *Tuscans and Their Families: A Study of the Florentine Catasto of 1427* (New Haven: Yale University Press, 1985), p. 94; Maria Serena Mazzi and Sergio Raveggi, *Gli uomini e le cose nelle campagne fiorentine del Quattrocento* (Florence: Olschki, 1983), pp. 71–72.

[6] Roberto Bizzocchi, *Chiesa e potere nella Toscana del Quattrocento* (Bologna: Il

pulpit meant that clerics, and especially the great preaching orders of Franciscans, Dominicans, and Augustinians, were responsible for cultural mediation and indoctrination on a scale that no other group could match.[7] Ecclesiastical institutions continued to be the leading patrons of the arts, as they had been ever since the fourth century; and even when laymen commissioned works of art, whether for placement in a church or for private devotional use, the form and content of those works were defined by established religious traditions.[8]

These traditions were nominally centered on the seven sacraments, which in this period lacked the clear definition, fundamental importance, and rigorous subjection to priestly control they received in the sixteenth century at the Council of Trent.[9] To be sure, in 1215 the

---

Mulino, 1987); *Strutture ecclesiastiche in Italia e in Germania prima della Riforma*, ed. Paolo Prodi and Peter Johanek (Bologna: Il Mulino, 1984); *Gli Sforza, la Chiesa lombarda, la corte di Roma: Strutture e pratiche beneficiarie nel ducato di Milano (1450–1535)*, ed. Giorgio Chittolini (Naples: Liguori, 1989); and *Storia d'Italia, Annali 9: La Chiesa e il potere politico dal Medioevo all'età contemporanea*, ed. Giorgio Chittolini and Giovanni Miccoli (Turin: Einaudi, 1986), especially the essay by Chittolini, "Stati regionali e istituzioni ecclesiastiche nell'Italia centrosettentrionale del Quattrocento," pp. 149–193.

[7] Roberto Rusconi, "De la prédication à la confession: Transmission et contrôle de modèles de comportement au XIIIe siècle," in *Faire croire: Modalités de la diffusion et de la réception des messages religieux du XIIe au XVe siècle*, ed. André Vauchez, Collection de l'Ecole Française de Rome, 51 (Rome: Ecole Française de Rome, 1981), pp. 67–85; "I francescani e la confessione," in *Francescanesimo e vita religiosa dei laici nel Duecento*, Atti dell'VIII Convegno Internazionale di Studi Francescani (Assisi: Società Internazionale di Studi Francescani, 1981), pp. 251–309; "'Ordinate confiteri': La confessione dei peccati nelle 'Summae de casibus' e nei manuali per i confessori (metà XII-inizi XIV secolo)," in *L'Aveu: Antiquité et Moyen Age* (Rome: Ecole Française de Rome, 1986), pp. 297–313; "Dal pulpito alla confessione: Modelli di comportamento religioso in Italia tra 1470 circa e 1520 circa," in *Strutture ecclesiastici*, pp. 259–315; and his collection of texts, *Predicazione e vita religiosa nella società italiana da Carlo Magno alla Controriforma* (Turin: Loescher, 1981).

[8] Michael Baxandall, *Painting and Experience in Fifteenth-Century Italy* (Oxford: Oxford University Press, 1972), pp. 40–56; Peter Burke, *The Italian Renaissance: Culture and Society in Italy* (Princeton: Princeton University Press, 1986), p. 89.

[9] Excellent surveys of late medieval religious life are provided by Francis Rapp, *L'Eglise et la vie religieuse en Occident à la fin du Moyen Age* (Paris: P.U.F., 2d ed. 1980), and Francis Oakley, *The Western Church in the Later Middle Ages* (Ithaca: Cornell University Press, 1979). Less good, at least for Italy, is Steven Ozment, *The Age of Reform, 1250–1550* (New Haven: Yale University Press, 1980). Giovanni Miccoli's long, densely argued, and provocative essay on "La storia religiosa" in the Einaudi *Storia d'Italia*, vol. 2: *Dalla caduta dell'Impero romano al secolo XVIII* (Turin: Einaudi, 1974), pp. 431–1079, has shaped all subsequent Italian scholarship on the

Fourth Lateran Council had enjoined annual confession and communion, generally at Easter.[10] But once a year is rather seldom, few people chose to communicate more frequently, and others doubtless communicated even less often.[11] Sinners were understandably reluctant to disclose their misdeeds, particularly when it meant speaking face to face with a parish priest who knew them all too well, and who stood at the center of gossip networks in the village or neighborhood. Although priests who betrayed the secrecy of confessions risked being removed from office, far too many people found themselves in the position of the unhappy parishioners of San Giorgio in Cortona, who complained that their priest's mistress had reprimanded them in public for things said privately to the priest in confession. Even wandering friars like Venturino da Bergamo, who would take their embarrassing knowledge of hidden sins with them when they left town, had to employ all sorts of ruses to extract full confessions.[12] And while one might suspect an element of satirical humor in Caesarius of Heisterbach's story of an adulterous priest confessing his sin to a servant in a stable, there continued to be churchmen such as the canon lawyer Andreas de Escobar, whose popular manual for confessors was printed forty-eight times in the fifteenth century, who seriously

subject. A cornucopia of information can be found in Etienne Delaruelle, E.-R. Labande, and Paul Ourliac, *L'Eglise au temps du Grand Schisme et de la crise conciliaire (1378–1449)*, vol. 14 of *Histoire de l'Eglise depuis les origines jusqu'à nos jours*, ed. Augustin Fliche and Victor Martin (Paris: Bloud & Gay, 1964), and in the collected essays of Etienne Delaruelle, *La piété populaire au Moyen Age* (Turin: Bottega d'Erasmo, 1975).

[10] *Conciliorum oecumenicorum decreta*, ed. Giuseppe Alberigo et al. (Bologna: Istituto per le Scienze Religiose, 1973), p. 245. See Nicole Bériou, "Autour de Latran IV (1215): La naissance de la confession moderne et sa diffusion," in Groupe de la Bussière, *Pratiques de la confession: Des pères du desert à Vatican II: Quinze études* (Paris: Cerf, 1983), pp. 73–92.

[11] On the practice of confession in the late Middle Ages, see (in addition to the studies of Roberto Rusconi) Thomas N. Tentler, *Sin and Confession on the Eve of the Reformation* (Princeton: Princeton University Press, 1977); Tentler, "The Summa for Confessors as an Instrument of Social Control," in *The Pursuit of Holiness in Late Medieval and Renaissance Religion*, ed. Charles Trinkaus with Heiko A. Oberman (Leiden: E. J. Brill, 1974), pp. 103–126; John Bossy, "The Social History of Confession in the Age of the Reformation," *Transactions of the Royal Historical Society*, ser. 5, 25 (1975): 21–38; and Hervé Martin, "Confession et contrôle social à la fin du Moyen Age," in *Pratiques de la confession*, pp. 117–134.

[12] For San Giorgio, Noemi Meoni, "Visite pastorali a Cortona nel Trecento," *Archivio storico italiano*, 129 (1971): 248–250; for Venturino da Bergamo, Lester K. Little, "Les techniques de la confession et la confession comme technique," in *Faire croire*, p. 95.

maintained that if no priest could be found, a dying penitent could confess to and receive absolution from a layman.[13] The Bianchi of 1399, by confessing their sins and receiving communion before setting out in procession, were performing an act of special devotion, and one that was frequently judged worthy of note by the chroniclers who recorded the progress of the movement.

The life-cycle sacraments—baptism, confirmation, marriage, and extreme unction—were also unevenly respected and insecurely kept under the control of the clergy. Virtually everyone was baptized, but the priest and the religious rite may well have been overshadowed by the godparents and the social rite of godparentage.[14] Nor was the intercession of a priest absolutely required. In the bull "Exultate Deo" of 1439, Eugenius IV affirmed the strict necessity of baptism, urged that infants be baptized as soon as possible after birth, and, if no priest was available and the child's death seemed imminent, allowed a lay man or woman to perform the baptism: even a pagan or a heretic could baptize, declared the pope, as long as he or she followed the form used by the church and intended to perform what the church performs.[15] It was, however, respect for his personal sanctity rather

---

[13] Caesarius of Heisterbach, *The Dialogue on Miracles*, trans. H. Von E. Scott and C. C. Swinton Bland (London: George Routledge & Sons, 1929), vol. 1, pp. 125–126 (bk. III, 2); Tentler, *Sin and Confession*, pp. 41, 66–67.

[14] So argues John Bossy, in his "Blood and Baptism: Kinship, Community and Christianity in Western Europe from the Fourteenth to the Seventeenth Centuries," in *Sanctity and Secularity: The Church and the World*, ed. Derek Baker (Oxford: Basil Blackwell, 1973), pp. 129–143; "Padrini e madrine: un'istituzione sociale del cristianesimo popolare in Occidente," *Quaderni storici*, 41 (1979): 440–449; "God-parenthood: The Fortunes of a Social Institution in Early Modern Christianity," in *Religion and Society in Early Modern Europe, 1500–1800*, ed. Kaspar von Greyerz (London: George Allen & Unwin, 1984), pp. 194–201; and *Christianity in the West, 1400–1700* (Oxford: Oxford University Press, 1985), pp. 14–19. In forming my impression of the social importance of baptism and godparentage, I have also relied on Bossy's "The Counter-Reformation and the People of Catholic Europe," *Past and Present*, 47 (May 1970): 51–70; Christiane Klapisch, "'Parenti, amici e vicini': Il territorio urbano d'una famiglia mercantile nel XV secolo," *Quaderni storici*, 33 (1976): 953–982 (English translation: Christiane Klapisch-Zuber, *Women, Family, and Ritual in Renaissance Italy*, trans. Lydia G. Cochrane [Chicago: University of Chicago Press, 1985], pp. 68–93); and three papers presented at the Nineteenth International Congress on Medieval Studies, Kalamazoo, Michigan, May 10–13, 1984: Joseph Lynch, "Spiritual Kinship in 13th and 14th Century Priests' Manuals;" Christiane Klapisch-Zuber, "Tentative Reflections on the Naming Function of Godparents in Medieval France and Italy;" and Natalie Zemon Davis, "Conflict and Community in Sixteenth Century Lyons."

[15] *Conciliorum oecumenicorum decreta*, pp. 542–543. The provisions concerning

than the pressure of urgent need that inspired the people of Gauldo Tadino to carry their infants to the cell of the hermit Marzio to be baptized by this uneducated layman.[16] No sense of urgency impelled anyone to seek confirmation, the most neglected of the sacraments. On those rare occasions when a bishop visited one of the rural parishes of his diocese, he might confirm hundreds of persons in a single ceremony, as Bishop Enoc Cioncolari of Cortona did at the village of Montanare in 1419—a sure sign that no one had been confirmed there for years.[17] Extreme unction, on the other hand, does not seem to have been willfully ignored, though the high incidence of sudden death meant that in many cases it could not be administered; and in the Apennine hill town of Castellarquato, none of the four priests charged with the care of souls could explain what effect it had when it *was* administered.[18]

Ecclesiastical rules governing marriage had to be ignored, since the broad way in which incest was defined made it nearly impossible for a peasant to find in his village a marriage partner who was not too closely related to him, or for a noble to find within his restricted and inbred group a spouse who was both socially and canonically acceptable. Nobles sometimes took the trouble to purchase dispensations from the incest rules, while peasants presumably ignored them.[19] And when the marriage was celebrated, the blessing of a priest could

---

baptism in this decree for the Armenians were repeated in the decree for the Copts, pp. 576–577.

[16] André Vauchez, "Frères Mineurs, érémitisme et sainteté laïque: Les Vies des saints Maio (†v. 1270) et Marzio (†1301) de Gualdo Tadino," *Studi Medievali*, ser. 3, 27 (1986): 376, where Marzio is referred to as an "idiota et simplex illiteratus," an ignorant man and a simple illiterate.

[17] Noemi Meoni, "Visite pastorali a Cortona nel Quattrocento," *Annuario dell'Accademia Etrusca di Cortona*, 22 (1985–1986): 180. For observations on the extent to which the sacrament of confirmation had fallen into disuse in France, see Paul Adam, *La vie paroissiale en France au XIVe siècle* (Paris: Sirey, 1964), p. 268.

[18] Enrico Cagnoni, "Un Esame di Curati nel 1449," *Bollettino storico piacentino*, 21 (1926): 118.

[19] Nobles sometimes ignored them as well: Giovanna Motta, *Strategie familiari e alleanze matrimoniali in Sicilia nell'età della transizione (secoli XIV-XVII)* (Florence: Olschki, 1983), pp. 18–19, mentions marriages between a brother-in-law and sister-in-law, second cousins, and an uncle and niece, while Gérard Delille has documented a systematic pattern of cross-cousin marriage in which the imperative of preserving the family patrimony overrode the wish to observe the ecclesiastical norms governing matrimony: Gérard Delille, *Famille et propriété dans le Royaume de Naples (XVe-XIXe siècle)*, Bibliothèque des Ecoles Françaises d'Athènes et de Rome, 259 (Rome: Ecole Française de Rome, 1985), pp. 217–309.

be relegated to a minor and peripheral role, as it was in Florence, while in the villages the church was useful principally as a place for feasting and dancing.[20] The religious aspect of marriage was so generally overshadowed by the social that not all theologians were agreed that marriage was a sacrament or that all marriages were sacramental, despite the authoritative affirmation of Thomas Aquinas.[21] In short, many people went through their lives without being confirmed, married without benefit of clergy, and met their deaths without receiving extreme unction. Unlike baptism, these sacraments were not considered indispensable.

Ordination touched directly only a fragment of the populace in any case, and around 1400 the validity of this sacrament was rendered uncertain by the prolongation of the Great Schism: with two rival hierarchies pressing their claims, how could one tell which set of clergy was properly ordained?[22] Nor was the ordained clergy a unified, homogeneous body. Of the clergy, the true specialists in the sacred were the members of the monastic and mendicant orders; they were the ones who were set off from the profane world by their training, appearance, and daily regimen. The secular clergy, in contrast, was thoroughly a part of the profane world. The great ecclesiastical lords lived very much like secular lords, to whom they were generally related; those bishops who did not live like great lords were usually members of the mendicant orders, and behaved like mendicants rather than bishops. The parish clergy lived very much like their parishioners: they dressed like them, talked like them, worked with them, ate and drank with them, gambled with them, fought with them, slept with them.[23] And in those cases in which the actual holder of the benefice was not on the spot, he hired someone else to

---

[20] Klapisch-Zuber, *Women, Family, and Ritual*, pp. 193–196; compare the observations concerning France in Adam, *La vie paroissale*, pp. 271–273.

[21] James A. Brundage, *Law, Sex, and Christian Society in Medieval Europe* (Chicago: University of Chicago Press, 1987), pp. 432–433, 496–497.

[22] Roberto Rusconi, *L'attesa della fine: Crisi della società, profezia ed Apocalisse in Italia al tempo del grande scisma d'Occidente (1378–1417)* (Rome: Istituto Storico Italiano per il Medio Evo, 1979), pp. 18–19.

[23] All this is cataloged in the strictures on clerical behavior issued at the Council of Trent; see *The Canons and Decrees of the Council of Trent*, trans. H. J. Schroeder (Rockford, Illinois: TAN, 1978), pp. 110–111, 152–153. For two regional studies of clerical culture and comportment, see Charles M. de La Roncière, "Dans la campagne florentine au XIVe siècle: Les communautés chrétiennes et leurs curés," in *Histoire vécue du peuple chrétien*, ed. Jean Delumeau (Toulouse: Privat, 1979), vol. 1, pp. 281–314, and Grado G. Merlo, "Vita di chierici nel Trecento: Inchieste nella diocesi di Torino," *Bollettino storico-bibliografico subalpino*, 73 (1975): 181–210.

do it for him—someone who was, if anything, even less distinguishable from his flock.

This social and cultural continuity between priest and parishioners ran counter to the efforts of canon lawyers and town governments to mark a clear boundary between the lay and clerical estates and to define their jurisdictional competencies and fiscal responsibilities. Their efforts were further complicated by the presence of persons and groups who had semiclerical status, in defiance of the legal precept that a person must be either lay or cleric. The many *conversi* and *oblati* affiliated with thirteenth-century monasteries and hospitals enjoyed clerical exemptions from taxation, military service, and communal courts, while continuing to live in the world and conduct business there. This glaring imbalance between rights and responsibilities made the *conversi*, like other privileged groups, the target of concerted efforts by town governments to eliminate exemptions and extend civic authority over all residents, and as a result the numbers of *conversi* declined precipitously in the fourteenth century. As they did, new groups emerged in their place, most notably the penitents and tertiaries affiliated with the mendicant orders.[24] In addition to these canonically defined and legally recognized groups, the cities and countryside of Italy harbored substantial numbers of individual hermits, recluses, and anchorites: in 1290, the commune of Perugia spent public funds to help support sixty-eight of them, while smaller cities hosted more modest, but still significant numbers of recluses.[25]

---

[24] Daniela Rando, "Laicus religiosus: Tra strutture civili ed ecclesiastiche: l'Ospedale di Ogni Santi in Treviso (sec. XIII)," *Studi medievali*, ser. 3, 24 (1983): 617–656; Duane J. Osheim, "Conversion, *Conversi*, and the Christian Life in Late Medieval Tuscany," *Speculum*, 58 (1983): 368–390. On the penitents and tertiaries, see, for instance, Fernanda Sorelli, "Per la storia religiosa di Venezia nella prima metà del Quattrocento: Inizi e sviluppi del terz'ordine domenicano," in *Viridarium Floridum: Studi di storia veneta offerti dagli allievi a Paolo Sambin*, ed. Maria Chiara Billanovich, Giorgio Cracco, and Antonio Rigon (Padua: Antenore, 1984), pp. 89–114; Mario Sensi, "Incarcerate e penitenti a Foligno nella prima metà del Trecento," in *I frati penitenti di San Francesco nella società del Due e Trecento*, ed. Mariano D'Alatri (Rome: Istituto Storico dei Cappuccini, 1977), pp. 291–308; Giovanna Casagrande, "Terziarie francescane regolari in Perugia nei secoli XIV e XV," in *La beata Angelina da Montegiove e il movimento del Terz'Ordine Francescano femminile*, ed. Raffaele Pazzelli and Mario Sensi (Rome, 1984), pp. 437–492; and the essays in *Prime manifestazioni di vita comunitaria maschile e femminile nel movimento francescano della penitenza (1215–1447)*, Atti del Convegno di Studi Francescani, Assisi, 30 giugno–2 luglio 1981, ed. Raffaele Pazzelli and Lino Temperini (Rome: Commissione Storica Internazionale T.O.R., 1982).

[25] Mario Sensi, "Incarcerate e recluse in Umbria nei secoli XIII e XIV: Un biz-

Far from living in isolation, these recluses—dependent as they were on charitable donations, yet unable to go about in search of them—were to be found pursuing their solitary existence in the most public locations, such as the Rubaconte bridge over the Arno, in Florence.[26] These common figures on the religious landscape owed their social identity, like the thaumaturgical powers sometimes ascribed to them, not to any formal act of profession or rite of ordination, but rather to their resolute pursuit of a distinctive manner of life.

The priest did perform one act that no lay person or non-ordained religious could: he transformed ordinary bread and wine into the body and blood of Christ. This miracle of transubstantiation was the focus of tremendous popular devotion; Richard Kieckhefer has even suggested that the eucharist was used more as a focus for devotion than as a sacrament.[27] Paradoxically, devotion to the eucharist could interfere with its sacramental use. Awe of the transformed eucharist contributed to the infrequency with which people actually received it: the more the eucharist was exalted, the more unworthy of it they felt. St. Catherine of Siena had to chide Ristoro Canigiani for the "foolish humility" that led him to abstain from communion—though the bloody hosts and other gory eucharistic phenomena experienced by Catherine herself and many other late medieval saints make it easy to understand Ristoro's misgivings and the general reluctance to partake of the eucharist.[28] Instead of participating in the ceremony, the

---

zocaggio centro-italiano," in *Il movimento religioso femminile in Umbria nei secoli XIII–XIV*, ed. Roberto Rusconi (Florence: La Nuova Italia, 1984), pp. 105–106.

[26] *The Society of Renaissance Florence: A Documentary Study*, ed. Gene Brucker (New York: Harper & Row, 1971), p. 232; Anna Benvenuti Papi, "*In castro poenitentiae*": *Santità e società femminile nell'Italia medievale* (Rome: Herder, 1990), pp. 182–183, 575–576, 594, and 596.

[27] Richard Kieckhefer, "Major Currents in Late Medieval Devotion," in *Christian Spirituality*, vol. 2: *High Middle Ages and Reformation*, ed. Jill Raitt with Bernard McGinn and John Meyendorff (New York: Crossroad, 1987), p. 100. Some of the many eucharistic devotions of the late Middle Ages are described on pp. 96–100 of Kiechkefer's essay; see also Delaruelle, Labande, and Ourliac, *L'Eglise au temps du Grande Schisme*, pp. 749–752. On the eucharist in general, see Dennis Steel Devlin, "Corpus Christi: A Study in Medieval Eucharistic Theory, Devotion, and Practice," Ph.D. dissertation, University of Chicago, 1975. See now Miri Rubin, *Corpus Christi: The Eucharist in Late Medieval Culture* (Cambridge: Cambridge University Press, 1991), which appeared too late for me to incorporate its findings in this overview.

[28] *Le lettere di S. Caterina da Siena, ridotte a miglior lezione, e in ordine nuovo disposte con note di Niccolò Tommaseo*, ed. Piero Misciattelli, 2d ed. (Siena: Giuntini & Ben-

laity passively but eagerly witnessed the priest's performance of the mass. Their regular attendance at mass was encouraged by faith in the protective power of the consecrated host, for it was widely believed that a person who had seen the body of Christ in the morning would be preserved from death for that day. This popular devotion to the eucharist inspired changes in liturgical ceremony: the prolonged or repeated elevation of the host, the use of monstrances, and the institution of Corpus Christi processions were all introduced to satisfy the laity's fervent desire to see the body of Christ.

The liturgy itself was often overshadowed by paraliturgical devotions. A voracious appetite for sermons made the fifteenth century one of the great ages of homiletics; and preachers like Giovanni Dominici, Vincent Ferrer, Bernardino da Siena, Manfredi da Vercelli, Roberto da Lecce, Bernardino da Feltre, and Girolamo Savonarola traversed Italy tirelessly to satisfy that demand.[29] Town governments competed with each other for the honor of booking these famous speakers for the Lenten season—a task the city of Florence once entrusted to Niccolò Machiavelli, who found the commission amusing—and audiences gathered to hear them with high expectations and critical attention.[30] The merits or demerits of various preachers were frequently debated in humanist dialogues: Giovanni Gioviano Pontano praised the preaching of Egidio da Viterbo in his *Aegidius*, while Poggio Bracciolini was severely critical of everyone but Bernar-

---

tivoglio, 1913), vol. 4, pp. 169–177 (let. 266, to Ristoro Canigiani). In addition to the brief remarks of André Vauchez, "Dévotion eucharistique et union mystique chez les saintes de la fin du Moyen Age," in his *Les laïcs au Moyen Age: Pratiques et expériences religieuses* (Paris: Cerf, 1987), pp. 259–264, see Caroline Walker Bynum, *Holy Feast and Holy Fast: The Religious Significance of Food to Medieval Women* (Berkeley and Los Angeles: University of California Press, 1987), esp. pp. 59–60, 63–64, and 141–142.

[29] In addition to the studies of Roberto Rusconi cited in n. 7, see Carlo Delcorno, *Giordano da Pisa e l'antica predicazione volgare* (Florence: Olschki, 1975), and the excellent introduction and selection of illustrative documents in Delcorno, *La predicazione nell'età comunale* (Florence: Sansoni, 1974). The anthropologically oriented overview by Ida Magli, *Gli uomini della penitenza* (Milan: Garzanti, 1977) should be balanced against the patiently assembled documentation provided by Mario Sensi, "Predicazione itinerante a Foligno nel secolo XV," *Picenum Seraphicum*, 10 (1973): 139–195, and the precise analyses of the conference on "Predicazione francescana e società veneta nel Quattrocento: Committenza, ascolto, ricezione," in *Le Venezie francescane*, 6 (1989): 7–270.

[30] Niccolò Machiavelli, *Lettere*, ed. Franco Gaeta (Milan: Feltrinelli, 1961), pp. 401–413.

dino da Siena, and mildly critical even of him, in his *De avaritia*.[31] The problem, as Cencio Romano put it in Poggio's dialogue, was that these preachers spoke without considering their audience. To satisfy such discerning listeners, more expert preachers tailored their sermons to the needs and tastes of varied audiences: monks, dignitaries of the papal court, or the crowd filling the piazza in front of the cathedral or town hall.[32] One measure of their success was the market for texts. Listeners sometimes recorded sermons almost word for word as they were given, and readers acquired copies of individual sermons or entire collections for private devotional purposes.[33] Members of the Bolognese confraternity of Santa Maria della Morte were advised to attend the sermons of respected preachers and write down pithy remarks and clarifications of difficult questions, so that they would be able to remember them.[34] In literate urban circles, at least, the circulation of written sermons thus supplemented the actual preaching of mendicant friars and parish priests, and the contribution of preaching to the devotional life of the parish was less seasonal and episodic than the Lenten campaigns of a Bernardino da Siena might suggest.[35]

[31] Giovanni Gioviano Pontano, *Aegidius*, in *I Dialoghi*, ed. Carmelo Previtera (Florence: Sansoni, 1943), pp. 248–249; Poggio Bracciolini, *De avaritia*, in his *Opera omnia*, ed. Riccardo Fubini (Turin: Bottega d'Erasmo, 1964), vol. 1, pp. 2–5. See John W. Oppel, "Poggio, San Bernardino of Siena, and the Dialogue *On Avarice*," *Renaissance Quarterly*, 30 (1977): 564–587.

[32] Gustavo Cantini, "San Bernardino da Siena perfetto predicatore popolare," in *San Bernardino da Siena: Saggi e ricerche pubblicati nel quinto centenario della morte (1444–1944)* (Milan: Vita e Pensiero, 1945); *Bernardino predicatore nella società del suo tempo*, Atti del XVI Convegno del Centro di Studi sulla Spiritualità Medievale, 9–12 ottobre 1975 (Todi: Accademia Tudertina, 1976); D. L. d'Avray, *The Preaching of the Friars: Sermons Diffused from Paris before 1300* (Oxford: Clarendon Press, 1985); Salvatore S. Nigro, *Le brache di San Griffone: Novellistica e predicazione tra '400 e '500* (Bari: Laterza, 1985); John W. O'Malley, *Praise and Blame in Renaissance Rome: Rhetoric, Doctrine, and Reform in the Sacred Oratory of the Papal Court, c. 1450–1521* (Durham: Duke University Press, 1979).

[33] Zelina Zafarana, "Per la storia religiosa di Firenze nel Quattrocento: Una raccolta privata di prediche," *Studi medievali*, ser. 3, 9 (1968): 1017–1113; Roberto Rusconi, "Reportatio," *Medioevo e Rinascimento*, 3 (1989): 7–36.

[34] Mario Fanti, *La Confraternita di S. Maria della Morte e la Conforteria dei condannati in Bologna nei secoli XIV e XV*, Quaderni del Centro di Ricerca e di Studio sul Movimento dei Disciplinati, 20 (Perugia: Centro di Ricerca e di Studio sul Movimento dei Disciplinati, 1978), p. 67.

[35] Zelina Zafarana, "Cura pastorale, predicazione, aspetti devozionali nella parrocchia del basso Medioevo," in *Pievi e parrocchie in Italia nel basso Medioevo*, pp. 493–539. This essay, like "Per la storia religiosa," has been reprinted in Zafarana,

Just as the audience for sermons included both laity and clerics, so too the preachers of the sermons could belong to either group. Of course, preaching on doctrinal matters was formally restricted to clerics, and the specialists in preaching remained the members of the mendicant orders; it was the mendicants whose preaching to the Bianchi of 1399 was singled out for special mention by the chroniclers. But preaching on morals was a different matter. In 1201 Pope Innocent III had permitted the lay Umiliati to preach, on condition that they would restrict themselves to moral exhortation, advocating a just life and active piety.[36] And this sort of moral sermonizing continued to be practiced by laymen of all sorts and conditions, from St. Francis of Assisi to the humanist Cristoforo Landino, until the Council of Trent stipulated that weekly preaching was the duty of the clergy having the care of souls, and only the clergy.[37]

Public processions, like preaching, were a fixture of religious life, and like preaching they involved a number of groups, both lay and clerical.[38] Lay confraternities and urban magistrates, parish priests and members of the regular orders, all shared in varying degrees in these processions. Some processions, like the Corpus Christi ones, became regular celebrations, part of the formal liturgical calendar; although laymen marched in them and the lay confraternities often organized them, they were led by clerics. Other processions were organized and staged by the confraternities independently of the liturgical

---

Da Gregorio VII a Bernardino da Siena: Saggi di storia medievale, ed. Ovidio Capitani, Claudio Leonardi, Enrico Menestò, and Roberto Rusconi (Florence: La Nuova Italia, 1987).

[36] Herbert Grundmann, Movimenti religiosi nel Medioevo (Bologna: Il Mulino, 1970), pp. 89–90.

[37] Gilles Gérard Meersseman, "Predicatori laici nelle confraternite medievali," in his Ordo fraternitatis: Confraternite e pietà dei laici nel medioevo (Rome: Herder, 1977), pp. 1273–1289; Gian Piero Pacini, "La predicazione laicale nelle confraternite," Ricerche di storia sociale e religiosa, n.s., 17/18 (1980): 13–27. Preaching by laywomen, on the other hand, was always suspect; one of the charges commonly leveled at heretical groups was that they allowed ignorant women to preach. On the question of female preaching among the early Waldensians, see Grado G. Merlo, "Sulle 'misere donnicciuole' che predicavano," in his Valdesi e valdismi medievali, II: Identità valdesi nella storia e nella storiografia: Studi e discussioni (Turin: Claudiana, 1991), pp. 93–112. On the contested choice of a language for preaching, see Vittorio Coletti, Parole dal pulpito: Chiesa e movimenti religiosi tra latino e volgare (Casale Monferrato: Marietti, 1983).

[38] On processions, see Richard C. Trexler, Public Life in Renaissance Florence (New York: Academic Press, 1980); and Edward Muir, Civic Ritual in Renaissance Venice (Princeton: Princeton University Press, 1981).

calendar and clerical control. Still other processions, such as those to welcome a visiting dignitary or install newly elected officials, adapted the symbolic vocabulary of religious processions to a secular purpose.[39]

On those occasions when the well-being of a community was threatened, special propitiatory processions were organized. These processions enjoyed the sanction and support of communal and ecclesiastical authorities, who cooperated in bringing sacred images out of their holy enceintes and into public view. In Perugia in 1476 (to cite one example among many), processions were made to assuage the angry God who had sent plague upon the city. Holy images were brought out of the churches and carried through the streets:

> And so for five days they went in a line with very great contrition, devoutly praying God to remove this pestilence from us, and also praying to his glorious mother and all the saints of the celestial court that they might intercede for us, and that it please God to revoke every harsh sentence and affliction and not heed our sins; and the holy Banner of the Madonna di San Francesco and other banners and images were brought out for these processions.[40]

When these processions failed to restore Perugia to health, a new and longer series of processions lasting eighteen days, including three of fasting, was declared at the urging of the Servite preacher Fra Bonaventura. A decade later, in 1486, another epidemic of plague in Perugia stimulated a new round of processions of white-robed penitents, led this time by the Franciscan Bernardino da Feltre.[41]

Plague was not the only catastrophe capable of evoking this sort of mass response. The image of the Virgin at Santa Maria dell'Impruneta was carried in formal procession to Florence in times of plague or political turmoil, but above all it was importuned for relief from bad

---

[39] Richard C. Trexler, *The Libro Cerimoniale of the Florentine Republic by Francesco Filarete and Angelo Manfidi: Introduction and Text* (Geneva: Droz, 1978).

[40] "E così andaro 5 dì a la fila con grandissima contritione e divotamente pregando eddio, che levi da noi questa pestilenzza, e anco pregando la sua gloriosa madre con tutti li santi e sante de la corte celestiale, a ciò che intercedano per noi, grati a dio che esso revocasse ogni ria sentenzza e flagello, e non guardasse a li nostri peccati, e a le dette processione for cavati el divoto Gonfalone de la Madona de S. francesco e altre gonfalone e figure." "Cronaca perugina inedita di Pietro Angelo di Giovanni (già detta del Graziani) Parte II (Anni 1461–1494)," ed. Oscar Scalvanti, *Bollettino della R. Deputazione di storia patria per l'Umbria*, 9 (1903): 102. Unless noted otherwise, all translations are mine.

[41] "Cronaca perugina," pp. 103–104, 245.

weather. This image was believed to control rain, which it was called on to bring in times of drought and moderate in times of flood.[42] In Cuneo in 1464, the extreme cold and the apocalyptic preaching of the Dominican friar Giovanni di Brancaccio da Napoli (in the church of San Francesco!) provoked processions by youths of both sexes, an influx of young women and widows into the ranks of the tertiaries, and the establishment of a confraternity of young flagellants dedicated to the recently canonized Dominican saint Catherine of Siena.[43]

Lay Confraternities

Such confraternities were among the most important religious institutions of late medieval Italy, so important that the late Middle Ages has been called the Golden Age of small pious associations.[44]

[42] Richard C. Trexler, "Florentine Religious Experience: The Sacred Image," *Studies in the Renaissance*, 19 (1972): 11–18. On Impruneta, see also two recent collections of essays: *L'Impruneta: Una pieve, un santuario, un comune rurale* (Florence: Francesco Papafava, 1988), and *Impruneta: Una pieve, un paese: Cultura, parrocchia, e società nella campagna toscana* (Florence: Salimbeni, 1983).

[43] *Chronicorum Cunei libri tres*, ed. Domenico Promis, in *Miscellanea di storia italiana*, 12 (Turin, 1871), p. 289.

[44] M. Fougères [Marc Bloch], "Entr'aide et piété: Les associations urbaines au moyen âge," *Mélanges d'histoire sociale*, 5 (1944): 106, building on the essay of Gabriel Le Bras, "Les confréries chrétiennes," reprinted in Le Bras, *Etudes de sociologie religieuse* (Paris: P.U.F., 1955 and 1956), pp. 423–462. The only book surveying medieval Italian confraternities is still Gennaro Maria Monti, *Le confraternite medievali dell'alta e media Italia* (Venice: La Nuova Italia, 1927), which is badly outdated. For example, whereas Monti noted only three confraternities in Liguria, within twenty years of the publication of his book more than a hundred had been identified: Domenico Cambiaso, "Casacce e confraternite medievali in Genova e Liguria," *Atti della società ligure di storia patria*, 71 (1948): 81–110. Monti's survey mentions approximately 500 confraternities of all types in northern and central Italy; but in 1969, when P. L. Meloni summarized a decade of work by the Perugian Centro di Documentazione sul Movimento dei Disciplinati, some 1,800 flagellant confraternities had already been identified, though the work of the Centro was still not complete—and the many non-flagellant confraternities were not even being counted in this census: Pier Lorenzo Meloni, "Topografia, diffusione, e aspetti delle Confraternite dei Disciplinati," in *Risultati e prospettive della ricerca sul movimento dei Disciplinati* (Perugia: Deputazione di Storia Patria per l'Umbria, 1972), pp. 16–22. The immense volume of specialized studies that have appeared since Monti's survey makes replacing his book a daunting and perhaps impossible task. Roberto Rusconi's "Confraternite, compagnie, e devozioni," in *Storia d'Italia, Annali*, vol. 9: *La Chiesa e il potere politico dal Medioevo all'età contemporanea*, ed. Giorgio

Though rigid classifications into categories are hard to maintain, groups of *laudesi* gathered primarily to sing vernacular hymns in honor of the Virgin Mary or the saints, while confraternities of *disciplinati* or *battuti* centered their meetings on the penitential rite of flagellation, which in their liturgy was framed by devotional songs and scriptural readings.[45] Other confraternities were dedicated principally to charitable activities or to the tending of a private cult. Confraternities were found in both urban and rural communities, and among a great variety of social groups. Villages normally supported only a single confraternity, which included all adult males who were active in the community; the rural confraternity, like that of San Rocco in Villa del Bosco or the one referred to simply as "the fraternity of the men of Villa Montecchi" near Cortona, was, in effect, a formal assembly of the men who gathered in the nave of the village church.[46] The passage from one large and inclusive confraternity to a number of smaller and more specialized ones may indicate a transition from town to city, as it did at Borgo San Sepolcro at the end of the thir-

---

Chittolini and Giovanni Miccoli (Turin: Einaudi, 1986), pp. 469–506, is a marvel of compression and the best guide to the current bibliography on medieval confraternities. Giancarlo Angelozzi, *Le confraternite laicali: Un'esperienza cristiana tra medioevo e età moderna* (Brescia: Queriniana, 1978), offers a selection of illustrative texts. For the period of the Catholic Reform and Counter-Reformation, see Christopher F. Black, *Italian Confraternities in the Sixteenth Century* (Cambridge: Cambridge University Press, 1989).

[45] As in the "Ordo ad faciendum disciplinam," preserved in two nearly identical versions in Assisi, Archivio Capitolare di San Rufino, mss. 20 and 21. See also the *Liber per la compagnia* of flagellants in Novara edited by Pier Giorgio Longo, *Letteratura e pietà a Novara tra XV e XVI secolo* (Novara: Associazione di Storia della Chiesa Novarese, 1986), pp. 287–420.

[46] On Villa del Bosco, see De Sandre Gasparini, *Contadini, chiesa, confraternita*. The "Fraternitas hominum de Villa Montechi" appears as the owner of three parcels of land, one of which was later sold, in Archivio Storico del Comune di Cortona, C. 7: Estimo dei beni ecclesiastici, fol. 205v. On rural confraternities in the Val d'Elsa, see Charles M. de La Roncière, "La place des confréries dans l'encadrement religieux du contado florentin: L'example de la Val d'Elsa," *Mélanges de l'Ecole Française de Rome, Moyen Age–Temps Modernes*, 85 (1973): 31–77, 633–671, with some corrections by La Roncière himself in "Les confréries en Toscane aux XIV et XV siècles d'après les travaux récents," *Ricerche per la storia religiosa di Roma*, 5 (1984): 50–64, esp. p. 51. For a comparison of the typology and evolution of confraternities in Florence and in its region, see La Roncière, "Les confréries à Florence et dans son contado aux XIVe et XVe siècles," in *Le mouvement confraternel au Moyen Age: France, Italie, Suisse* (Rome: Ecole Française de Rome, 1987), pp. 297–342.

teenth century.[47] In the great metropolis of Florence, the number of confraternities multiplied from six in the mid-thirteenth century to thirty-three in the middle of the fourteenth; over the next century the number tripled again, to ninety-six—and this despite the brutal plague-driven reduction in Florence's population by more than 50 percent between 1340 and 1440. Cortona, tiny by comparison with Florence, nonetheless had seven flagellant confraternities and eight of *laudesi* on its fifteenth-century tax rolls.[48] The multiplicity of urban confraternities allowed people to choose among many alternatives, or even to enroll in more than one: Lorenzo the Magnificent, for instance, was an active member of half a dozen Florentine confraternities.[49] Confraternities, too, could choose special identities for themselves in an urban setting. Some enrolled only youths.[50] A few, like a fourteenth-century flagellant confraternity in Catania, were exclusively female.[51] Most, however, were formed and led by adult males,

[47] James R. Banker, *Death in the Community: Memorialization and Confraternities in an Italian Commune in the Late Middle Ages* (Athens: University of Georgia Press, 1988). According to Banker, Borgo San Sepolcro remained a unified community, with a single parish and a single confraternity, until around 1300; the first hint of a multiplication of parishes comes in the 1290s (p. 24), and new confraternities are documented early in the following century. See also Banker, "Death and Christian Charity in the Confraternities of the Upper Tiber Valley," in *Christianity and the Renaissance: Image and Religious Imagination in the Quattrocento*, ed. Timothy Verdon and John Henderson (Syracuse: Syracuse University Press, 1990), pp. 302–327, esp. p. 311.

[48] For Florence, see John Henderson, "Penitence and the Laity in Fifteenth-Century Florence," in *Christianity and the Renaissance*, p. 233. See also Massimo D. Papi, "Per un censimento delle fonti relative alle confraternite fiorentine: Primi risultati," in *Da Dante a Cosimo I*, ed. Domenico Maselli (Pistoia: Tellini, 1976), pp. 92–121; and Papi, "Confraternite ed ordini mendicanti a Firenze: Aspetti di una ricerca quantitativa," *Mélanges de l'Ecole Française de Rome, Moyen Age–Temps Modernes*, 89 (1977): 723–732. For Cortona: Archivio Storico del Comune di Cortona, C. 7: Estimo dei beni ecclesiastici, fols. 192–206. According to the Catasto of 1427, Cortona had a population of around 3,250, which is likely to have risen slightly in the course of the fifteenth century. Herlihy and Klapisch-Zuber, *Tuscans and Their Families*, pp. 56 and 58.

[49] Ronald F. E. Weissman, *Ritual Brotherhood in Renaissance Florence* (New York: Academic Press, 1982), pp. 117 and 169–170.

[50] Richard C. Trexler, "Ritual in Florence: Adolescence and Salvation in the Renaissance," in Trinkhaus, *The Pursuit of Holiness*, pp. 200–264.

[51] Carmellina Naselli, "Notizie sui Disciplinati in Sicilia," in *Il Movimento dei Disciplinati nel settimo centenario dal suo inizio* (Perugia: Deputazione di Storia Patria per l'Umbria, 1962), p. 321. In Cortona, the Compagnia della Croce Santa, which allowed both men and women to join, reserved all offices to the female members.

who sometimes limited their membership to the nobility, or to practitioners of a particular craft.[52]

If some confraternities were homogeneous, composed entirely of one class or trade group, many more of them mixed persons of widely varying social strata.[53] This heterogeneity could be jealously guarded: Ettore Vernazza failed in his attempt to make the Genoese Compagnia della Misericordia an exclusively noble confraternity.[54] Indeed, the association of great and small, powerful and weak in confraternities made them ready vehicles for the formalization of those patron-client relationships that permeated Italian society and politics. For this reason, wary governments kept close watch on the confraternities. In 1419, the Florentine Signoria dissolved all but a few confraternities, and placed the remaining ones under government supervision. Seven years later it ordered a fresh inquiry into the political activities of pious confraternities.[55] The Venetians exercised more regular control over their confraternities: all flagellant confraternities had to obtain government approval for their annual election of new members and an official license to take part in the Good Friday procession.[56] Such watchfulness was not based on idle fears; the confraternities could indeed serve as bases for political action, or as covers for it.

Biblioteca del Comune e dell'Accademia Etrusca de Cortona, ms. 411: Capitoli della Compagnia della Croce Santa posta in San Francesco di Cortona, fol. 12.

[52] Lia Sbriziolo, "Per la storia delle confraternite veneziane: Dalle deliberazioni miste (1310–1476) del Consiglio dei Dieci: Scolae comunes, artigiane, e nazionale," *Atti dell'Istituto veneto di scienze lettere ed arti*, 126 (1967–1968): 413–415, discusses the problem of the relation between trade guilds and confraternities. See in general Richard Mackenney, *Tradesmen and Traders: The World of the Guilds in Venice and Europe, c. 1250–c. 1650* (Totowa, New Jersey: Barnes & Noble, 1987), pp. 4–7, 44–77.

[53] This may have changed in the sixteenth century, when confraternities formed according to social status, occupation, or neighborhood became more common: Weissman, *Ritual Brotherhood in Renaissance Florence*, pp. 197–235.

[54] Giovanna Balbi, "La Compagnia della Misericordia di Genova nella storia della spiritualità laica," *Momenti di storia e arte religiosa in Liguria* (Genoa: n.p., 1963).

[55] Gene A. Brucker, *Renaissance Florence* (New York: John Wiley and Sons, 1969), p. 208; Brucker, *The Civic World of Early Renaissance Florence* (Princeton: Princeton University Press, 1977), pp. 479–480.

[56] Lia Sbriziolo, "Per la storia delle confraternite veneziane: Dalle deliberazioni miste (1310–1476) del Consiglio dei Dieci: Le scuole dei Battuti," in *Miscellanea Gilles Gérard Meersseman* (Padua: Antenore, 1970), pp. 715–763. William B. Wurthmann, "The Council of Ten and the *Scuole Grandi* in Early Renaissance Venice," *Studi Veneziani*, n.s., 18 (1989): 15–66, covers the same ground as Sbriziolo, but makes no mention of her study.

Matteo Villani described how a group of Romans, fed up with the unrestrained factional violence of their city, met in the guise of a confraternity to try to restore order: "Finally, not able to find any other way in which the people could assemble, on the day after Christmas, following the practice of a confraternity dedicated to the Madonna, many good *popolani* assembled as planned in Santa Maria Maggiore and there decided that they wanted a Captain of the People; and then and there in unity they elected Giovanni Cerroni."[57] And during the Savonarolan period in Florence, confraternities functioned as vehicles for political organization and for the articulation of political dissent.[58]

Confraternities often became institutions of considerable economic importance as well.[59] Their devotional activities involved outlays for the construction and decoration of chapels, the purchase of furnishings, and the preparation of processions, as well as the procuring of smaller items like candles and robes. But most of the economic activity of the confraternities was concerned with their works of charity.[60] They comforted in their last hours those condemned to death and saw to their burial; they staffed hospitals, cared for the ill, and sheltered pilgrims; they distributed food to the poor, supported widows, orphans and foundlings, provided dowries for needy girls, and buried the indigent. Many restricted their charitable activities to their own members, providing a kind of social insurance for the less well

[57] "Ultimamente non trovando altro modo come a consiglia il popolo si potesse radunare, il dì dopo la natività di Cristo, per consuetudine d'una compagnia degli accomandati di Madonna santa Maria, s'accolsono avvisatamente molti buoni popolani in sancta Maria Maggiore, e ivi consigliarono di volere avere capo di popolo: e di concordia in quello stante elessono Giovanni Cerroni." Matteo Villani, *Cronica*, ed. Francesco Gherardi Dragomanni (Florence: S. Coen, 1846), vol. 1, p. 173.

[58] Lorenzo Polizzotto, "Confraternities, conventicles, and political dissent: The case of the Savonarolan 'Capi rossi'," in *Politica e vita religiosa a Firenze tra '300 e '500, Memorie domenicane*, n.s., 16 (1985): 235–283.

[59] Giuseppe Mira, "Primi sondaggi su taluni aspetti economico-finanziari delle Confraternite dei Disciplinati," in *Risultati e prospettive*, pp. 229–260, remains the only general treatment of medieval confraternities in economic terms, and studies of the economic activities of individual confraternities are rare. For one good example, an examination of an account book of the confraternity of Sant'Antonio di Padova, see Beatrice Varanini, "Spunti per una indagine sull'economia della confraternita (Anni 1484–1488)," in *Liturgia, pietà, e ministeri al Santo* (Vicenza: Neri Pozza, 1978), pp. 235–243. Banker, *Death in the Community*, also uses financial records to treat the economic activities of the confraternities in Borgo San Sepolcro.

[60] Luciano Orioli, *Le confraternite medievali e il problema della povertà: Lo statuto della compagnia di Santa Maria Vergine e di San Zenobio di Firenze nel secolo XIV* (Rome: Edizioni di Storia e Letteratura, 1984).

off among them; others aided any needy person. Some tried to prop up elites suffering the unpleasant effects of downward mobility, giving money to the *poveri vergognosi*—impoverished persons of good background who were too proud to beg.[61] All these activities demanded considerable sums. In meeting their expenses, the confraternities depended on income from ordinary sources, such as membership fees and revenue from the confraternal patrimony, and from extraordinary sources: fines, special offerings of members, grants on the part of public authorities, and especially bequests—the obligatory bequests of members and the voluntary bequests of both members and non-members. Many confraternities amassed large endowments, though some, like the Florentine Compagnia de' Buonomini di San Martino, had a policy of maintaining no capital, and immediately sold any property received in gift or bequest and distributed the proceeds.[62] The Buonomini's reputation for giving away all they were given won them an impressive flow of donations. They also received communal encouragement and support derived from tax revenues, and operated for a while as a kind of semipublic charity through which the commune channeled charitable subventions, much as Or San Michele had done in the mid-fourteenth century.

Confraternities were also influential cultural institutions. They built and decorated oratories and chapels, the most spectacular of which belonged to the *scuole grandi* of Venice, the city's largest and wealthiest confraternities. The Scuola di San Rocco spent so much on its lavishly appointed hall, with its gilded ceiling and paintings by Tintoretto, that one critic charged it with neglecting its duty to care for Christ's poor.[63] They organized elaborate processions and staged dramatic performances; the Compagnia de' Magi put on some of the most striking theatrical productions in Florence, and in 1425 the

[61] Richard C. Trexler, "Charity and the Defense of Urban Elites in the Italian Communes," in *The Rich, the Well Born, and the Powerful*, ed. Frederic Cople Jaher (Urbana: University of Illinois Press, 1973), pp. 64–109; Amleto Spicciani, "The 'Poveri vergognosi' in Fifteenth-Century Florence: The First Thirty Years' Activity of the Buonomini di S. Martino," in *Aspects of Poverty in Early Modern Europe*, ed. Thomas Riis (Stuttgart: Klett-Cotta, 1981), pp. 119–182.

[62] Trexler, "Charity and the Defense of Urban Elites," pp. 95–98.

[63] Brian Pullan, *Rich and Poor in Renaissance Venice: The Social Institutions of a Catholic State, to 1620* (Cambridge: Harvard University Press, 1971), pp. 130–131. On art and the Venetian *scuole*, see *Le scuole di Venezia*, ed. Terisio Pignatti (Milan: Electa, 1981), and William Brooks Wurthmann, "The *Scuole Grandi* and Venetian Art, 1260–c. 1500," Ph.D. dissertation, University of Chicago, 1975.

Compagnia di Sant'Agnese spent 61 percent of its annual budget on its production of an Ascension play.[64] Members of confraternities wrote and sang vernacular hymns; indeed, some groups even hired professional singers in order to be sure of putting on a first-rate show.[65] They also invited leading men of letters to deliver sermons: Donato Acciaiuoli, Cristoforo Landino, and Alamanno Rinuccini gave sermons before the prestigious Confraternity of the Bigallo in Florence, and Acciaiuoli, Landino, and other humanists of the Medici circle preached to the Compagnia de' Magi.[66]

But these social, political, economic, and cultural functions were all secondary to the confraternities' essential, spiritual purpose. They were the institutional means par excellence by which laymen participated in religious life on an equal footing with clerics. While many confraternities carefully preserved their ties to the mendicant or monastic orders that had given birth to them, other confraternities that originally had met under the supervision of religious orders and in quarters provided by those orders quickly established their independence and moved into meeting places of their own construction.[67]

---

[64] Rab Hatfield, "The Compagnia de' Magi," *Journal of the Warburg and Courtauld Institutes*, 33 (1970): 107–161; Cyrilla Barr, "A Renaissance Artist in the Service of a Singing Confraternity," in *Life and Death in Fifteenth-Century Florence*, ed. Marcel Tetel, Ronald G. Witt, and Rona Goffen (Durham: Duke University Press, 1989), p. 106.

[65] Sbriziolo, "Per la storia delle confraternite veneziane: Le scuole dei Battuti," pp. 757–760. On the musical performances of lay confraternities, see Cyrilla Barr, *The Monophonic Lauda and the Lay Religious Confraternities of Tuscany and Umbria in the Late Middle Ages*, Early Drama, Art, and Music Monograph Series, 10 (Kalamazoo: Medieval Institute Publications, 1988), and Blake Wilson, *Music and Merchants: The Laudesi Companies of Republican Florence* (New York: Oxford University Press, 1992). In 1590, the Scuola di San Marco in Venice spent more on musicians than it gave to paupers in almshouses—the sort of practice that had earned the Scuola di San Rocco a stinging rebuke in 1553: Pullan, *Rich and Poor in Renaissance Venice*, pp. 127 and 189.

[66] Hatfield, "The Compagnia de' Magi"; Marvin B. Becker, "Aspects of Lay Piety in Early Renaissance Florence," in Trinkhaus, *The Pursuit of Holiness*, pp. 190–195; Paul Oskar Kristeller, "Lay Religious Traditions and Florentine Platonism," in his *Studies in Renaissance Thought and Letters* (Rome: Edizioni di Storia e Letteratura, 1956), pp. 99–122; Ronald F. E. Weissman, "Sacred Eloquence: Humanist Preaching and Lay Piety in Renaissance Florence," in Verdon and Henderson, *Christianity and the Renaissance*, pp. 250–271.

[67] It may well be that ownership of a meeting place was connected with the devotional orientation of the confraternity. All seven of the flagellant confraternities of Cortona owned an oratory or a *domus* that could serve as a meeting place, while the *laudesi* confraternities, none of which owned an oratory, were all affili-

They thus ceased to be clients of ecclesiastical patrons and became instead patrons of ecclesiastical clients. They hired clerics to say mass or preach, and they sought episcopal or papal approval of their devotions mainly in order to win indulgences and so augment the spiritual rewards of their activities. The Paduan confraternity of San Giovanni Evangelista was typical of these autonomous organizations.[68] This confraternity, made up largely of artisans, was dedicated to the burial of those condemned to death, to the maintenance of the Ospedale del Camposanto, and to the practice of flagellation. Throughout the fifteenth century it showed no tie with any religious order; it was an independent lay association, assisted by a chaplain hired from among the secular clergy. It received some support from the town government, which recognized that its modest financial resources were insufficient to allow it to perform its worthy charitable tasks.

When a confraternity chose to maintain its ties to a monastic institution, the relationship could be stormy. From 1260 at the latest, and perhaps as early as 1224, a lay confraternity was associated with the Benedictine monastery of San Giovanni Battista del Venda, located in the Euganean hills not far from Padua.[69] Twice a year, on the feast of the nativity of John the Baptist on June 24 and of his beheading on August 29, the men and women of the confraternity climbed up the Venda from Padua and held their celebrations in a house next to the monastery. These celebrations apparently included throngs of people not formally connected with the confraternity, who joined in revelry which lasted all night. The only thing that kept these confraternal celebrations from provoking the ire of the monks was the dismal condition of the monastic community: the stable group of nine or ten monks in the first half of the fourteenth century had been reduced in the wake of the Black Death to three monks in 1351 and a solitary one by 1363. The building itself was in disrepair, and this scene of material and spiritual desolation could hardly have been greatly disturbed by the confraternity's revels. In 1380, however, what was left of the

---

ated with various churches. Archivio Storico del Comune di Cortona, C. 7: Estimo dei beni ecclesiastici, fols. 192–206.

[68] Giuseppina De Sandre Gasparini, "La confraternita di S. Giovanni Evangelista della Morte in Padova e una 'riforma' ispirata dal vescovo Pietro Barozzi (1502)," in *Miscellanea Gilles Gérard Meersseman*, pp. 765–815.

[69] Paolo Sambin, "Il monastero di S. Giovanni Battista del Venda dalle origini alla riforma olivetana e la omonima confraternita," in his *Ricerche di storia monastica medievale* (Padua: Antenore, 1959).

monastery was turned over to the reformed congregation of Monte Oliveto, and the revived and newly strict monastery soon came into conflict with the confraternity over these celebrations. In the first two decades of the fifteenth century, both Bishop Pietro Marcello of Padua and Doge Tommaso Mocenigo of Venice had to intervene in order to smooth over the conflicts. But their solutions did not last: fresh complaints were registered in 1433, 1467, and 1469, as the confraternity stubbornly refused to either relinquish its traditional gathering place or restrain its festivities there.

Relations with the secular clergy could be prickly as well, particularly when the confraternities arrogated to themselves some of the rights normally assigned to the parish church. In 1401, members of a flagellant confraternity in Verona obtained from Boniface IX permission to celebrate mass on Sundays and feast days at their own oratory, to select a chaplain who would preach for them and hear their confessions, and to be buried on the confraternity's premises.[70] These privileges allowed the flagellants to pursue a more active devotional life and a more demanding penitential regimen than was usual, and provided a means by which they could satisfy the religious needs that were not met by the ministrations of the parish clergy. Such ample privileges were obviously very desirable, and over the following decades they were claimed by other confraternities that wished to exercise similar control over their own devotional lives. Just as obviously, they infringed on the prerogatives of the secular clergy, which reasserted the institutional obligation that parishioners confess their sins, hear mass, take communion, and receive burial at their parish church. By 1427 the congregation of the clergy as a body, and not just individual parish priests, was taking vigorous action against the flagellant confraternities, denouncing the papal privilege as obtained under false pretenses and defending in the courts its control over the administration of the sacred. Stirred by this challenge to its liturgical and sacramental hegemony, the clergy of Verona displayed a sharpened awareness of its rights and its duties.

The confraternities, in short, were independent lay institutions, formed and directed by lay men and women for their own devotional purposes, even when clerics were admitted as members. Some of

[70] Giuseppina De Sandre Gasparini, "Confraternite e 'cura animarum' nei primi decenni del Quattrocento: I disciplinati e la parrocchia di S. Vitale in Verona," in *Pievi, parrocchie, e clero nel Veneto dal X al XV secolo*, ed. Paolo Sambin (Venice: Deputazione di Storia Patria per le Venezie, 1987), pp. 305–319.

them were more convivial than devout, like the Aretine Compagnia di Sant'Antonio, whose major expenditures were for wine for the annual feast,[71] or the Paduan confraternity of San Giovanni Battista del Venda—though even in the latter case it may be unfair to judge the group only on the basis of monastic complaints about its behavior on festive occasions. Most of them staged public events—feasts, processions, performances—only once or twice a year. They met for private devotions far more frequently. At these private meetings, the members heard mass or listened to sermons: that is, they duplicated what they normally experienced in church, but on their own terms and often with the participation of lay preachers. They also performed devotional exercises—private prayer, the singing of hymns, flagellation—according to the specific bent of the confraternity. Virtually all confraternities, however, made a practice of having their statutes read aloud to the assembled members at every meeting, or at least with some frequency.[72] In Assisi, the prior of the flagellant confraternity of Santo Stefano was required to have the fraternity's notary read and expound the statutes at least three times during his three months in office, so that no one would be ignorant of them; and this provision, like the rest of Santo Stefano's statutes, was copied two years later by the confraternity of San Lorenzo.[73] Santo Stefano's statutes needed exposition, since they were in Latin, and San Lorenzo's decision to translate them into the local vernacular when it made them its own was surely inspired by the wish to render them

[71] Archivio di Stato d'Arezzo, Compagnie religiose, II: Compagnia di S. Antonio, 11: Saldi, 1442–1458. Between December 1, 1445 and January 13, 1448, the account book records few expenditures that exceed £1. What stand out are payments of £26 s.7 d.8 "for a cask of wine that the confraternity got for the feast" (fol. 26v: January 27, 1446), £15 s.8 for "wine sold to the confraternity for the feast" (fol. 27v: January 20, 1447), and £19 "for partial payment for a cask of wine bought for the feast" (fol. 28: January 6, 1448). No other single payment for those years reaches even £7.

[72] Gilles Gérard Meersseman, "La riforma delle confraternite laicali in Italia prima del Concilio di Trento," in *Problemi di vita religiosa in Italia nel Cinquecento: Atti del Convegno di storia della chiesa in Italia* (Padua: Antenore, 1960), pp. 27–28.

[73] "Statuto della fraternita dei disciplinati di S. Stefano," ed. Enrico Menestò, in *Le fraternite medievali di Assisi: Linee storiche e testi statutari,* ed. Ugolino Nicolini, Enrico Menestò, and Francesco Santucci (Perugia: Centro di Ricerca e di Studio sul Movimento dei Disciplinati, 1989), p. 265; "Statuto della fraternita dei disciplinati di S. Lorenzo," ed. Francesco Santucci, in Nicolini, *Le fraternite medievali di Assisi,* p. 297. Stefano Brufani offers a sensitive and insightful commentary on the influential 1327 statutes of Santo Stefano in "La fraternita dei disciplinati di S. Stefano," pp. 45–86 of the same volume.

more easily intelligible to the assembled brethren. The desire to have the rules that governed their devotional assemblies written in the language they spoke drove a more general shift from Latin to the vernacular, of which San Lorenzo in Assisi was a precocious example. In Padua, for instance, at the end of the fourteenth century and the beginning of the fifteenth, confraternities ceased to write their statutes in Latin—and all of the vernacular statutes contain the stipulation that they be read aloud at regular intervals, coupled with specific penalties if this obligation is not fulfilled.[74] The goal of this practice was stated explicitly in the 1502 statutes of the confraternity of San Giovanni Evangelista della Morte: "While the statutes are being read, we wish everyone to remain silent with their heads bowed and their ears pricked up, and they should seek to understand what is read and put it into practice: we assure them that by acting in this manner they will become so familiar with the statutes that they will know them by heart just like everything else, and they will progress from virtue to virtue."[75]

The statutes thus became, in all probability, the single text most familiar to the confraternity members and the most influential in shaping their spirituality.[76] All statutes contained dry lists of rules and of election procedures, exactly calibrated penalties for infractions of the rules, and instructions for the keeping of proper records: after all, these were the formal regulations governing a religious corpora-

---

[74] *Statuti di confraternite religiose di Padova nel Medio Evo*, ed. Giuseppina De Sandre Gasparini (Padua: Istituto per la Storia Ecclesiastica Padovana, 1974), p. xxiii. A typical example is rubric 26 of the 1392 statutes of the confraternity of S. Nicola da Tolentino, on pp. 251–252: "We also decree and require that the present stewards and any future ones must have the notary of the said confraternity read the confraternity's statutes and rules at the general assembly, so that the brethren of the said confraternity may be familiar with all the things they must do for the salvation of their souls. And this must be done throughout their term of office, on pain of the sacrament and a fine of s.60."

[75] De Sandre Gasparini, *Statuti di confraternite religiose di Padova*, p. 206: "Et mentre che se lezerano, volemo che tuti stiano in silentio cum el capo basso et le rechie drette e cerchino de intender quello firà lecto et de meterlo in practica: facendo in questo modo, li promettemo che se li farano familiari, in modo che li haverano a memoria chussì chomo ogni altra chossa, et anderano de virtù in virtù."

[76] One sign of how familiar they were was the appearance of parodies such as Machiavelli's *Capitoli per una compagnia di piacere*: Niccolò Machiavelli, *Il teatro e tutti gli scritti letterari*, ed. Franco Gaeta (Milan: Feltrinelli, 1965), pp. 201–205. However, for some reservations about the view that statutes were the primary force in shaping confraternal spirituality, see Roberto Rusconi, "Pratica cultuale ed istruzione religiosa nelle confraternite italiane del tardo Medio Evo: 'Libri da compagnia' e libri di pietà," in *Le mouvement confraternel au Moyen Age*, pp. 140, 148.

tion. But they often took the trouble to explain the reasons for the rules and evoke the spirit in which they should be observed. This was particularly true of confraternities founded or reformed in the late fourteenth and fifteenth centuries, when many sets of statutes came to resemble little devotional tracts—and in the process became too long to be read in their entirety at a single meeting, which was why the Paduan confraternity of San Giovanni Evangelista della Morte stipulated that its statutes be read in such a manner that in the course of a year they would be read through at least four times.[77] The confraternal statutes propounded to their members the practical elaboration of a moral theology of prayer, penitence, and good works. Those of the Battuti di San Domenico in Bologna, redacted September 19, 1443, exhorted the brethren to fulfill the duties incumbent on them as sober citizens and good Christians:

> Because we are men of the world and have charge of goods and families, we cannot always remain busy in the service of God like monks. Nonetheless, we should call our Lord to mind in the morning and the evening and at mealtime. For Solomon says: "Mane semina semen tuum et vespere non cesset manus tua, quia nescis quid magis oriatur, hoc aut illud, et si utrumque simul melius erit;" that is, in the morning when you rise from bed, begin to perform good works, and in the evening do not omit to perform some good works before you go to bed, for you do not know whether what you did in the morning was acceptable to God, and so therefore do good in the evening, and if both the one and the other are received by God, so much the better for your soul.
>
> We desire, therefore, dearest brethren, that when you rise in the morning you raise your mind to God and devoutly make the sign of the holy cross and say a Pater noster and an Ave Maria with the lesser Credo, fixing your mind on not offending God in your neighbor and on wishing to refer to His honor and glory every good thing that may happen to you that day, and pray Him that He may give you that grace. You should also do this same thing in the evening before you go to bed, being sorrowful, beating your breast, and lamenting for every evil thought, evil word, and evil deed done that

[77] De Sandre Gasparini, *Statuti di confraternite religiose di Padova*, p. 206.

day against God and your neighbor, asking for His forgiveness and determining to do better from now on than in the past.[78]

This text recognized that laymen lived in different circumstances and faced different social obligations than monks, and it accordingly attempted to define a manner of religious life for laymen as laymen. It insisted on the social virtues of charity and humility, and called for regular self-scrutiny to see that those virtues were being practiced. It also enjoined frequent recitation of simple prayers and of a basic profession of faith, which it assumed the brethren would know. The Perugian Compagnia di San Tommaso d'Aquino similarly asked its members to recite the Our Father and Hail Mary eighteen times a day, distributed over the seven canonical hours of worship, and stipulated that they all learn the Ten Commandments and the Apostles' Creed; the prior was charged with teaching the brethren these elements of the faith, and to make his catechetical task easier, the constitutions of the fraternity provided doggerel synopses of the commandments in both Latin and the vernacular.[79]

This rare reference to a formal, if fairly rudimentary catechesis conducted within a confraternity highlights the role of these groups in religious instruction, which went far beyond the regular iteration of the confraternal statutes. Their devotional activities impelled the confraternities to acquire and employ a variety of religious writings— psalters, hymnals, liturgical texts, instructions for ritual celebrations, and handbooks for those involved in comforting the dying—which could constitute substantial libraries. With the advent of printing, confraternities began to sponsor the reproduction of these devotional works in inexpensive pamphlets of a few leaves, often illustrated with woodcuts and designed for wide distribution.[80] Through the written word as well as their ritual performances, confraternities assisted in the circulation of religious messages.

[78] Meersseman, *Ordo fraternitatis*, p. 671.

[79] Olga Marinelli, *La Compagnia di San Tommaso d'Aquino di Perugia*, Temi e testi, 8 (Rome: Edizioni di Storia e Letteratura, 1960), pp. 47–48: "Volemo che ciaschuno de la Chompagnia inpare lo Credo de li doddicie Apostoglie e ancho li diecie chomandamente de la leggie de Dio. E volemo ch'el priore sia hobligato de farle inparare a tute lo Credo e li chomandamente e acioché almancho s'enparano per praticha." For the specified hours of prayer, see p. 49.

[80] Rusconi, "Pratica cultuale ed istruzione religiosa," pp. 133–153.

Popular Devotional Movements

Many of these confraternities grew out of the devotional movements that punctuated the history of late medieval Italy. The most
dramatic and influential, that of the flagellants or Disciplinati of 1260,
was sparked by a hermit, Fra Raniero Fasani of Perugia.[81] For eighteen years, according to his legend, Raniero practiced the penitential
exercise of self-flagellation alone in his cell. Finally, an obscure vision, interpreted for him by his patron saint, brought to Raniero a
warning and a promise. Because of the innumerable sins of humanity—in particular sodomy, usury, and heresy—God wished to destroy the world; but the Virgin Mary was willing to intercede with
her son, if men showed their repentance. Raniero's private and solitary flagellation must now become public and collective.[82]

Raniero took this message, along with an unopenable letter from
the Virgin Mary which attested to his account, to Perugia. There the
bishop received him and proclaimed his message from the steps of
the communal palace, inaugurating thereby the movement of the Disciplinati. In this first, local stage of the movement, Perugians followed Raniero's lead and adopted public ritual flagellation as a penitential act. Not everyone joined in; there were onlookers as well as
actors in this spectacle. But the devotion was perceived as general:
many shops closed, feuding families sought reconciliation, and for six
weeks, from the middle of April through the month of May, the
tenor of life was transformed.

The second stage of the movement—its spread starting in October
first to Rome, then through the Po valley, and finally beyond the
Alps—was the work not of Fra Raniero, but of the anonymous flagellants who propagated the rite by their example. The devotion, rather
than the devotees, went from town to town. As it spread, the quality
of its spirituality changed in accordance with local tendencies. In

---

[81] On the flagellant movement, see Arsenio Frugoni, "Sui flagellanti del 1260,"
Bullettino dell'Istituto Storico Italiano per il Medio Evo, 75 (1963): 211–237, and *Il Movimento dei Disciplinati.*

[82] The legend of Fra Raniero is published as an appendix to Emilio Ardu, "Frater
Raynerius Faxanus de Perusio," in *Il Movimento dei Disciplinati,* pp. 93–98. The
papers in *Settimo centenario della morte di Raniero Fasani,* Atti del Convegno Storico,
Perugia 7–8 dicembre 1981 (Perugia: Centro di Ricerca e di Studio sul Movimento
dei Disciplinati, 1984) shed light on the Perugian setting, but have little to say
about Fra Raniero himself.

Italy, the songs of the Disciplinati expressed a devotion to the merciful Virgin who protects mankind from divine wrath, whereas in Germany the emphasis was passional and flagellation was interpreted as an imitation of the sufferings of Christ. In much of Italy the secular and religious authorities supported and participated in the devotion, while in Germany it was above all the poor who tried thus to work out their own salvation, in despite of opposition from the ecclesiastical and political hierarchy.[83]

The Disciplinati did not vanish after their initial dramatic sweep through Italy. Hundreds of flagellant confraternities were founded, though connections between the movement and the confraternities remain vague. In most cases the confraternities appeared long after the movement had passed, fruit more of the memory of that flamboyant rite than of immediate fervor.[84] It was these confraternities, which engaged in regular and frequent meetings in the privacy of their own chapels and in less frequent public processions, that firmly established the flagellation of devout laymen as the premier form of public penitence, ready to be employed whenever disaster threatened the community or an apocalyptic preacher stirred religious enthusiasm.

For instance, flagellation played a part in the "pilgrimage" to Rome led by Venturino da Bergamo in 1335.[85] Venturino, a Dominican, began preaching a penitential devotion at Bergamo late in 1334; early the following year he extended his preaching into the countryside. He and an estimated 3,000 followers left Bergamo in early February, on a circuitous pilgrimage to Rome. They passed by Milan, Lodi, Cre-

[83] Public flagellation seems to have had different ecclesio-political meanings in Germany and in Italy. On fourteenth-century flagellants in Germany, see Richard Kieckhefer, "Radical Tendencies in the Flagellant Movement of the Mid-Fourteenth Century," *Journal of Medieval and Renaissance Studies*, 4 (1974): 157–176. Etienne Delaruelle compared the flagellant processions in the Low Countries in 1349 with the Bianchi processions of 1399 in "Les grandes processions de pénitents de 1349 et 1399," in *Il Movimento dei Disciplinati*, pp. 109–145, and reflected on why the flagellants of 1349 did not spread from Germany and the Low Countries to France in "Pourquoi n'y eut-il pas de flagellants en France en 1349?" in *Risultati e prospettive*, pp. 292–304; both articles are reprinted in Delaruelle, *La piété populaire*, pp. 277–327.

[84] Mario Fanti, *Gli inizi del movimento dei Disciplinati a Bologna e la Confraternita di Santa Maria della Vita*, Quaderni del Centro di documentazione sul movimento dei Disciplinati, 8 (Perugia: Centro di Documentazione sul Movimento dei Disciplinati, 1969).

[85] Clara Gennaro, "Venturino da Bergamo e la 'peregrinatio' romana del 1335," in *Studi sul Medioevo cristiano offerti a Raffaello Morghen* (Rome: Istituto Storico Italiano per il Medio Evo, 1974), pp. 375–406.

mona, Mantua, Ferrara, Bologna, Florence, Siena, Orvieto, and Viterbo before arriving at Rome on March 21. Their numbers supposedly increased en route to about 10,000, though good estimates of
the number of people involved were rendered difficult by their practice of traveling in small groups in order to facilitate provisioning and
avoid conflicts with local authorities. Venturino and his followers
were only partly successful in this. Several cities closed their gates to
them, although the government of Milan did allow its citizens to go
outside the city walls to hear him preach, and the government of
Ferrara permitted Venturino alone, without his followers, to enter the
city. But elsewhere, as in Cremona, Bologna, and Florence, they were
received with enthusiasm.

Venturino devised for his followers distinctive clothing, closely
modeled on the Dominican robes but enriched with symbolic insignia. Over white tunics they wore mantles of dark purple or black, the
color of penitence. Their hoods were marked with the tau cross—the
sign of penitence, according to Venturino, though this symbol was
not clearly understood by all witnesses. The fronts of their habits
bore on the left breast a white dove with three olive leaves in its
beak, and on the right a red and white cross. For Venturino's followers as for the fraternities of penitents, donning these robes was
the exterior sign of their interior conversion; it marked their separation from civic life and assumption of a quasi-clerical status.[86] To sig-
nify their refusal of the civic duty to bear arms and rejection of secular calls to violence, they used no iron tips on their pilgrim staffs, and
each small party marched behind a cross crying "peace and mercy."

At first Venturino enjoyed the support of his order. He stayed in
Dominican houses wherever he went. His constant companion, Niccolò da Faenza, was also a Dominican. At least six other Dominicans
joined him, with the permission of their provincials. His followers'
dress, as we have seen, was very similar to the Dominican habit. And
Venturino's pilgrims practiced flagellation in the privacy of Dominican churches, before the altar, rather than in the streets and public
squares.

This changed after Venturino's arrival in Rome. He began his usual
round of preaching, including delivering a sermon in the Cam-
pidoglio before the Roman senate. Here, apparently, he declared that

---

[86] On the change of dress ("mutatio habitus") of the penitents as an indicator of
their change of status, see Meersseman, *Ordo fraternitatis*, pp. 283–286.

no one could be a worthy pope unless he resided in Rome and sat upon the throne of St. Peter.[87] Perhaps he was unnerved at the reaction to this remark, with its evident challenge to the legitimacy of the Avignon papacy, or by the untoward attention that his presence and preaching were attracting in this Lenten season. At any rate, he suddenly fled Rome on Passion Sunday, less than two weeks after his arrival and even before all of his followers had managed to gather there. From this point dates the mutual separation between Venturino and his order, which was trying to preserve its autonomy from papal interference and had come to see Venturino as a liability in this struggle. He did not ask permission of his superior, as he should have, before going to Avignon to appear before the pope. On his arrival in Avignon he stayed with the Franciscans, rather than with his fellow Dominicans—who were already moving to denounce him. One of his inquisitors was the vice-procurator of his order; and in June of 1335 the chapter general of the Dominican order, meeting in London, condemned Venturino and his pilgrimage.

The pope, too, condemned Venturino, sentencing him to perpetual exile and forbidding him to preach or to hear confession. The grounds for this sentence were twofold: Venturino's declaration that the true pope could be based only in Rome, and his creation without papal approval of a new order with new insignia. Venturino took this sentence in good grace; it does not seem that he ever seriously questioned papal authority, and indeed it was on his own initiative that he presented himself before Benedict XII in Avignon. He spent several years quietly in exile in Provence, and died while promoting a crusade against the Turks.

Another Dominican, Manfredi da Vercelli, led a movement similar to that of Venturino, though it differed in several important respects: it was smaller, longer-lived, and more extreme in its religious precepts and social implications.[88] Manfredi was a flamboyant preacher, much given to apocalyptic sermons in the manner of St. Vincent Fer-

---

[87] "Diceva che non era niuno degno papa se non stesse a Roma alla sedia di san Piero." Giovanni Villani, *Cronica* (Florence: Il Magheri, 1823), vol. 6, p. 61 (bk.XI, ch. 23).

[88] Raymond Creytens, O.P., "Manfred de Verceil O.P. et son traité contre les fraticelles," *Archivum Fratrum Praedicatorum*, 11 (1941): 173–208; Roberto Rusconi, "Fonti e documenti su Manfredi da Vercelli ed il suo movimento penitenziale," *Archivum Fratrum Praedicatorum*, 47 (1977): 51–107; and Rusconi, "Note sulla predicazione di Manfredi da Vercelli e il movimento penitenziale dei terziari manfredini," *Archivum Fratrum Praedicatorum*, 48 (1978): 93–135.

rer. He proclaimed that the Antichrist was about to come, and suggested that he might even have been born already. Since the end was so near, all marriage ties were dissolved and wives could—and should—leave their husbands to live in Manfredi's company in perpetual penitence and avid preparation for the apocalypse. Because of his advanced age, Manfredi was not widely suspected of illicit sexual relations with these women, though male kinfolk of the women complained that their estates were passing into his hands.

Manfredi began this line of preaching in Piedmont and Liguria in 1417 or 1418. Late in 1418 he moved to Lombardy, where he attracted most of his following. He and his company—400 to 1,000 people, half of them women, dressed in white tunics and black mantles like Dominican tertiaries—moved gradually southward, arriving in Florence in May 1419. He enjoyed the support of the Florentine government, and with its protection he was able to stay there for five years, despite his penchant for religious polemic. During his sojourn in Florence he was attacked by Martin V and excommunicated by Amerigo Corsini, bishop of Florence, and by Leonardo Dati, master general of the Dominicans; this second excommunication was later revoked. He studied the teachings of the Fraticelli to be better able to preach against this Franciscan sect and confute its spokesmen in debate. And he clashed repeatedly with the great Franciscan preacher Bernardino da Siena. Bernardino attacked Manfredi for his teachings about marriage and the imminent coming of the Antichrist; Manfredi in turn accused Bernardino of idolatry for his devotion to the name of Jesus and labeled him the messenger of the Antichrist. Finally, late in 1424, Manfredi was summoned to Rome, perhaps at the instigation of Bernardino and his partisans, perhaps because of alarm at reports that his followers believed him to be the angelic pope.[89]

Manfredi announced his pleasure at going to Rome: there martyrdom awaited him and he would witness the final triumph over the Antichrist. But his fate was not so dramatic. He seems to have spent his years in Rome quietly, with no particular following. He composed a treatise against the Fraticelli, the fruit of his work in Florence. He has been suspected of promoting the citation before the papal court of his old enemy, Bernardino da Siena, in 1427. After that year noth-

---

[89] On the history of such attitudes and expectations, see Bernard McGinn, "Angel Pope and Papal Antichrist," *Church History*, 47 (1978): 155–173.

ing further is heard of him, though Antonino Pierozzi says he did not die until the pontificate of Eugenius IV (1431–1447).

Unlike these other movements, the Bianchi of 1399 had no charismatic leader to provide them with a visionary interpretation of the Christian tradition and no permanent core group of disciples to enact that vision in exemplary fashion for all to imitate. As a result, they were less distinctive, peculiar, or innovative. They wore simple white robes, rather than the elaborately symbolic outfits of Venturino's followers. They introduced no new devotional practice, as did Raniero Fasani's flagellants. They espoused no eschatological message calling for the loosing of ordinary social bonds, as did Manfredi's supporters. They were generally indifferent to theological issues, and so presented no ideological challenge to orthodoxy.

The Bianchi introduced no new devotional practices, but rather organized themselves around what was already familiar to them: the traditional institutions and practices of their religious culture, which I have tried to describe in this chapter. They ate a Lenten diet and sang responsively and prayed in unison, all common devotional practices. They arranged themselves like the secular church on parade, organizing their processions by parishes, with the banner of the parish at the head of each group of parishioners and the local bishop at the head of them all. They undertook a typical novena, dedicating themselves to nine days of devotions. During their nine days on the road they observed the same devotional practices that they did at home: they visited churches, heard mass, and listened to sermons. When they returned home, they deposited the crucifixes they had carried in chapels to be the objects of local cults like so many others, and they founded confraternities to tend those cults. Their one distinctive feature—and the one that the confraternities tried to preserve—was the dress they adopted: the white robes that gave the movement its name. But even this was only mildly distinctive, for white robes were also worn by confraternities that had nothing to do with the movement of the Bianchi. And without some distinguishing trait that could be cherished and preserved, the movement of the Bianchi was almost certain to vanish with hardly a trace in a culture that already had a plenitude of religious institutions.

The Bianchi's reliance on already extant institutions and practices thus vitiated attempts to perpetuate their devotional movement.[90] But

[90] On these attempts, see below, Chapter 6.

by indicating in their behavior which of the vast repertoire of devotional forms were most immediately meaningful to them, the Bianchi inadvertently provided the historian of religious life with an exceptionally clear picture of the popular religious culture of late medieval Italy. In contrast to the oblique approach adopted by a number of recent studies, in which sex crimes are used to define the bounds of "normal" sexuality and the reverence or revulsion excited by certain exceptional individuals serves to suggest more widely shared ideals and aspirations, the mass participation in the Bianchi processions and the very ordinariness of the Bianchi's behavior afford an access to popular culture that is more direct and results that are, perhaps, more persuasive.[91] And unlike the mosaic of this chapter, built with discrete tesserae culled from scattered places and times, the picture traced by the Bianchi is by its nature an integrated one, one which allows us to see in clear outline the contours of medieval religious culture at a given moment, along with the distinctive shading that that culture acquired in particular locales.

[91] I have in mind such studies as Guido Ruggiero, *The Boundaries of Eros: Sex Crime and Sexuality in Renaissance Venice* (Oxford: Oxford University Press, 1985), and Judith C. Brown, *Immodest Acts: The Life of a Lesbian Nun in Renaissance Italy* (Oxford: Oxford University Press, 1986).

CHAPTER TWO

THE ORIGINS OF THE BIANCHI

A new light has dawned
New grace and new life,
   A new dress and new habit.
              —from a devotional song of the Bianchi

THE PEASANT HAD barely resumed his labors after his midday meal when he was accosted by a young pilgrim who asked him for bread. He regretfully told the stranger that he had just lunched on what little he had. However, at the pilgrim's insistence, he searched in his bag, where to his surprise he found three pieces of bread. The pilgrim, instead of accepting the bread he had requested, told the peasant to take the three pieces and throw them into the spring at the foot of a tree nearby. The peasant protested that he had worked these fields for twenty years and knew that there was no spring for more than a mile. But when he considered how he had found three pieces of bread in a bag which he knew was empty, he stopped objecting and set off for the tree. There he found not only the promised spring, but also a weeping woman dressed all in white. She tried to dissuade the peasant from his mission, twice sending him back to the pilgrim. Her first message to the pilgrim was simply that a woman did not want him to do this thing; her second, that his mother forbade it. But the pilgrim insisted, and he sent the peasant back to the spring a second time and a third. Finally the peasant threw one of the pieces of bread past the woman, who tried to block his way, and into the spring.

As soon as he had done this, the woman broke down and disclosed to the peasant the true meaning of this strange drama in

Epigraph: Giovanni Sercambi, *Croniche,* ed. Salvatore Bongi, Fonti per la storia d'Italia, vols. 19–21 (Rome: Istituto Storico Italiano, 1892), vol. 2, p. 300.

43

which he had become involved. She was the Virgin Mary and the noble young pilgrim was her son Jesus, who was infuriated at the sinfulness of the world and wished to destroy it despite her pleas for mercy. The peasant had just helped to enact this doom: because he had thrown one piece of bread into the spring, one third of humankind must perish; if he had cast in all three pieces, the entire world would have been destroyed.

The peasant, horrified at this revelation, fell to his knees and asked Mary what could be done. She replied that there was no remedy to be found,

> unless you go from city to city, and from town to town, and from village to village, and preach this event and by preaching move all of Christendom to follow this pattern: let every man, woman, and child, priests and friars and people of all sorts dress themselves in white linen as I am dressed, or like the Flagellants, with head covered and with a red cross on the heads of the women and on the shoulders of the men, and beat themselves, and go for nine days in procession with a crucifix carried before them, beating themselves and crying "misericordia, misericordia, misericordia, pace, pace, pace" as loudly as they can. And they must not sleep in a walled town or remove their robes for these nine days, or lie in a bed; and every morning they must enter some city or town and visit at least three churches and hear the mass sung solemnly in one of them, and listen to sermons. And you must not eat meat, and on the first Sunday fast on bread and water; and go barefoot singing loudly that hymn or sequence which goes "Stabat mater dolorosa, iuxta crucem lacrimosa, dum pendebat filius" and other good hymns and prayers. All Christendom must do this for nine days and nights, and I likewise will plead with Him day and night; and perhaps Christ my son, who is full of mercy and grace, will revoke this sentence—at least for those who do all this. Go and proclaim this through all the land and do what I have told you. Do it with good heart and good conscience, lamenting and crying day and night through every city, town, and village, with all of Christendom as I told you, and repent and forgive each other and make peace and concord.

So that the peasant might be believed and his story accepted, the Virgin Mary gently laid her hand on his cheek and left its outline there. And he then returned to the town and announced what he had seen, done, and learned, gathering at first a small group of disciples and then an infinite number of followers.

This is the story of the origin of the Bianchi. The Bianchi sang a versified form of it in their processions; their preachers told it when they introduced the devotion to a new town.[1] Chroniclers learned it from these sources and recorded it along with the other particulars of this dramatic outburst of devotion. Luca Dominici of Pistoia (from whom I have paraphrased my version) and Giovanni Sercambi of Lucca give long and detailed accounts that differ only slightly, while other chroniclers report it more summarily.[2] Giovanni Conversini of Ravenna simply alludes to the story, as if it were already familiar to all of his readers.[3]

The story appears to fit the pattern of an origin legend: it explains and justifies the movement by providing it with a sacred paradigm, and details the practices which the Bianchi are to follow. They must don white robes marked with a red cross and go in procession with a crucifix at their head, beating themselves and crying for peace and mercy; they must follow a Lenten diet, visit three churches and hear mass daily; they must maintain these devotions for nine days; and they must not remove their robes or sleep in a bed or within a walled town for the duration of the procession. For the most part, the Bianchi adhered to this behavioral charter. The behavior prescribed by the origin story generally agrees with their actions as described by diarists, chroniclers, and other contemporary observers. However, certain significant contrasts can be noted between the behavior prescribed by the origin story and that described by the chroniclers. Flagellation is emphasized in the origin story but almost absent from accounts of the Bianchi; peacemaking appears as an afterthought in Mary's list of injunctions, but is among the most prominent of the Bianchi's described activities. The origin story seems calculated to establish the credentials of the peasant who receives the revelation— the charismatic leader of lower-class origin who wears on his face the physical sign of divine election. Norman Cohn has stressed the role

---

[1] One such song is "Venne Gesù a colui," in Le Laude dei Bianchi, ed. Bernard Toscani (Florence: Libreria Editrice Fiorentina, 1979), pp. 69–81; another is "Del segno ch'è aparito," in Giovanni Sercambi, Croniche, ed. Salvatore Bongi (Rome, Instituto Storico Italiano, 1892), vol. 2, pp. 294–300.

[2] Luca Dominici, Cronaca della venuta dei Bianchi e della moria, 1399–1400, ed. Giovan Carlo Gigliotti (Pistoia: Alberto Pacinotti, 1933), pp. 50–55; Sercambi, Croniche, pp. 291–294.

[3] Giovanni Conversini da Ravenna, La processione dei Bianchi nella città di Padova (1399), ed. and trans. Libia and Dino Cortese (Padua: Centro Studi Antoniani, 1978), p. 17. Giovanni Conversini was not at all convinced of the veracity of this story, which he considered as implausible as it was familiar.

of this sort of charismatic leader, who is often a renegade cleric, in the millenarian movements of the Middle Ages.[4] Yet this central figure of the origin legend never makes an appearance in the Bianchi processions. The few mentions of him are all tentative and dubious; no one claims to have actually seen this mysterious peasant.

Even when the Bianchi are described as performing the actions prescribed by the origin story, the manner in which they perform them differs from the tone of the paradigmatic model. That model sanctions a movement of penitential character and eschatological orientation, in which the harsh ascesis of flagellation and fasting offers a means of escaping from imminent destruction. But in their actions the Bianchi eschew ascetic practices. Flagellation is virtually absent, and fasting is practiced in moderation. They stress devotion rather than penitence, practical solutions to the problems of this world rather than personal preparation to enter the next.[5]

Such disparities between mythic paradigm and ritual enactment have received little attention from historians, who have tended to see myth and ritual as perfectly congruous, and both of them as congruous with the society that produces them.[6] But as Jonathan Z. Smith has recently pointed out, "ritual is incongruent with the way things are or are likely to be, for contingency, variability and accidentality have been factored out. . . . Ritual gains its force where incongruency is perceived."[7] In the case of the Bianchi, we are confronted with a double incongruency: between their mythic mandate and its ritual performance, and between the ritualized harmony of the processions and ordinary social relations. The two incongruencies call for different explanations, though they yield the same insight.

The origin story appears to be a pastiche of commonplace elements. The descriptions of Jesus as pilgrim and Mary as sorrowful and compassionate intercessor are perfectly ordinary, and the triple repetition of actions is a stock motif in European folklore. What we have here, apparently, is a more or less free-floating legend which was appropriated by the Bianchi and used to provide plausible super-

---

[4] Norman Cohn, *The Pursuit of the Millennium*, revised edition (New York: Oxford University Press, 1970).

[5] I will return to the question of the spirituality of the Bianchi in Chapter 4.

[6] Edward Muir, *Civic Ritual in Renaissance Venice* (Princeton: Princeton University Press, 1981), is one widely praised example of this approach.

[7] Jonathan Z. Smith, "The Bare Facts of Ritual," *History of Religion*, 20 (1980–1981): 127, 125. This essay is reprinted in revised form in Smith, *Imagining Religion: From Babylon to Jonestown* (Chicago: University of Chicago Press, 1982), pp. 53–65.

natural sanction for the movement and a convenient explanation of its ritual practices.[8] Such appropriation of texts, tales, and motifs occurred regularly, and it just as regularly produced odd disparities which testified to derivation from another context. Thus, for example, when two flagellant confraternities of Assisi patterned their statutes on those of the earlier confraternity of St. Stephen, they even retained Stephen's epithet "protomartyr"—applying it inaptly to their own patrons, St. Lawrence and St. Antoninus.[9] We should no more be disturbed than were the Bianchi by the disparities between the conventional story they appropriated and the ritual actions they performed. We can, however, use these disparities as a way of identifying certain features of the Bianchi movement as particularly characteristic of it, for those were the features that did not fit perfectly within the conventional mold of the story. By the end of the fourteenth century, the origin story suggests, penitential flagellation was commonly held to be a normative practice of religious movements; the behavior of the Bianchi, which substituted peacemaking for flagellation, indicates that strife and its elimination lay at the center of the Bianchi movement.

The Longing for Blessed Peace

Pacification was urgently needed and fervently desired, for everyday life was intensely competitive and often violent. The incongruency between ordinary social relations and the ritualized harmony of the Bianchi processions focused attention on the gap between the way things were and the way they ought to be. The Bianchi forced people to reflect on how they treated their neighbors, on their readiness to yield to sudden anger and cling to enduring hatreds. At the same time, they demonstrated that hatred and violence could be re-

[8] Robert E. Lerner, *The Powers of Prophecy: The Cedar of Lebanon Vision from the Mongol Onslaught to the Dawn of the Enlightenment* (Berkeley and Los Angeles: University of California Press, 1983), traces the repeated appropriation of one short text.

[9] Stefano Brufani, *La vita religiosa in Assisi dal 1316 al 1367* (Assisi: Porziuncola, 1982), p. 92; *Le fraternite medievali di Assisi: Linee storiche e testi statutari*, ed. Ugolino Nicolini, Enrico Menestò, and Francesco Santucci (Perugia: Centro di Ricerca e di Studio sul Movimento dei Disciplinati, 1989), pp. 256, 290, and 380.

nounced. They called on people to close the gap between the normal and the normative, quotidian strife and ritual harmony. In their words and their deeds, the Bianchi invited imitation. Their example proclaimed that it was possible to transform society and enact a holy peace.

The Bianchi were far from the first group to apply religious sanctions to the pacification of society. Starting around 990, diocesan synods and lay associations tried to limit violence and promote what they called the Peace of God.[10] Peace was also promoted by wandering preachers like that Fra Alberto da Mantova who in 1207 brought an end to ninety-five mortal feuds in Faenza, twenty-eight in Imola, and others in Bertinoro, Forlimpopoli, and elsewhere in northern Italy.[11] The work of peacemaking became something of a specialty of the mendicant orders, starting with St. Francis himself: in August of 1222, he preached in Bologna with such force that "many factions of nobles, among whom the wild fury of old hatreds had caused much bloodshed, were in fact peacefully reconciled."[12] In 1233 both Franciscans and Dominicans eagerly placed themselves at the head of the devotional movement known as the Alleluia; with the support of the crowds of devotees, they reconciled enemies, made peace between warring cities, and called for the release of prisoners, the restitution of usurious profits, and the moral reform of society. To institutionalize and perpetuate these reforms, they took a leading part in the revision of the statutes of Parma, Bologna, Vercelli, and other towns of the Po valley in 1233 and 1234.[13]

[10] In addition to the classic pages of Marc Bloch, *Feudal Society*, trans. L. A. Manyon (Chicago: University of Chicago Press, 1961), pp. 412–420, and Georges Duby, "Laity and the Peace of God," in *The Chivalrous Society*, trans. Cynthia Postan (Berkeley and Los Angeles: University of California Press, 1977), pp. 123–133, see *The Peace of God: Social Violence and Religious Response around the Year 1000*, ed. Thomas Head and Richard Landes (Ithaca: Cornell University Press, 1992).

[11] *Corpus chronicorum Bononiensium*, ed. Albano Sorbelli, in *Rerum Italicarum Scriptores*, new edition (henceforth *RIS²*), 18, part 1, tome 2, p. 69, *Cronaca A*.

[12] "ut multe tribus nobilium, inter quas antiquorum inimiciciarum furor immanis multa sanguinis effusione fuerat debachatus, ad pacis consilium reducerentur." Thomas of Spalato, *Historia pontificum Salonitanorum et Spalatinorum*, ed. L. de Heinemann, *Monumenta Germaniae Historica, Scriptorum*, 29 (Hanover, 1892), p. 580. Translation from Lester K. Little, *Religious Poverty and the Profit Economy in Medieval Europe* (Ithaca: Cornell University Press, 1981), pp. 162–163.

[13] André Vauchez, "Une campagne de pacification en Lombardie autour de 1233," *Ecole Française de Rome, Mélanges d'archéologie et d'histoire*, 78 (1966): 503–549; Vito Fumagalli, "In margine all''Alleluia' del 1233," *Bullettino dell'Istituto Storico*

The friars, however, had no monopoly on the application of religious sanctions to the work of peacemaking. It was a group of Bolognese nobles who formed the lay order of the Frati Gauduti in 1260; they set themselves the task of ending the fratricidal strife between rival factions, and swore to present themselves armed only with a rod of office in the midst of any fighting that might break out.[14] And when all other efforts to pacify the Florentine Black and White Guelfs had failed, the layman Dino Compagni summoned the leaders of these factions to the church of San Giovanni and persuaded them to swear an oath of reconciliation on the holy font where they had been baptized.[15]

In the fourteenth century, such efforts at pacification became an increasingly prominent feature of religious movements.[16] The groups that gathered around Venturino da Bergamo, Giovanni Colombini, and other religious leaders all included peace as part of their programs, though what exactly each meant by peace could and did vary. Some had clear eschatological expectations, and considered peace on earth a sign and promise of the Kingdom of God. Others linked peace and penitence; for them, only true contrition and moral conversion could turn men from their long-standing enmities. In the sermons he preached in the town square of Siena in 1427, Bernardino of Siena defined interior peace as the shadow of God's peace, and freedom from sin as the necessary precondition for social pacification.[17] For many the requisite penance took the form of pilgrimage—and pilgrimage could mean war rather than peace, when it was assimilated with a crusade and the penitents fought under the sign of the cross. Others steadfastly refused to bear arms: the followers of Ven-

---

Italiano per il Medio Evo, 80 (1968): 257–272; Daniel A. Brown, "The Alleluia: A Thirteenth Century Peace Movement," Archivum Franciscanum Historicum, 81 (1988): 3–16; Augustine Thompson, Revival Preachers and Politics in Thirteenth-Century Italy: The Great Devotion of 1233 (New York: Oxford University Press, 1992).

[14] Antonio De Stefano, "Le origini dei Frati Gauduti," Archivum Romanicum, 10 (1926): 305–350, esp. p. 328.

[15] Dino Compagni, Cronica (Turin: Einaudi, 1968), p. 77.

[16] Clara Gennaro, "Movimenti religiosi e pace nel XIV secolo," in La pace nel pensiero, nella politica, negli ideali del Trecento, Convegni del Centro di studi sulla spiritualità medievale, 15 (Todi: Accademia Tudertina, 1975), pp. 93–112. On the Bianchi in particular, see Diana M. Webb, "Penitence and Peace-Making in City and Contado: The Bianchi of 1399," in The Church in Town and Countryside, ed. Derek Baker (Oxford: Basil Blackwell, 1979), pp. 243–256.

[17] Bernardino da Siena, Prediche volgari sul Campo di Siena, 1427, ed. Carlo Delcorno (Milan: Rusconi, 1989), pp. 1263, 1269.

turino took this principle so seriously that they even removed the usual metal tips from their pilgrims' staffs. Nearly all of these groups called for political and economic measures that would reduce social tensions and foster the cause of peace; they sought the release of prisoners, the repatriation of exiles, the renunciation of usury, and so on. Only the Bianchi, however, at the end of the century, made peace and the institutional means of achieving peace the core of their message. The insistence with which the call for peace recurred in their preaching and their songs is echoed in Coluccio Salutati's description of them: "With crucifix in hand, in the name of Jesus Christ and the most holy company of Bianchi they plead for peace, they pray for peace, they answer peace, and as if with one voice they all cry for peace, clamor for peace."[18]

The Bianchi's dedication to peacemaking was evident in their behavior. Virtually all of their chroniclers stressed the many peace agreements they arranged, and some also noted the specific parties to the agreements.[19] Like other religious movements, the Bianchi pressed for the release of prisoners and the repatriation of exiles as concrete signs of the abandonment of old rancor. They did their best to disarm the populace, collecting the weapons which lay too ready at hand. One witness wrote in admiration of the Bianchi of Prato: "Just think that they arranged so many peace compacts that the weapons they were given—a sword here, a knife and helmet there—could not have been carried by two mules."[20] Even their miracles served the cause of peace, stimulating the hesitant to embrace their enemies and afflicting those who refused to do so. When ser Filippo di ser Lazzaro di Giovanni Lazzerini made peace with some enemies in Lucca, his action was attributed to divine inspiration.[21] Such recon-

---

[18] "Habentes enim crucifixum in manibus per Christum Iesum et Alborum sanctissimam societatem pacem petunt, pacem orant, pacem replicant et omnes simul una voce pacem vociferant, pacem clamant." Coluccio Salutati, *Epistolario*, ed. Francesco Novati (Rome: Istituto Storico Italiano, 1891–1911), vol. 3, p. 359.

[19] For instance, Buonaccorso Pitti, *Cronica* (Bologna: Romagnoli dall'Acqua, 1905), pp. 111–112, who says that "we Pitti made peace with Antonio and Geri, sons of Giovanni Corbizi and nephews of that Matteo del Ricco who was killed in Pisa, and with Matteo, son of Paolo Corbizi; and ser Antonio di ser Chello drew up the contract."

[20] "Ragonate che feciono fare tante pacie che l'arme che fue loro donato—chi ispada, chi choltello e chi pianella—noll'arebe portate ii muli." Archivio Datini di Prato, no. 864, lett. Firenze-Barcellona, Associazione "ai veli" Francesco Datini e Domenico di Cambio, September 27, 1399. See also Dominici, *Cronaca*, pp. 91, 111.

[21] Dominici, *Cronaca*, p. 145.

ciliation of inveterate enemies was considered to be the greatest and most convincing miracle performed by the Bianchi.[22]

At times these miracles of persuasion were supplemented by threats. Accounts of the Bianchi are replete with stories of what happened to those who violated the peace of the Bianchi. To cite but one dramatic example, Giovanni Sercambi tells how one of the Bianchi, while praying in a church in Vezzano, was murdered by an enemy who seized this opportunity to strike down his unarmed foe; the murderer was immediately consumed by a miraculous fire which left nothing behind, not even a bone or some ashes.[23]

In general, the Bianchi were received most enthusiastically in those cities which were reputed to be particularly violent, such as Pistoia or Genoa. By the time of Dante and of Dino Compagni, the Pistoiese had achieved a well-deserved reputation for fratricidal passions, which they indulged despite the best efforts of their Florentine rectors to restrain them, since "the Pistoiese are by nature disagreeable, cruel, and savage men."[24] But even the Pistoiese chronicler Luca Dominici considered the Genoese truly exceptional in their propensity for violence: "To tell the truth, Genoa and its countryside were in worse shape than any city in this land; they killed each other like animals, and more than 10,000 of them have been slain. And in these circumstances, blessed be he who could instead go to the house of his enemy and make peace with him."[25] The Genoese chronicler Giorgio Stella shared this desire for a blessed respite from violence. He saw the Bianchi in these terms, and described their advent in Genoa as a sudden turning from discord and civil strife to peace and reconciliation.[26]

The movement of the Bianchi, then, satisfied a widespread desire for peace; it held out the possibility that religiously inspired harmony would replace rivalry and factional strife. But it did not spring up spontaneously in all these scattered sites, in Genoa and Pistoia, Florence and Orvieto and all the other places where people donned white

[22] Francesco di Montemarte, *Cronaca*, ed. Luigi Fumi, in *RIS²*, 15, part 5, p. 267.
[23] Sercambi, *Croniche*, p. 314.
[24] Compagni, *Cronica*, p. 74. See also Dante Alighieri, *Inferno* XXIV, 126.
[25] "In verità Genova e il contado stava peggio che città di questo paese e uccidevansi insieme come bestie; ed èvene de' morti più di X mila: e testeso e in questo punto beato colui che piuttosto poteva ire a casa del suo inimico a renderli pace." Dominici, *Cronaca*, p. 55.
[26] Giorgio Stella, *Annales Genuenses*, ed. Giovanna Petti Balbi, in *RIS²*, 17, part 2, p. 236.

robes in the pious hope of a lasting reconciliation with their neighbors. It began in one corner of the Italian peninsula, from which it spread in precise lines of diffusion.

The Bianchi in Liguria

The several versions of the origin legend all locate the revelation to the peasant in a more or less distant land: Provence, Spain, even Scotland.[27] Even the version that places it closest to Italy, that of Luca Dominici, says that this marvelous encounter happened on the other side of the mountains, in the Dauphiné.[28] While differing in the precise location, they concur in claiming that it was someplace far, far away: such events do not occur here at home.[29] Since their point is simply to set the revelation to the peasant in a strange land where strange events might plausibly occur, there is no reason to expect that these identifications of the locus of revelation are accurate; indeed, there is no evidence of Bianchi devotions in any of these other lands. The actual origins of the Bianchi must be sought in the area in which they were first reported: the mountainous hinterland of the Ligurian coast.

This was an area of fragmented political authority and persistent factional violence; Giorgio Stella identified it as a place characterized by exceptionally bitter hatred.[30] It was also an area showing signs of religious ferment, to which the tensions of the Great Schism contributed. Throughout western Europe, the rift which since 1378 had split the church provoked feelings of uneasiness among believers, and these tensions were felt unusually directly and forcefully in Liguria and Piedmont. For the most part, the rival popes kept to their own obediences and refrained from actively disputing areas to which they

[27] Sercambi, *Croniche*, p. 291, says England; the author of the *Annales Forolivienses* in *Rerum Italicarum Scriptores* (henceforth *RIS*), 22, col. 200, says Scotland; Jacopo Delaito, *Annales Estenses*, in *RIS*, 18, col. 956, says Spain. As so often, the most sensible opinion comes from Leonardo Bruni: "It's true place of origin is obscure." *Historiarum Florentini populi libri XII*, ed. Emilio Santini and Carmine di Pierro, in *RIS²*, 19, part 3, p. 278.
[28] Dominici, *Cronaca*, pp. 50–51.
[29] The accounts of miracles associated with the Bianchi also tend to place the more incredible and outlandish miracles in more distant locales. See Chapter 4.
[30] "Odiossissime erant inimicitie." Stella, *Annales Genuenses*, p. 238.

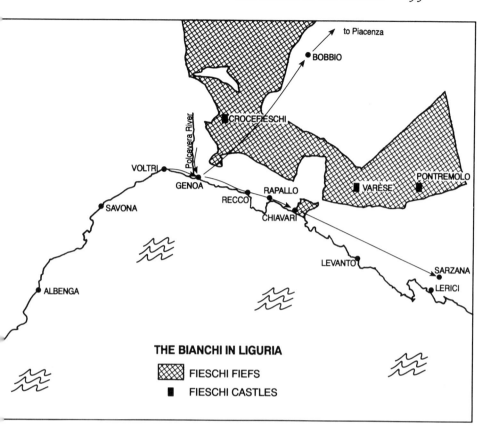

THE BIANCHI IN LIGURIA

▨ FIESCHI FIEFS

■ FIESCHI CASTLES

could lay no effective claim.[31] Liguria and Piedmont, however, formed one of the border areas between the two obediences to which both popes laid claim and accordingly appointed bishops. In some dioceses it took decades to disentangle the competing hierarchies: Ventimiglia, for instance, saw a long series of rival bishops, including one schismatic bishop appointed as late as 1420 by Benedict XIII.[32]

Even before the Schism, the church had often found its religious authority difficult to assert in the mountains. Episcopal visitations and diocesan synods were rare here, as they were elsewhere in Italy. But few other areas of the peninsula, if any, were as troubled by

---

[31] Denys Hay, *The Church in Italy in the Fifteenth Century* (Cambridge: Cambridge University Press, 1977), pp. 28–30.

[32] Girolamo Rossi, "Un vescovo scismatico della chiesa ventimigliese," *Archivio storico italiano*, ser. 5, 12 (1893): 139–148.

heresy. Heretics enjoyed the protection of the local nobility and were so bold as to invade churches and murder inquisitors with impunity. In 1365 the inquisitor Pietro di Ruffia was slain in the Franciscan friary of Susa; in 1374 his successor Antonio Pavonio was struck down as he left the church of Bricherasio.[33] With the advent of the Schism, ecclesiastical institutions decayed even further. The Dominican order, and with it inquisitorial responsibilities, was split.

Despite, or perhaps because of these troubles, the Clementine inquisitors were very active. Late in 1394 or early the following year, at Villastellone in the district of Chieri, they arrested a Carmagnolese blacksmith named Giacomo di Ristolassio. Giacomo declared himself to be a follower of a certain Fra Angelo della Marca, who dressed in a white robe and hooded tunic. He followed Fra Angelo's teachings in awaiting an imminent apocalypse, rejecting the sacraments, indulgences, and penances of the church, venerating the cross, and insisting on the personal sanctity of the true pope. He refused to abjure those of his beliefs which were declared heretical, and on March 10, 1395, he was turned over to the secular authorities and executed.[34]

Feelings of religious tension and concern were not restricted to isolated heretics, and as the schism persisted and the end of the century approached, these feelings were expressed more widely. Four years after the execution of Giacomo di Ristolassio, on March 5, 1399, severe weather and the impending turn of the century provoked in Chieri a general outburst of religious fervor, as men and women donned white robes and spent the day in procession, crying "Misericordia."[35]

The largest and best documented of these eruptions of popular fervor took place a full year before the appearance of the Bianchi. On June 6, 1398, a crowd of flagellants approached Savona. This crowd worried the Savonese authorities, who feared that the Adorno family would use it as a cover for an attempt to seize the city. They promptly secured the city gates and sent out the bishop with two doctors of theology to make inquiries. People in the procession told stories of miracles they had witnessed, and as a sign of these miracles

---

[33] Grado G. Merlo, *Eretici e inquisitori nella società piemontese del Trecento* (Turin: Claudiana, 1977), pp. 150–155.

[34] Giuseppe Boffito, *Eretici in Piemonte al tempo del gran scisma (1378–1417)*, extract from *Studi e documenti di storia e diritto*, 18 (1897) (Rome: Tipografia Poliglotta, 1897). The record of the case against Giacomo di Ristolassio is edited on pp. 13–24.

[35] *Chronicon Parvum Ripaltae*, ed. Ferdinando Gabotto, in *RIS²*, 17, part 3, p. 34.

they displayed a host purportedly consecrated by the bishop of Marseille. Under questioning, they admitted that they had not actually seen the host being consecrated, but had received it from two Provençals. Further inquiries revealed that the crowd included no one from Provence, or even from the town of Albenga, which lay between Provence and Savona. The bishop, dubious, ordered the crowd to disperse, while detaining some priests who had accompanied it. He sent a letter to the bishop of Marseille to try to ascertain the truth of the matter; unfortunately, the results of his inquiry are unknown.[36] But in the eyes of the merchant who reported this episode, the mere fact that these flagellants brought in their wake a swirl of violence and threats of further disorder was enough to discredit them.

Tensions resulting from the Great Schism and the concomitant desire for a reformed and reunited church headed by the one true pope also played a part in the movement of the Bianchi. These feelings emerge clearly in a second, less widely diffused legend of their origin. According to this story, a peasant plowing his field saw an angel bearing a book appear between the horns of his ox. The angel instructed the peasant to preach to the people, calling them to penitence, fasting, and prayer, and gave him the book as a tangible proof of the veracity of his message. The book itself had miraculous powers: it could only be opened on the high altar of St. Peter's in Rome, by the hand of another angel. This book was said to contain God's plan for the future of the world and of the church: the new century was supposed to bring universal peace and the triumph of the church, which was to have new leaders and a new way of life.[37] The shadowy bearer of this wondrous book (no writer claims to have actually seen him or it) was reported to be headed for Rome, performing many miracles on the way and attracting a large group of followers. Among his followers was said to the man who was to be the new pope, since the Schism would soon be healed by God's grace.[38] The very vague-

---

[36] Archivio Datini di Prato, no. 660, lett. Genova-Firenze, comp. Datini, June 8, 1398.

[37] Sercambi, *Croniche*, pp. 302–303; Dominici, *Cronaca*, p. 56. This story, too, is composed of conventional elements, such as the unopenable book. The story of the origin of the flagellant movement, for instance, mentions a similar book: see Emilio Ardu, "Frater Raynerius Faxanus de Perusio," in *Il Movimento dei Disciplinati*, pp. 93–98.

[38] "E dicesi esservi tra loro chi de' esser nuovo papa; perchè si dice qui tosto

ness of this figure—if he existed at all—may have helped keep the Bianchi from direct confrontation with the ecclesiastical authorities, to whom he would have posed a challenge and a threat, while even the rumor of his existence coalesced the widespread hopes for the renewal, unification, and purification of the church.

The first certain word of the Bianchi movement proper came from the mountainous areas to the west and north of Genoa. First came reports of peacemaking and miracles in Voltri, the Oltregiogo, and the Polcevera, where bitter enmity was suddenly transformed into peace and harmony.[39] Then, on the morning of Saturday, July 5, 1399, an estimated 5,000 men, women, and children arrived at the gates of the city. They came from the valley of the Polcevera, a stream that enters the Mediterranean just to the west of Genoa. They marched in good order, singing the "Stabat Mater" and bearing crosses; with them were their parish priests, dressed like their parishioners in white. Nobles and leading citizens who lived in the countryside marched in the procession accompanied by their followers.[40] Also in the crowd was a boy who had reportedly been resurrected in the church of Sant'Ambrogio in Voltri. The presence of this living testimony to God's power, the sight of all this piety, and the sound of the cries for peace and mercy brought tears to the eyes of many Genoese, who had reacted with derision to earlier reports of this devotion. The participation of nobles and worthy citizens in the procession that approached Genoa may also have contributed to the polite reception accorded it. But if the Bianchi were not barred from Genoa, as the enthusiastic crowd of flagellants had been barred from Savona the year before, neither were they immediately welcomed to the heart of the city. The procession passed through Genoa from west to east, ending at the basilica of Santa Maria del Monte in the

---

questo scisma si leverà via con la grazia di Dio." Dominici, *Cronaca*, p. 56. Ser Luca does not merely distance himself from this story by his frequent uses of "si dice," "it is said"; he expresses his doubts openly when this personage is reported to be at Bologna with his book and his followers: "But if not all of this is clear, they are in the area of Bologna and have to pass this way; when they do and I can find out the truth from them, I will let you know." ("Ma perché non si fa chiaro ogni cosa, ellino sono appresso a Bologna e hanno a capitare in queste parti; quando ci saranno ciò che da loro saperò di verità, tel diro"; p. 118). But ser Luca apparently never learned anything more definite; he said no more on the subject.

[39] Stella, *Annales Genuenses*, p. 238. Except where indicated, I base my account of the Bianchi in Genoa on Stella, pp. 236–241. See also Sercambi, *Croniche*, pp. 305–309.

[40] Stella, *Annales Genuenses*, p. 239.

valley of the Bisagno, about one kilometer to the east of the city. There both the Bianchi and the gawkers they attracted heard mass before dispersing.

Two days later, on July 7, the devotion shifted from the periphery of the city to its sacred center. Jacopo Fieschi, the archbishop of Genoa, convoked his clergy in the cathedral church of San Lorenzo, and there he personally celebrated mass and urged the populace to adopt the new devotion. Religious excitement ran high among the crowd that spilled out of San Lorenzo, which was too small to accommodate all the worshipers. Wondrous lights were seen there and in Santa Maria de Coronata, and the mere sight of the resurrected boy from Voltri cured a man who had been crippled for fifteen years. This man, though resident in Genoa, was a native of San Biagio di Polcevera—the area from which the Bianchi had come to Genoa.[41]

For several days the Genoese prepared to adopt the Bianchi devotion by confessing their sins and forgiving their enemies. Then, at dawn on July 10, a huge crowd assembled to hear mass and receive the eucharist. Afterward, all of them—nobles and *popolani*, wives, maidens, brides, and widows, children, and a great part of the slaves—set off in procession, dressed in the prescribed white robes. Former enemies went bound to one another by belts or cords, in graphic demonstration of the new bonds of reconciliation. At the head of the procession were the white-robed clergy, led by Archbishop Fieschi. Too old and ill to go on foot, he rode a horse which was itself draped in white. Nothing like this had ever been seen before; 20,000 participants were counted, though there were some who said the number was even greater.[42] The procession of Bianchi, bearing the bodily remains of John the Baptist and other relics, followed the route normally taken by the Corpus Christi procession. Its course took it to the monastery of San Tommaso and to that of San Giovanni di Pavarano, on the left bank of the Bisagno.

General processions like this one were staged in the city for nine days. For those nine days the people of Genoa put aside their work, as if each day were Sunday. Sunday itself, however, was set apart from the nine days of the Bianchi devotion, for July 13 was given over to a special procession by the seventeen flagellant confraternities

[41] Stella, *Annales Genuenses*, p. 239.
[42] Archivio Datini di Prato, no. 661, lett. Genova-Firenze, comp. Datini, July 13, 1399.

of Genoa. The distinct character of this procession is evident: it included only men, the more than 1,400 members of the flagellant confraternities; it involved public flagellation, which is not mentioned elsewhere in Stella's account; and it did not count toward the requisite nine days of Bianchi devotions. The Bianchi processions apparently followed itineraries which highlighted each of the major churches of Genoa in turn, defining the sacred geography of the civic entity. On one day the Franciscans paraded their relics, as the relics of the cathedral had been carried in the initial procession, and on their day the Dominicans did the same. In the monastery of San Siro, the bodies of the early Genoese bishops Romolo, Felice, and Valentino were displayed.[43]

While these processions made the rounds of the urban churches, other processions left Genoa to propagate the devotion along the Riviera di Levante to Recco, Chiavari, and Rapallo. These columns of Bianchi set out several days after the urban processions had begun, for their imminent departure was still being anticipated on July 13, when an agent of Francesco Datini of Prato wrote from Genoa: "The procession is supposed to go to Recco, and the people there are pleased about it. This thing is so devout that it looks to us as if it will spread through the entire Riviera, and it seems to us that it will bring peace everywhere: may it so please Our Lord."[44] His expectations were borne out in practice, as the people of these towns in turn adopted the devotion and made peace between the Guelf and Ghibelline factions.

In Genoa, the nine days of processions, which had begun on July 10, ended on July 19. The following day, a Sunday, the body of St. Siro and other relics were carried on a circuit of the city. Archbishop Fieschi and the governor of the city participated in this procession, but the mass of the populace did not join in as eagerly as before: this official procession, not part of the ordained nine, was noticeably smaller than the great procession of July 10. On Monday, Genoa finally returned to business as usual.

---

[43] The feast-day of San Felice had just been celebrated, on July 9. Domenico Cambiaso, "L'anno ecclesiastico e le feste dei santi in Genova nel loro svolgimento storico," *Atti della Società ligure di storia patria*, 48 (1917): 187.

[44] "A Reccho si de' ire a procesione, e quelli di là ne son contenti. È la cosa sì devota che per tutto la Riviera ci pare passerà la cosa, e parci sarà cagione di metter pace per tutto: così piaccia a nostro Signore." Archivio Datini di Prato, no. 661, lett. Genova-Firenze, comp. Datini, July 13, 1399.

The course of the Bianchi devotion in Genoa shows many features which we shall see repeated in other cities. Typical of the devotion were the movement from periphery to center, the shift from initial mockery to enthusiasm, the stress on orderliness and moderation, the participation of people from all levels of society, of leading church-men and laymen as well as the lower classes, the prominent involve-ment of women, the coordination of intraurban and interurban pro-cessions, the cessation of normal economic activity, and the emphasis on peacemaking. Typically absent were any apocalyptic message and widespread flagellation, though the clear-cut restriction of this peni-tential practice to members of flagellant confraternities and to a par-ticular day is unique to Genoa.

Also unique to Genoa is the central role played by a single man, Archbishop Jacopo Fieschi.

Jacopo Fieschi was no stranger to either the religious tensions of the Schism or the factional violence of Genoa, from both of which he had suffered. He was the first bishop of Ventimiglia to have his claim to the see disputed, when Clement VII named Bertrando Inpati to that see in 1380.[45] And from the time he was translated to the arch-diocese of Genoa in 1382, his family associations embroiled him in the violent politics of his city.

The Fieschi, like the Doria, the Grimaldi, and the Spinola, were one of the old noble families excluded from the principal communal offices by the governmental reform of 1339. All of these families strove for alternative positions of honor and authority, but the strat-egy adopted by the Fieschi set them apart from the others.[46] The Doria, the Grimaldi, and the Spinola were all prominently involved in commerce and in the Casa di San Giorgio, the financial institution which controlled most of the communal revenues and many of the Genoese colonies; the Fieschi were not. Instead, the Fieschi found other bases for their power. As Jacques Heers says, they were all captains or churchmen, and occasionally both at once.[47] Their vast

[45] Hay, The Church in Italy, p. 30.

[46] Jacques Heers, Gênes au XVe siècle: Activité économique et problèmes sociaux (Paris: SEVPEN, 1961), pp. 538 and 666. On the social organization of Genoese families, see also Diane Owen Hughes, "Urban Growth and Family Structure in Medieval Genoa," Past and Present, 66 (February 1975): 3–28, and "Kinsmen and Neighbors in Medieval Genoa," in The Medieval City, ed. Harry A. Miskimin, David Herlihy, and A. L. Udovitch (New Haven: Yale University Press, 1977), pp. 95–111.

[47] Heers, Gênes, pp. 532–534, 609.

fiefs in the Apennines along the Riviera di Levante provided armies of dependents, with which they could even wage war on Genoa. Their castles guarded the crucial Apennine passes and overlooked Genoa itself. And within the city, their control of high ecclesiastical office placed them among the leaders of the Guelf party and enabled them to meddle directly in Genoese politics.

In the late fourteenth and early fifteenth centuries the political leaders of the Fieschi family were Luca Fieschi and Cardinal Ludovico Fieschi. These two men were the Fieschi protagonists when the struggle over the dogeship provoked street fighting in August 1394. Cardinal Ludovico joined Antonio Guarco and Pietro Campofregoso in forcing Nicolò da Zoagli to resign the dogeship. Luca Fieschi added armed might to the prestige of his kinsman's title: he led 600 friends and followers to Genoa and fortified himself in the Fieschi palace in Carignano, next to the basilica of Santa Maria in via Lata. This position proved too strong for his Ghibelline foes, who turned instead to an easier target. At the start of September they burned the archiepiscopal palace, where many Guelfs had taken refuge with Archbishop Jacopo. Luca then retreated from the city to his rural possessions, and the Fieschi palace in Carignano which he abandoned was also put to the torch. This palace was evidently rebuilt before long, for in August 1398 fighting again swirled around it. It was not until the very end of 1409 that Luca and Cardinal Ludovico seemed thoroughly discomfited. An expedition from Genoa forced them to surrender Portofino, where they had used the church of San Giorgio as their fortress, and chased them from the Riviera di Levante; the cardinal's palace on the heights overlooking Recco was razed. But within a year, Luca Fieschi and several hundred armed followers again threatened the very gates of Genoa.[48]

Jacopo Fieschi generally kept himself aloof from these conflicts. He could not always escape their consequences, as the burning of the archiepiscopal palace in 1394 demonstrated. But even on that occasion, it was his kinsman Luca who was acting the belligerent, leading troops to Genoa and fortifying his palace, while Jacopo opened his residence to those seeking asylum. Jacopo also kept himself aloof from ecclesiastical politics. As long as he lived, Genoa remained quietly in the Roman obedience. Unlike Cardinal Ludovico, his kinsman, Archbishop Jacopo was no warrior-prelate; ceremonial leadership of

[48]Stella, *Annales Genuenses*, pp. 210–212, 231, 293–294, 301–302.

religious processions was more to his liking. When Genoa suffered from an epidemic of plague in 1384, he led his clergy in parading the relics and imploring divine mercy.[49] After the capable and well-liked doge Leonardo Montaldo died in that epidemic, Jacopo ignored the terrors of the plague and again led his clergy in procession, escorting the doge's coffin to its resting place in the cathedral.

When the Bianchi appeared in Genoa, they thus found a man who was perfectly placed to lend decisive support to a religious plea for unity and concord, and who was inclined to exercise his influence in favor of a familiar and congenial kind of ritual performance. Instead of opposing this outburst of religious enthusiasm and doing his best to quell it, as had the bishop of Savona, Jacopo Fieschi welcomed it and put himself at the head of the procession. His actions catalyzed the inchoate religious ferment of the Ligurian hinterland into a major devotion. It was under his personal sponsorship that the movement of the Bianchi conquered the city of Genoa. And it was his family connections that facilitated the growth of the movement, for once serving the cause of peace rather than war. While Archbishop Fieschi was leading the Bianchi processions inside Genoa, other columns of Bianchi propagated the devotion outside the city walls, spreading it through the Fieschi fiefs southeast of the city, toward Tuscany, and carrying it over the Fieschi-controlled passes to the northeast, into Lombardy.

[49] Stella, *Annales Genuenses*, p. 190.

CHAPTER THREE

THE SPREAD OF THE

BIANCHI DEVOTION

Nothing like it was ever seen. On the first day 20,000 of them were counted, both men and women, all from the city; and there are those who say the number was even greater. Many miracles have been reported; the one that seems to me greatest and most striking is the making of peace and forgiveness of injuries. People think this thing comes from God. They are supposed to go to Recco in procession, and the people over there are pleased. This thing is so devout that it looks to us as if it will spread along the entire coast, and it seems to us that it will bring peace everywhere: may it so please Our Lord.

—a businessman in Genoa, writing to
a colleague in Florence

THE BIANCHI MOVEMENT spread from Genoa as a linked series of local processions. Rather than making a pilgrimage to a specific shrine, a "center out there" in Victor Turner's evocative phrase, parties of Bianchi undertook a nine-day circuit of the surrounding area. At each place they visited, they urged people to imitate them, to adopt the devotion and spread it to yet other locales.[1] But the processions were contiguous, not continuous: there was no significant carry-over of personnel, whether leaders or simple participants, from one local procession to the next. As a result, the several Bianchi pro-

---

Epigraph: Archivio Datini di Prato, no. 661, lett. Genova-Firenze, comp. Datini, letter of July 13, 1399.
[1] Victor W. Turner, "The Center Out There: Pilgrim's Goal," *History of Religions*, 12 (1972–1973): 191–230.

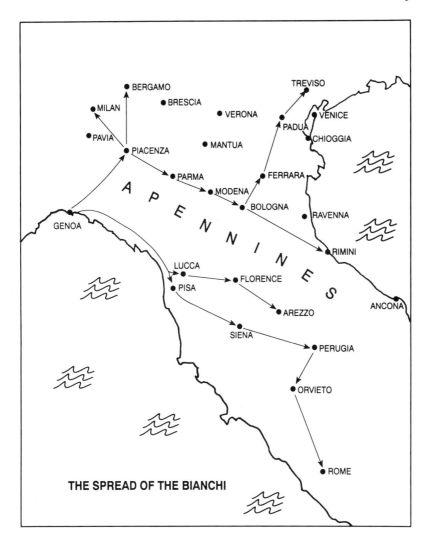

THE SPREAD OF THE BIANCHI

cessions displayed a range of modulations within the loose framework of the devotion. Their behavior was shaped by local conditions
and local concerns. Local religious customs and institutions helped
give a distinctive form to each Bianchi procession, as did political
structures and economic conditions, military threats and epidem-
iological dangers, the unchangeable facts of geography and the un-
predictable quirks of weather. The Bianchi processions thus appear as

so many variations on a single grand theme. In their overall consistency they reveal the common elements of religious culture and shared concerns of social praxis; in their subtle modulations they demonstrate the variety, fluidity, and responsiveness of late medieval religious life.

The Bianchi spread from Genoa in two great streams. One flowed through the Po valley from west to east before washing up on the shores of the Venetian lagoon. The other meandered southward through Tuscany, Umbria, and Lazio to Rome. Smaller rural devotions proliferated at the edges of these great urban processions, and in their wake swirled a welter of private or secondary devotions. Tracing these devotions produces a picture that is complex and unavoidably detailed, for it is only by close attention to the details that we can determine how the movement spread, whose energies it engaged, what needs it met, and what concerns it evoked. As Aby Warburg aptly said, God is to be found in the details.

The Po Valley

About a week after the Bianchi appeared at Genoa, groups of Bianchi began to arrive in Piacenza, on the other side of the Apennines. The chronicler Giovanni de' Mussi mentions the arrival of a party from Bobbio and then, on July 13, of some 4,000 Bianchi from the Valtidone and beyond the Trebbia—that is, from the river valleys along which paths led south and west toward Genoa.[2] This route was not commonly used; indeed, at this period it was almost completely neglected in favor of routes farther west, which connected Genoa with Milan by way of Novi Ligure or Voltri and Ovada.[3] The problems with the easterly route were partly physical: it followed streams like the Bisagno, which became dangerous torrents after a storm. But they were also political: the Scoffera pass was controlled by the Fieschi, who could obstruct traffic at this key point whenever they wished. The Bianchi, however, carried the approval of Jacopo Fieschi and so did not need to worry about finding the pass closed to them.

---

[2] Giovanni de' Mussi, *Chronicon Placentinum*, in *RIS*, 16, cols. 558–559.
[3] Jacques Heers, *Gênes au XVe siècle: Activité économique et problèmes sociaux* (Paris: SEVPEN, 1961), pp. 431–432.

The Bianchi from the valleys of the Tidone and the Trebbia were drawn to Piacenza in part by the desire to visit an image of the Virgin Mary which had recently performed some striking miracles.[4] The Bianchi, however, were not permitted to enter Piacenza and visit this image; both the party from Bobbio and the later, and larger, group from the Valtidone were kept outside the city walls, and the people of Piacenza had to go outside to greet them, hear mass, and listen to their preaching. As at Genoa, the Bianchi devotion soon moved from the periphery to the center of the city. Piacentine men and women of all ranks donned white robes and went barefoot in procession from church to church, praying and singing the "Stabat Mater." At the same time, another group went to Fiorenzuola to propagate the devotion.

Piacenza was the center from which the Bianchi spread north of the Apennines, as Genoa was the starting point for their diffusion south of the Apennines. The mountains kept the two patterns of diffusion distinct; only occasionally did smaller parties of Bianchi cross the divide. The behavior of the Bianchi and the reception they evoked, while broadly similar, show distinct emphases on the two sides of the mountains. The actions of the Piacentine authorities, who, unlike the Genoese, shut their gates to the Bianchi, typified the more wary response of civic authorities in the Po valley. Their wariness was due above all to a concern for public health. The doom threatened by the Bianchi origin legend—the sudden destruction of one-third of humankind—pressed close upon those who had known the appalling mortality of the late fourteenth century; and in the summer of 1399 an epidemic of plague which had only begun to touch Tuscany, and would not reach major proportions there until the following year, was already raging in the Po valley. Authorities here had good reason to shut their gates to crowds of foreigners, who might be carrying with them the terrible disease. At the same time, they also had reason to welcome a movement that promised to resolve differences and end internecine strife. Less than a month before the arrival of the Bianchi, a brawl in Piacenza during the feast of John

---

[4] In particular, one citizen of Piacenza was freed of a curvature of the spine that had kept him bent like a hoop. The chronicler Giovanni de' Mussi himself, as well as a hundred others, bore witness to this cure. Mussi, *Chronicon Placentinum*, cols. 558–559.

the Baptist had resulted in the death of a man and the banishment of many knights from both factions.[5]

The Piacentine authorities were not entirely free to act as they wished, for Piacenza was part of the territory ruled by Giangaleazzo Visconti, duke of Milan. The Visconti holdings in this period can only loosely be called a state; they were rather a congeries of properties, each immediately subject to Giangaleazzo.[6] This dominion, which at its height stretched over most of the Po valley and included pockets of Tuscany and Umbria, was assembled piecemeal, by conquest, diplomacy, and purchase; it was never melded into a coherent whole, and it rapidly dissolved into its component parts after Giangaleazzo's death.[7] In a very real sense, the ruler was the state.

Giangaleazzo Visconti built and maintained his dominion with ceaseless personal attention. While he left the daily operations of government—the normal administration of justice, collection of taxes, and preservation of public order—to the traditional institutions of each of his subject territories, he was constantly alert to the situation of his subjects and ready to interfere directly in response to their appeals or the dictates of his policy. The mechanism by which he made his wishes known was the stream of letters that issued from his busy personal chancery.[8] These letters were sometimes concerned with those small matters, such as the granting of personal favors,

---

[5] Giovanni Agazzari, *Cronica civitatis Placentiae*, in *Monumenta historica ad provincias Parmensem et Placentinam pertinentia* (Parma: Pietro Fiaccadori, 1862), p. 55.

[6] The string of Giangaleazzo's titles reveals the direct and distinct relationship between him and each of his subject territories: duke of Milan, count of Pavia and Vertus, lord of Pisa and Siena, and so on. D. M. Bueno de Mesquita, *Giangaleazzo Visconti: A Study in the Political Career of an Italian Despot* (Cambridge: Cambridge University Press, 1941), esp. pp. 45–58, stresses Giangaleazzo's efforts to centralize and integrate his dominion, though in so doing he reveals the limited success of that policy. Giorgio Chittolini, "Infeudazioni e politica feudale nel ducato visconteo-sforzesco," in his *La formazione dello stato regionale e le istituzioni del contado, secoli XIV e XV* (Turin: Einaudi, 1979), pp. 36–100, demonstrates the persistance of feudal ties and noble privileges, and describes Visconti rule in terms of the competing claims of ruler, subject cities, and feudal magnates. For some telling criticisms of the thesis that a "modern state" developed in this period, see Lauro Martines, *Lawyers and Statecraft in Renaissance Florence* (Princeton: Princeton University Press, 1968), pp. 464–476.

[7] On the Visconti lordship over Perugia, which, as elsewhere, left preexisting civic institutions substantially intact, see Hermann Goldbrunner, "Il dominio visconteo a Perugia," in *Storia e cultura in Umbria nell'età moderna (secoli XV-XVIII)*, Atti del VII Convegno di Studi Umbri, Gubbio, 18–22 maggio 1969 (Perugia: Centro di Studi Umbri, 1972), pp. 423–455.

[8] Caterina Santoro, *Gli uffici del comune di Milano e del dominio visconteo-sforzesco (1216–1515)* (Milan: Giuffre, 1968).

that were the daily business of governance.[9] More commonly, they dealt with matters basic to the stability of Giangaleazzo's regime. In them he fixed the amounts of revenue needed and apportioned the fiscal burden, granted tax relief when necessary, set monetary policy, announced the acquisition of new territories, and enacted measures meant to preserve public order. Everyday administration, left in the hands of local bureaucracies, was constantly being interrupted by directives from the ducal chancery, which itself never developed into a coherent central government. The continual mutual interference of local and ducal bureaucracies undermined the stability of both, and the smooth functioning of Visconti rule depended ultimately on the constant personal attention of the Visconti ruler.

An epidemic of plague could not fail to draw Giangaleazzo's attention, and in fact a great many of the ducal letters from the second half of 1399 and throughout 1400 are concerned with the plague.[10] Giangaleazzo took the usual steps to preserve public health and then, when they failed, to restore it. He issued general restrictions on travel and followed them with specific bans on contact with places known to be infected. He ordered the posting of guards at the city gates to enforce the travel restrictions, and even specified that they be burly men. He set aside houses in which plague victims were to be gathered and quarantined, and allocated funds to support these plague-houses. He commanded that the residences of the plague-stricken be aired and fumigated, and that their bedding be cleaned and exposed to the beneficent rays of the sun.[11]

Giangaleazzo was also concerned about the movement of the Bianchi, since religious processions from city to city within his lands hampered his efforts to restrict travel and impose an effective quarantine. Although he strove to meet the demands of both pious observance and public health, in this situation they proved fundamentally irrec-

---

[9] Many of the letters conferring minor sinecures came not from Giangaleazzo but from his wife, Caterina; on one occasion she made an appointment on the recommendation of her wet nurse. See *I registri dell'ufficio di provvisione e dell'ufficio dei sindaci sotto la dominazione viscontea*, ed. Caterina Santoro (Milan: Castello Sforzesco, 1929), letts. 6, 126, 141, 146, 147, 153, 229 (the wet nurse), 238, 241, and 265.

[10] Biblioteca Ambrosiana, Milano, Fondo Trotti, 245: Registrum litterarum 1397–1400, henceforth referred to as BA, Registrum litterarum. Santoro published a calendar of these letters in *I registri*, pp. 69–120.

[11] On these measures, see Aldo Bottero, "La peste in Milano nel 1399–1400 e l'opera di Gian Galeazzo Visconti," *Atti e memorie dell'Accademia di Storia dell'Arte Sanitaria*, ser. 2, 7 (1942): 17–28.

oncilable; his actions in defense of public health often conflicted directly with the free circulation of the Bianchi processions and the propagation of the movement. On July 13, the very day that the Bianchi from the Valtidone and the valley of the Trebbia arrived at Piacenza, Giangaleazzo issued a general caution on communication with infected areas.[12] He did not, however, move immediately to quash the religious enthusiasm of his subjects. He tried instead to direct and regulate it so that it would pose the least possible threat to public health. These ducal orders shaped definitively the unfolding of the Bianchi devotion in the Po valley. As the Bianchi spread from Piacenza in three directions—northwest toward Milan, due north toward Bergamo, and southeast toward Parma and Bologna—the development of the movement in each of these directions bore the impress of Giangaleazzo's actions.

In going northwest from Piacenza, the Bianchi were heading toward the heart of Giangaleazzo's dominions, and so drew his special attention. Giangaleazzo normally resided at Pavia, and he was particularly careful to see that no threat of infection approached that city. A chronicler as far away as Pistoia reported the duke's order that no one who had been in any place infected with plague be allowed in Pavia; according to the report that reached this chronicler, when the people in one household fell sick, the building and its contents were burned and all those who had been in contact with its residents were expelled from the city.[13] In these circumstances, it was hardly likely that Giangaleazzo would permit the Bianchi to enter Pavia, and indeed there is no notice of their having been there. The Bianchi apparently avoided Pavia and made their way to Milan via Lodi, where the jurist Antonio Maraviglia, who governed Lodi on Giangaleazzo's behalf, himself donned the white robes, perhaps inspired by the many terrifying astrological signs that he reported.[14]

The Bianchi devotions in Milan elicited Giangaleazzo's most detailed injunctions. On August 19 he granted permission for the people of Milan, moved by laudable devotion to the Virgin Mary, to participate in the processions. To minimize the danger of contagion, however, he instructed the residents of the city to keep themselves separate from those who lived in the surrounding area while they all

[12] BA, Registrum litterarum, fol. 118r; Mussi, Chronicon Placentinum, col. 559.

[13] Dominici, Cronaca, p. 131.

[14] Bernardino Corio, L'Historia di Milano (Padua: Paolo Frambotto, 1646), pp. 551–552.

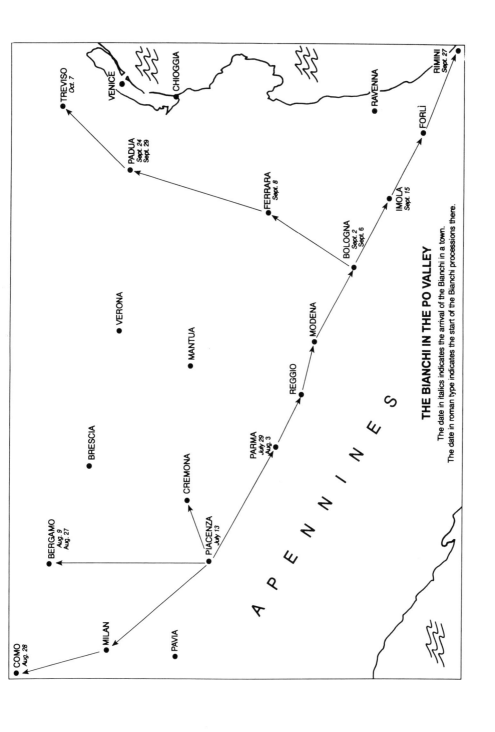

THE BIANCHI IN THE PO VALLEY

The date in italics indicates the arrival of the Bianchi in a town.
The date in roman type indicates the start of the Bianchi processions there.

went about visiting churches.[15] Two days later he suspended all court cases in Milan for two weeks, freeing the lawyers, witnesses, plaintiffs, and defendants involved in those cases to participate in the processions.[16] The plague, however, was already at the city gates. On September 6, just after the suspension of court cases expired, Giangaleazzo wrote to the governing council in Milan and to his vicar there, ordering them to cut all communication between Milan and plague-stricken Monza, just a few kilometers to the north. His decree was cried through the streets of Milan the next day.[17]

In this troubled situation, it was impossible for the Bianchi processions to move freely from city to city. Giangaleazzo had no objection to processions as such; there is no indication that he feared any riot or rebellion from such a large assembly of people in a time of tension.[18] In the midst of the plague, on September 22, 1399, and again on January 28, 1400, the duke proclaimed three days of processions and festivities to celebrate his acquisition of Siena and Perugia; the two letters of proclamation are virtually identical to the one of February 22, 1399, before the plague, which announced his purchase of Pisa.[19] And on September 9, 1399, he suspended all court cases so that the lawyers, litigants, and witnesses could join his son Giovanni Maria in a special procession to implore divine mercy for the plague-threatened city.[20] But all these processions were intraurban, and thus did not threaten to spread the infection. The Bianchi, on the other hand, circulated from city to city, and so could not be tolerated for long by a ruler concerned about a spreading epidemic. For the same reason, in December 1399 the duke postponed the celebration of the festival of Sant'Ambrogio, which normally brought large numbers of foreigners to Milan; and the following spring he rearranged the fair usually held at Arona on the calends of June.[21]

---

[15] BA, Registrum litterarum, fol. 122v.

[16] BA, Registrum litterarum, fols. 122v–123r.

[17] BA, Registrum litterarum, fols. 128v–129r.

[18] As we shall see later, however, other rulers, such as Boniface IX, were reported to be troubled by just such fears.

[19] BA, Registrum litterarum, fols. 103v (Pisa), 131v (Siena), and 162v (Perugia).

[20] BA, Registrum litterarum, fol. 130r. Tognetti, "Sul moto dei bianchi," pp. 304–305, uses Santoro's summary rather than the actual document and so mistakenly construes this procession as an extension of the Bianchi devotions beyond the usual nine days.

[21] BA, Registrum litterarum, fols. 141v and 184v.

By the time Giangaleazzo halted travel between Milan and Monza, however, the Bianchi had already spread north to Como. There, on August 28, the bishop of Como, Lucchino Borsano, led his people in the celebration of this devotion.[22] But the Comascan processions did not head toward other cities. Instead, they looped out from Como to visit three rural churches each day. Sunday, August 31, was the one day on which they did not visit rural churches, but gathered instead in the town piazza; as at Genoa, this special Sunday procession, different from the rest, did not count among the nine days of Bianchi devotions. In a pattern that we shall see repeated at other dead ends in the diffusion of the Bianchi movement, the rural churches visited by the processions here were all located in towns in the immediate vicinity of Como. Grandate, Lucino, Cardano, Lunate, Albate, Trecallo, Breccia—none was more than six or seven kilometers away. The radiation of the Bianchi to the northwest of Piacenza ended with these processions around Como.

In going due north, the Bianchi avoided Pavia and Milan and so did not arouse Giangaleazzo's immediate concern. They filtered through a series of small towns—Soncino, Gallignano, Antegnate, Fontanella, Covo, Romano, and Cologno—and when some 1,200 Bianchi from these towns, accompanied by their parish priests, arrived at Bergamo around vespers on August 9, they received a warm welcome, with abundant food and drink.[23] The next day the people of Bergamo went outside the city gates to hear the many masses sung for these Bianchi and the sermon of a preacher who spoke "of arranging peace between Christians and of certain miracles performed in various places."[24] Afterward, the visiting Bianchi returned to the south by a slightly different route, passing the devotion to Treviolo and Albegno.

This visit greatly impressed the people of Bergamo, especially the clergy and the prominent citizens—or at least the chronicler was impressed with how the leaders of society responded, for he noted the eager participation of nobles, jurists, doctors, and many other worthy

---

[22] Benedetto Giovio, *Historiae patriae sive Novocomensis libri duo*, in *Thesaurus antiquitatem et historiarum Italiae*, ed. Joannus Georgius Graevius and Petrus Burmannus, 4, part 2 (Leiden: Petrus Vander Aa, 1722), cols. 42–43.

[23] *Chronicon Bergomense guelpho-ghibellinum*, ed. Carlo Capasso, in *RIS²*, 16, part 2, pp. 94–95.

[24] "De pace tractanda inter Christianos et de certis miraculis factis in pluribus locis." Capasso, *Chronicon Bergomense*, p. 94.

men, along with their wives. On Sunday, August 17, they marched through the city to the church of Sant'Alessandro, where they heard mass and listened to a sermon by the Dominican Iacopo de Uris. On Monday, the procession ended at the cathedral church of San Vincenzo, where another Dominican, Oprandino de Cene, preached the sermon. Tuesday's procession ended at the church of Santa Maria Maggiore, which contains a crucifix venerated since the mid-fourteenth century; this time the preacher was a Franciscan, Luigi de Scalve. Wednesday the procession went through the newer neighborhoods outside the walls and Iacopo de Uris preached again, at Santo Stefano. The local chronicler, Castello de' Castelli, estimated that 6,000 persons or more participated in Wednesday's procession.[25]

These processions, however, were intended merely to advertise the Bianchi devotion and inspire the people of Bergamo to join it. After a week to allow word to spread and everyone to prepare, the true Bianchi processions began on August 27. People from the city, suburbs, and district of Bergamo, both the hill country and the valleys, gathered on Monte Fara. They were covered from head to toe in white robes—the first mention of the ceremonial garb in the processions at Bergamo.[26] The familiar figures of Iacopo de Uris, Oprandino de Cene, and Luigi de Scalve were joined by other Dominicans and Franciscans, by Fra Pietro da San Pellegrino, by the Augustinian Hermits, the canons and clerics of Sant'Alessandro and San Vicenzo, the bishop of Milan, and the whole clergy of Bergamo in a notable demonstration of ecclesiastical concord. Evidently the Bianchi inspired the regular and secular clergy, and even the Dominicans and Franciscans, to set aside *their* rivalries and grudges and unite in sponsoring this movement. The secular authorities joined the ecclesiastical in sanctioning the Bianchi devotion: Giangaleazzo Visconti's vicar in Bergamo, Giovanni da Castiglione, issued a license and safe-conduct allowing those placed under bans to join the procession. Again, a number of prominent citizens—jurists, procurators, knights, and their wives—lent their social stature to the peacemaking and the devotion. Giovanni da Romano, an Augustinian friar, preached the sermon, which climaxed with the formalization of many peace agreements. Everyone then set off in orderly columns, two by two, toward

---

[25] Capasso, *Chronicon Bergomense*, p. 95.
[26] "Omnes induti et indute de lanzolis et aliis pannis lini, coperti de toto corpore." Capasso, *Chronicon Bergomense*, p. 95.

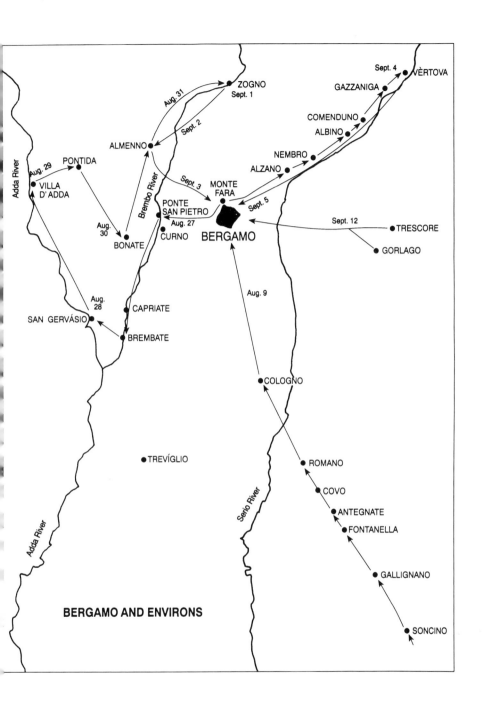

BERGAMO AND ENVIRONS

Ponte San Pietro, about six kilometers west of Bergamo. They spent the night there at Ponte San Pietro and the nearby hamlets of Curno and Margolda.

During the following days the procession of Bianchi moved through the countryside around Bergamo, covering the modest distance of ten to fifteen kilometers a day. On August 28, the Bianchi followed the course of the Brembo south to the hamlets of San Gervasio, Capriate, Brembate, and Grignano. On August 29, they followed the Adda upstream to Pontida and Villa d'Adda. They stayed there both that night and the following one, as the day of Saturday, August 30, was taken up with peacemaking. The night of August 30 one of the leaders of the devotion, Oprandino de Cene, died in Bonate di sotto, which suggests that the procession had turned downstream. On the last day of August it moved north once more, to Almenno; that cluster of towns was the Bianchi's base for Sunday, Monday, and Tuesday. On Monday, September 1, a party of 600 Bianchi traveled up the Brembo to Zogno, to make peace among the people of that area. This party rejoined the main body at Almenno, and then on Wednesday, September 3, the whole group returned to Monte Fara, just outside of Bergamo, where another multitude of peace compacts were celebrated. From there they set out once again, this time following the course of the Serio to the northeast, spending the night around Alzano and Nembro. September 4, the final day of the devotion, was spent making peace in the towns of the Serio valley: Alzano di sopra and di sotto, Nembro, Albino, Desenzano, and Comenduno. A party of 1,000 went a bit further upstream to Gazzaniga and Vértova. In this area the peace compacts involved not just feuding families, but whole villages: the men of Albino di sotto had apparently fallen out with nearly all of their neighbors, since peace agreements had to be arranged between them and the towns of Albino di sopra, Comenduno, and Desenzano. On September 5, the Bianchi of Bergamo once again congregated on Monte Fara, where they celebrated still more peace compacts and heard one last sermon by the Franciscan Luigi de Scalve. He asked them to say a Pater Noster and an Ave Maria every day in memory of this event, and enjoined them to keep the peace. This officially closed the devotion of the Bianchi in Bergamo.[27]

---

[27] Castello de' Castelli, to whom this chronicle was attributed and who actually seems to have written this part of it, went to confession the next day and arranged an indulgence from a papal vicar for the benefit of his sick wife. Castello appar-

The Bianchi devotions in Bergamo took place at nearly the same time as those in Como, and on the same pattern. No effort was made to transmit the devotion to another major city, such as Brescia; the processions kept to the immediate area of Bergamo. They followed the river valleys to the southwest, the northwest, the north, and the northeast, penetrating no more than twenty to twenty-five kilometers into the surrounding hills. These processions, together with the party that came from the south to introduce the devotion, covered nearly all of the district of Bergamo. The only area missed lay to the east, but that was soon rectified. On September 12, a week after the main processions ended, a party of 1,000 Bianchi, including people from the city and from the mountain district, gathered on Monte Fara to celebrate peace compacts concluded between various noble clans of Trescore and Gorlago, fifteen kilometers to the east.

This was the last flurry of Bianchi activity in Bergamo. Giangaleazzo Visconti quickly stifled any impulse to perpetuate the processions. On September 16, in execution of a ducal letter, public cry was made through the streets of Bergamo: "Let no person be so bold as to go in white robes to make processions, under pain of ten gold florins for each and every instance. And this is in order that no assembly be held, on account of the disease."[28] Once again, Giangaleazzo's objection was to interurban processions, which violated quarantine restrictions, not to processions as such. Indeed, just two weeks later, from September 28 to 30, the clergy of Bergamo staged three days of processions, on Giangaleazzo's express orders, to celebrate his acquisition of Siena.[29] By that time, in any case, it was too late for any of Giangaleazzo's actions to make much difference to the health of his dominions. The plague bacillus, sublimely indifferent to ducal decrees, was already devastating Bergamo and its district, as it continued to do through the fall and into the following summer.[30]

---

ently stayed home to care for her, since he does not claim to have participated in the processions himself; perhaps this is why he instead took the trouble to confess and receive absolution for himself and his wife. It was their son, Guglielmo, who represented the family in the Bianchi devotions. Capasso, *Chronicon Bergomense,* pp. 95 and 98.

[28] "Quod nulla persona amodo audeat ire cum vestibus albis, pro faciendo processiones, sub pena florenorum X auri pro quolibet et qualibet vice. Et hoc ut non fiat congregatio propter morbum." Capasso, *Chronicon Bergomense,* p. 98.

[29] Capasso, *Chronicon Bergomense,* p. 99.

[30] Capasso, *Chronicon Bergomense,* p. 100.

The third direction in which the Bianchi spread from Piacenza, toward the southeast, was the most successful. Here they were moving directly away from Giangaleazzo Visconti, and so met with no restrictions or resistance from ducal representatives. Perhaps as a result, the movement spread in this direction with remarkable rapidity. The main party of Bianchi arrived at Piacenza on July 13; it was probably a few days later that the Piacentine devotions began. At that time the Piacentine Bianchi went to pass the devotion on to Fiorenzuola, and the people of Fiorenzuola in their turn passed it on to the next town.[31] The movement passed from Fiorenzuola to Borgo San Donnino (the modern Fidenza), and from there to Parma. The Bianchi from Borgo San Donnino reached Parma on July 29, barely two weeks after the first dated mention of the Bianchi devotions in Piacenza and well before the start of the processions in Bergamo, Milan, and Como.[32]

By the time it reached Parma, the Bianchi movement already displayed the careful organization and formal correctness that characterized its progress along the Via Emilia. When the Bianchi of Parma set out for Reggio on August 3, they carried with them their own food supplies, in forty white-draped carts.[33] From Reggio the movement spread to Modena, and from Modena to Bologna.[34] This step

---

[31] Mussi, *Chronicon Placentinum*, col. 559.

[32] Anonymous addition to Fra Giovanni de' Cornazani, *Istoria di Parma*, in *RIS*, 12, col. 752.

[33] Cornazani, *Istoria di Parma*, col. 752.

[34] Our sources for Modena are not very useful. Alessandro Tassoni, *Cronaca modenese*, ed. L. Vischi, T. Sandonnini, and O. Raselli, in *Monumenti di storia patria delle provincie modenesi*, 15 (Modena: Società tipografica, 1888), p. 303, wrote long after the fact and transmitted little. Lodovico Vedriani, *Historia dell'antichissima città di Modona*, part 2 (Modena, 1667), p. 375, did more extensive research, but made the movement of the Bianchi conform to a post-Tridentine stereotype of popular religious movements that is remarkably similar to that of Norman Cohn's *The Pursuit of the Millennium*. The most promising source is the long poem by Gerardo Anechini, which was written by November 2, 1399, and edited by Vincenzo Licitra, "Gerardo Anechini cantore dei Bianchi," *Studi medievali*, ser. 3, 10 (1969): 399–459. But Anechini devoted so much care to phrasing his Latin hexameters in the proper antique manner (going so far as to transform the objects of devotion of this Christian movement into the Roman pantheon) that he did not bother to give any precise information on the actual progress of the devotion in Modena. And since dates were inimical to his poetic models, he left us in the dark about exactly when the events which so excited him occurred. See the remarks of Giuseppina De Sandre Gasparini on this text, in *Rivista di storia della chiesa in Italia*, 26 (1972): 195–199.

For Bologna, in contrast, we have a fine set of chronicles: Pietro di Mattiolo,

was prepared by ambassadors, fifty of whom arrived in Bologna on August 25, on horses robed like their riders in white.[35] They obtained the desired safe-conduct and permission to make the procession, and returned home the next day. A week later, on September 2, the procession of Modenese Bianchi appeared in Bologna. They marched in columns two by two, carrying white banners and singing *laude*. The procession was divided into parish groups; each parish carried the insignia of its patron saint and led a white-draped cart loaded with provisions.[36] They camped for the night outside the city, by the bridge over the Reno, and the populace of Bologna went out to see them and hear mass. The next morning, the Bianchi of Modena headed for home, except for a group that wanted to accompany the Bolognese in their devotions and then proceed on to Rome.[37]

On September 6, the Bolognese in their turn adopted the Bianchi devotion and began nine days of visiting churches in procession. So that these rounds could be made "ordenadamente e devotamente," in a manner both orderly and devout, the communal government had four banners made, one for each quarter of the city. The parishes of Bologna prepared banners of their own, and so the processions were organized: each parish troop followed its banner, and the parishes were grouped behind the banner of their quarter.[38] The rural communities of the *contado*, the subject territory, marched behind their own banners.

While these processions were going on within the city, preparations were made to carry the devotion its next stage down the Via Emilia. Ambassadors were sent to the lord of Imola, Luigi Alidosi, to secure his permission and a safe-conduct for the procession. At the end of the nine days of intraurban processions, on September 15, the great column left Bologna for Imola, grouped like the earlier processions by quarter and parish.[39] The Bolognese, like the communities of

---

Cronaca Bolognese, ed. Corrado Ricci (Bologna, 1885; rpt. Bologna: Forni, 1969), pp. 46–51; *Corpus chronicorum Bononiensium,* ed. Albano Sorbelli, in *RIS²,* 18, part 1, tome 3, pp. 465–469; and Girolamo Borselli, *Cronica gestorum civitatis Bononie,* ed. Albano Sorbelli, in *RIS²,* 23, part 2, p. 66.

[35] Pietro di Mattiolo, *Cronaca,* pp. 46–47.

[36] *Cronaca Bolognetti,* in Sorbelli, *Corpus chronicorum Bononiensium,* p. 466.

[37] Pietro di Mattiolo, *Cronaca,* p. 48.

[38] Pietro di Mattiolo, *Cronaca,* pp. 48–49.

[39] The chroniclers differ on the date of their departure. Matteo dei Griffoni says they left on September 16; *Cronaca A* says they went on September 6, the day that

the contado, all brought along carts loaded with bread, wine, and other provisions, according to the number of people in the commune.[40] They camped outside of Imola, and Luigi Alidosi generously sent food to supplement what they had brought; everyone was free to take whatever was needed.[41] The people of Imola came out to see them, hear mass, and listen to a sermon by Alberto da Ozano, who had gone along expressly to preach this devotion to the people of the city of Imola and its contado, and to inform them about how it should be performed.[42]

This meticulous organization of the Bianchi progress down the Via Emilia was prompted by several considerations. One, though unstated, was undoubtedly fear of the plague and worries for public health. In Bologna, deaths were already frequent before the advent of the Bianchi, and after their passage the pages of Pietro di Mattiolo's chronicle are given over almost entirely to noting the deaths of prominent citizens. Fear of the plague probably explains why the Bianchi in this region always camped outside the gates of the cities they visited. Another preoccupation was fear of attack in this unstable region, which had recently been ravaged by the condottiere Giovanni da Barbiano and his cavalry.[43] Pietro di Mattiolo even mentions that an armed escort accompanied the Bolognese Bianchi to protect their goods and persons.[44] This is the only notice we have of such an escort, but the need for some sort of protection is evident in the care with which the Bianchi in this region obtained safe-conducts and official permission to visit a neighboring town. The final concern was for food supplies. Bad weather in the spring and early summer had damaged crops and provoked worries about local food shortages. At the end of April, Piacenza was hit by a freak snowstorm and late frost; the unseasonable weather destroyed about half the grain and grapes, and the ensuing food shortage was held to be responsible for the

---

the processions started within the city; Pietro di Mattiolo, *Cronaca Bolognetti,* and *Cronaca B* concur in saying September 15.

[40] Pietro di Mattiolo, *Cronaca,* p. 50.

[41] *Cronaca Bolognetti,* p. 468.

[42] Pietro di Mattiolo, *Cronaca,* pp. 49–50.

[43] Museo Correr, Venezia, ms. Cicogna 1115 (35), fol. 58v. This anonymous chronicle also records pillaging by Giovanni da Barbiano in the territory of Modena. On the violent traditions of the Romagna, see John Larner, *The Lords of Romagna: Romagnol Society and the Origins of the Signorie* (Ithaca: Cornell University Press, 1965), pp. 58–75.

[44] Pietro di Mattiolo, *Cronaca,* pp. 50–51.

spread of disease.[45] Bologna, too, was hit by bad weather. On August 31, in the week between the visit of the Modenese ambassadors and the arrival of the Modenese Bianchi, the government of Bologna received petitions for relief because of damage suffered in a tempest on June 13; this storm had so devastated the crops that "they expect to be able to harvest little or nothing."[46] These worries about food supplies clearly lay behind the care with which the Bianchi here carted along their own victuals. Though their hosts would give what they could, the Bianchi in Emilia could not count on receiving charity sufficient for their needs, and so they saw to their own provisioning. The impersonal constraints of disease, war, and hunger, rather than the will of any ruler, molded the Bianchi devotions in this region.

After Imola, we know little of the Bianchi's progress through the Romagna. The Bolognese chroniclers simply say that the movement passed from Imola to Faenza, and from Faenza to Forlì; clearly, what happened after the Bolognese Bianchi turned back from Imola was of little interest to them. And decades later, when the Dominican friar Girolamo dei Fiocchi, who had said mass before the Bianchi in Forlì, finally got around to writing down his recollections of that event, all that he could remember was that they had come through town sometime in September (of 1400, as he recalled), and that they had made such an uproar during the mass that he had been thoroughly unnerved.[47]

By the end of September, the movement had reached Rimini. There, according to one chronicler, the lord of Rimini, Carlo Malatesta, and his brother-in-law Francesco Gonzaga donned the white robes on September 27 and set off to accompany the Bianchi as far as Fano.[48] This was apparently the group that Carlo's brother, Galeotto Belfiore, the ruler of Borgo San Sepolcro, joined on September 29. On its way back from Fano the party stopped at Cattolica, a few kilometers south of Rimini; from Cattolica, Galeotto Belfiore wrote to his vicar in Borgo San Sepolcro on October 6, announcing a general par-

[45] Mussi, *Chronicon Placentinum*, col. 558.

[46] "Nichil vel parum sperant posse reccipe[re]." Archivio di Stato di Bologna, Provvisioni in Capreto, vol. 6 (Liber G-H), 1398–1400, fol. 63v.

[47] Girolamo da Forlì, *Chronicon*, ed. Adamo Pasini, in *RIS²*, 19, part 5, pp. 4–5.

[48] Broglio di Tartaglia da Lavello, *Cronaca Universale*, ed. Aldo Francesco Massèra, in *RIS²*, 15, part 2, pp. 190–191. See also Baldo Branchi, *Cronaca Malatestiana*, in the same volume, p. 174.

don for all convictions up to September 29, the day on which he had joined the Bianchi.[49] But Galeotto Belfiore's letter takes us across the Apennines to Tuscany; it is the last sure notice we have of the Bianchi in the Romagna.

Elsewhere in the Po valley, the development of the Bianchi devotion was neither as clear nor as well documented as this progress down the Via Emilia. For Cremona we have merely an undated general notice to the effect that 1399 was the year of the Bianchi.[50] For Mantua, our information is no better. The humanist historian Platina was no doubt delighted to get paid by two patrons for the same piece of work, and his history of Mantua simply repeats the general sketch of the Bianchi that he had already given in his biographies of the popes—and largely in the same words, right down to his claim to have heard these vague but sonorous phrases from his father, who saw the men in white.[51]

Early in September, the Bianchi movement entered Ferrara. According to the local chronicler Jacopo Delaito, the devotion was brought by four messengers who arrived on September 1.[52] The following day, Sunday, September 2, one of these four preached of the apparition of the Virgin to the peasant, of the miracles which followed, and of the spread of the devotion, and he persuaded the people of Ferrara to adopt it in their turn. Afterwards a great procession

---

[49] Gino Franceschini, "Anna Montefeltro-Malatesta," in *Studi Riminesi e bibliografici in onore di Carlo Lucchesi* (Faenza: Fratelli Lega, 1952), p. 95.

[50] *Cronaca di Cremona*, in *Biblioteca Historica Italica*, 1 (Milan, 1876), pp. 167–168.

[51] Platina, *Historia urbis Mantuae Gonziacaeque familiae*, in *RIS²*, 20, cols. 791–792; *Liber de vita Christi ac omnium pontificum*, ed. Giacinto Gaida, in *RIS²*, 3, part 1, pp. 293–294. See also the equally imprecise Antonio Nerli, *Breve chronicon monasterii Mantuani*, ed. Orsini Begami, in *RIS²*, 24, part 13, p. 13, and Bonamente Aliprandi, *Cronica di Mantova*, in Ludovico Antonio Muratori, *Antiquitates Italicae medii aevi*, 5 (Milan, 1741), cols. 1216–1217.

[52] Jacopo Delaito, *Annales Estenses*, in *RIS*, 18, cols. 956–958. Delaito's account presents several problems. For one thing, September 2 was not a Sunday, as Delaito says, but a Tuesday. Did he mean Sunday, or September 2? Perhaps he (or his copyist) slipped and left the V off VII; September 7 *was* a Sunday, and the day before the procession to Belfiore. This hypothesis would fit the pattern of a delay of a few days between the first appearance of the Bianchi in a town and the adoption of the devotion there. Adding to the uncertainty, another source says that the devotion was brought to Ferrara not by four ambassadors, but by a large crowd of Bianchi, and that they arrived on September 10, not September 1: Museo Correr, Venezia, ms. Cicogna 1115 (35), fols. 59r–v. Given these difficulties, I have generally given only those particulars on which the two sources concur.

was staged, with the participation of the entire clergy and of men and women of all ages and conditions. On September 8, the feast of the Nativity of the Virgin, the Ferrarese cycle of Bianchi processions seems to have begun. On that day the fifteen-year-old marquis Niccolò d'Este and his wife, Gigliola da Carrara, the bishop of Ferrara and the patriarch of Jerusalem (both of the noble Ferrarese family de' Roberti), many nobles and courtiers, the whole clergy, and a great multitude of people went to the Este park of Belfiore, where the bishop of Modena, Dionigi Restani, preached. In the following days, similar processions went through the city and the surrounding area, visiting churches, while the four Bianchi who had carried the devotion to Ferrara set off to bring it to Padua, the March of Treviso, and the Friuli.

Delaito's account of the transmission of the Bianchi devotion by a small party resembling formal ambassadors is echoed by events in Padua. There, too, the Bianchi devotion was brought by messengers—"oratores dictae albae societatis"—who came from Ferrara on September 24.[53] Giovanni Conversini da Ravenna, chancellor to Francesco da Carrara, tells us that these ambassadors were specifically invited by Francesco, who had heard rumors of the Bianchi and wanted to know more.[54] He sent to Ferrara, where his daughter Gigliola had herself taken part in the processions.[55] In response, a priest arrived mounted on a white-draped horse. The priest was followed the next day, September 24, by five more Bianchi, and these ambassadors spent the next few days preaching the devotion to a steadily growing audience. On September 29 the formal Bianchi processions

[53] *Liber regiminum Padue*, ed. A. Bonardi, in *RIS²*, 8, part 1, pp. 375–376. Bartolomeo Gatari, *Cronaca Carrarese*, ed. Antonio Medin and Guido Tolomei, in *RIS²*, 17, part 1, p. 466, says that the devotion was introduced on October 23 (an evident error) by two doctors of theology.

[54] Giovanni Conversini da Ravenna, *La processione dei Bianchi nella città di Padova (1399)*, ed. and trans. Libia Cortese and Dino Cortese (Padua: Centro Studi Antoniani, 1978), p. 63. Libia and Dino Cortese have used Giovanni Conversini's account to describe the Bianchi processions in "Trecento padovano e religiosità popolare," *Il Santo*, 25 (1985): 173–194, while renouncing any attempt at analysis. For a topographical study of the processions in Padua, based on Giovanni Conversini's memoir, see Ada Francesca Marcianò and Maria Spina, "La processione dei Bianchi a Padova, 1399: Una fonte per lo studio della città tra Medioevo e Rinascimento," *Storia della città*, 4 (1977): 3–30, and, more elaborately, Ada Francesca Marcianò, *Padova 1399: Le processioni dei Bianchi nella testimonianza di Giovanni di Conversino* (Padua: Centro grafico editoriale, 1980).

[55] Delaito, *Annales Estenses*, col. 957.

began; the Bianchi in Padua were organized like those in Bologna according to quarters of the city, and within each quarter according to parish. To a certain extent, the Bianchi processions in Padua were coordinated with the ecclesiastical calendar: on October 4, the feast-day of St. Francis, they went to the church of San Francesco; and on October 7, feast-day of Santa Giustina, they brought the Bianchi devotions to a close at the church dedicated to that Paduan virgin and martyr. The processions kept to the city and the area immediately around it; no effort was made to spread the devotion elsewhere.

In fact, an official bar had been placed to the further spread of the Bianchi devotion in this direction. A month earlier, on September 10, the Venetian Council of Ten had instructed the podestà at Chioggia to turn back any Bianchi that came his way with the intention of going to Venice.[56] That is precisely what his colleague Remigio Soranzo did at Treviso on October 7, when he dispersed a group of people who tried to stage a Bianchi procession at that Venetian outpost on the mainland.[57] Though Padua was not yet subject to Venetian rule, it too had a Venetian podestà, Jacopo Gradenigo, and we may surmise that the wishes of the Council of Ten were known to him. There was no place for the Bianchi to go from Padua; the borders of Venice were closed to them.

Central Italy

Compared to developments in the north, the progress of the Bianchi devotion south of the Apennines seems different in many respects: it is more festive, less regularized, less orderly in its spread. Some of these differences may be more apparent than real, due to disparities in the documentation. We have, alas, no record for the Po valley equal to the Tuscan chronicle of Luca Dominici in precision of detail; if we did, perhaps we would find that some of the differences between developments north and south of the mountains were not so marked as they seem. But many of the contrasts were quite real,

---

[56] Archivio di Stato di Venezia, Consiglio dei Dieci, Misti, 8 (1392–1407), fol. 53r. This measure was published by Emmanuele Antonio Cicogna, *Delle inscrizioni veneziane* (Venice: G. Orlandelli, 1824–1853), vol. 6, pp. 142–143.

[57] Luigi Pesce, *La Chiesa di Treviso nel primo Quattrocento* (Rome: Herder, 1987), p. 48.

and resulted from the different circumstances of the two regions. In the first place, Tuscany and Umbria were still largely free of the plague, and the Bianchi processions there were characterized, at least initially, by hope and joy, not by terror; in the plague-stricken Po valley, in contrast, there was little occasion for rejoicing. In addition, Tuscany and Umbria were fragmented into a multitude of small, independent states; the unfolding of the Bianchi processions there was not molded by the will of a single dominating power, as the course of the movement in Lombardy was shaped by Giangaleazzo Visconti. Finally, central Italy was physically as well as politically fragmented, a region of broken terrain in which there were always several alternate routes between any two points; the Bianchi processions wandered through the hilly countryside, rather than following one clear highway such as the Via Emilia. The result was a pattern of development far more diffuse than that to the north.

We do not know exactly when the Bianchi started to spread from Genoa through the Riviera di Levante; the outset of the procession in that direction was still being awaited on July 13.[58] Sometime in the second half of July, the devotion spread to the string of strife-torn towns perched between the mountains and the sea: Recco, Rapallo, and Chiavari, "where enmities were extremely fierce."[59] Its entrance into Tuscany can be traced by plotting the miracles that marked its progress, at Vezzano, Lerici, and Sarzana. These miracles, as recounted by Giovanni Sercambi, served to validate the movement and overcome resistance. The case of Sarzana is typical. About 1,000 Bianchi arrived at that fortress town to find it prepared to resist them: the viscount who represented the duke of Milan there had ordered his garrison to seal the gates. But the troops were evidently less firm in their opposition than was their captain, for the Bianchi were allowed to enter without hindrance. They went to the central piazza, where their prayers caused a dry elm to burst forth in fresh green leaves. This was enough to convert the bishop of Luni, who promptly urged the people of Sarzana to adopt the devotion. It took a second miracle, however, to convince the stubborn viscount: when he tried to carve some cooked salt meat for his dinner, the cured meat bled unstint-

---

[58] "A Reccho si de' ire a processione, e quelli di là ne son contenti." Archivio Datini di Prato, no. 661, lett. Genova-Firenze, comp. Datini, letter of July 13, 1399.
[59] "Ubi erant acutissima odia." Stella, *Annales Genuenses*, p. 240.

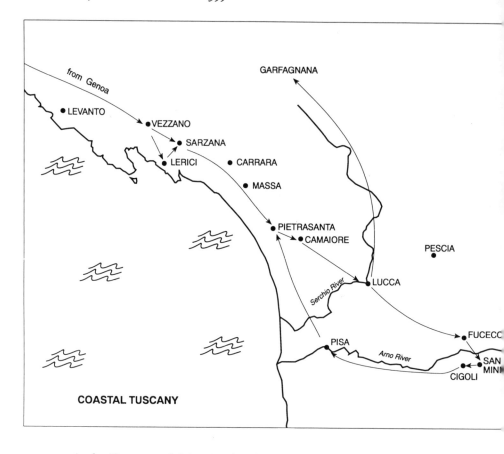

ingly. Because of this miracle, the viscount donned the white robes and joined the procession together with all his companions.[60]

The Sarzana Bianchi went to Pietrasanta, in the territory of Lucca; they converted that town without incident, and most of them then turned back. A party of about sixty, however, continued on toward Lucca, passing Camaiore on August 6, and entering Lucca two days later. Trailed by a crowd of curious Lucchesi, they went immediately to the cathedral church of San Martino to see the Volto Santo, the famous portrait of Christ crucified attributed to Nicodemus.[61] The pilgrims left Lucca that same evening, continuing their circuit to the

---

[60] Sercambi, *Croniche*, p. 315.

[61] On the cult of this image, see *Lucca, il Volto Santo e la civiltà medioevale* (Lucca: Maria Pacini Fazzi editore, 1984).

southeast toward Fucecchio, San Miniato, and the shrine of the Virgin at Cigoli, and then returned home by way of Pisa, where they also introduced the devotion.[62] According to a Dominican chronicler, this unusually wide ranging party of Bianchi was led by Fra Tommaso di ser Michele de Nodica, prior of the Dominican convent in Sarzana, who thus became "the root and origin of so much good in Tuscany."[63] Nor was Fra Tommaso the only Dominican to be so active in promoting this devotion. In contrast with the rest of Italy, where the Bianchi had no particular affiliation with any one religious order, the Bianchi movement took root in this corner of Tuscany thanks in good part to the initiative and support of the Dominicans.

The Bianchi of Pietrasanta followed the same route to Lucca. The vicar allowed only 220 of them to embark on this procession: many more were eager to go, "but so that Pietrasanta would not be left short, he did not want more people to leave at that time."[64] They were at Camaiore on August 8 and then, after having passed by Montemagno, they approached Lucca on the evening of Saturday, August 9. That night they lodged outside the walls, at San Piero. On Sunday morning they entered the city, visited the Volto Santo in San Martino and the churches of San Frediano and Sant'Agostino, heard mass at San Salvatore, and there preached the devotion to the assembled crowd of Lucchesi. At vespers they visited San Romano and San Michele, and then marched forth through the Porta di Borgo. They headed north along the valley of the Serchio to San Pellegrino, and spread the Bianchi devotion through the Garfagnana.[65]

The stage was thus set for the diffusion of the Bianchi devotion throughout central Italy. The group from Sarzana had introduced the devotion to both Lucca and Pisa, and from those two cities welled two main currents of diffusion. From Lucca, the devotion spread east along the Valdarno to Pistoia, Prato, Florence, and Arezzo. From Pisa, it coursed southwards to Volterra, Siena, Perugia, Orvieto, and Rome.

---

[62] Sercambi, *Croniche*, pp. 316–318.

[63] "Et sic Frater Thomas fuit radix et principium Tusciae circa tot bona." Domenico da Peccioli, *Chronica antiqua conventus Sanctae Catharinae de Pisis*, ed. Francesco Bonaini, in *Archivio storico italiano*, vol. 6, part 2 (1845): 577–578.

[64] "Ma perchè Pietrasanta non rimanesse sfornita, non volse che più n'uscissero per quella volta." Sercambi, *Croniche*, p. 318.

[65] Sercambi, *Croniche*, pp. 318–320.

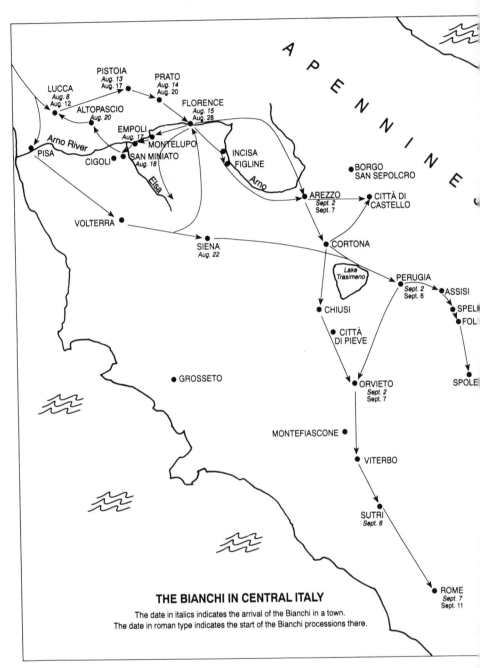

THE BIANCHI IN CENTRAL ITALY

The date in italics indicates the arrival of the Bianchi in a town.
The date in roman type indicates the start of the Bianchi processions there.

Feelings in Lucca were divided at first. On August 10, the day that the party from Pietrasanta left, a number of citizens and a few friars set up a cross in the Dominican church of San Romano and proclaimed that the white robes and the processions were very pious things.[66] They passed the word that everyone who wanted to take part in the devotion should confess and receive communion; the next day was to be spent in preparation for a departure on August 12. When the ruling council (anziani, or Elders) of Lucca learned of these plans, they ordered a halt: no one was to go out on procession. But more than a thousand Bianchi set out hurriedly, before this ban could be put into effect. Their route took them to Lunata, Pescia, Montecatini, and Serravalle; along the way their numbers swelled as the rural populace joined their procession, and when they spent the night of August 12 in the Valdinievole near Pistoia, they numbered approximately 2,000. On August 13 they entered Pistoia, where they were exceptionally well received, and that evening they went on toward Prato.[67] On August 14 they visited the Girdle of the Virgin in Prato, and then proceeded to Campi, where they spent the night. On August 15 they entered Florence, but were received with skepticism and even derision, despite their performing a miraculous cure in the Franciscan church of Santa Croce. They thought it best to leave Florence, and after lodging that night across the Arno at Monticelli turned toward home, passing through Lastra (August 16), Montelupo and Empoli (August 17), San Miniato and Santa Croce (August 18 and 19), Altopascio and Capannori (August 20), before returning to Lucca on August 21.[68]

While this group of Bianchi was making its rounds, the Elders of Lucca tried to mollify those whom they had prevented from going by staging a series of internal processions.[69] They met on August 13 to make their plans, and decided to begin their devotions on August 15, the feast of the Assumption. The Elders and the bishop marched in this procession, along with 1,200 men and 1,600 women.[70] Since it

---

[66] Sercambi, Croniche, p. 348. Again, Dominicans take the lead in promoting the devotion.

[67] Sercambi, Croniche, pp. 349–351; Dominici, Cronaca, pp. 57–61.

[68] Sercambi, Croniche, pp. 351–360. Dominici, Cronaca, p. 60, offers a slightly different chronology: he says that the Lucchesi entered Florence on August 16, instead of August 15, and returned home on August 20, not August 21.

[69] Sercambi, Croniche, pp. 353–354, 356–357.

[70] The preponderance of women in this internal procession suggests that mostly

was a Marian feast, they proceeded to the church of Santa Maria For-isportam; they then accompanied the bishop back to San Martino and dispersed for the night. Each day they repeated this pattern: visit a church, and then escort the bishop home. They heard mass at each of the major churches of Lucca in turn: San Frediano, San Salvatore, San Michele, San Francesco, San Romano, Santa Maria dei Servi, San Giovanni, and on August 23, the last of the nine days of the devotion, the cathedral church of San Martino.

The devotion had evidently taken root in the surrounding area, for each day parties of Bianchi came to Lucca. On August 15, 100 Bianchi arrived from Montetignoso to the north, followed the next day by 225 from Massa.[71] On August 17, nearly 500 Bianchi from Camaiore arrived; this group was on its way back from Florence, where it had overcome the resistance of the Florentines by performing a miracle in the Palazzo della Signoria, in the presence of the priors.[72] A party of Pisans came on August 18; 125 Bianchi from the lands of the cathedral chapter and ten times that number from the vicariate of Coreglia, in the Garfagnana, on August 19; groups from Barga and Gallicano, in the same region, on August 20; groups from Pisa on the following three days; and 600 Bianchi from the Valdinievole on August 23.[73] These parties came from areas to the north, the east, and the south of Lucca; the whole region had adopted the Bianchi devotion.

The Lucchesi who had been prevented from going on the procession to Florence were not satisfied with the internal processions, and so the Elders decided to let them go out a portion at a time.[74] On August 23, the last day of the internal processions, a party of 1,800 Bianchi assembled in San Frediano, took the crucifix from that church, and set out to the southwest. Their circuit took them to Pisa, Cascina, Montopoli, Cigoli, San Miniato, Santa Croce, Santa Maria al Monte, Vicopisano, Buti, and Pontetto. They stopped at small towns on their way to make peace, and often stayed at monasteries—the Certosa di

---

men went on the external one—although Giovanni Sercambi marvels that "it seemed like a divine miracle that good honest women and wives of solid citizens went out from the city like crazy women, not caring whether they left fathers, husbands, or children or worrying about the heat and the strain, to follow the crucifix." Sercambi, *Croniche*, pp. 349–350.

[71] Sercambi, *Croniche*, p. 354.

[72] Sercambi, *Croniche*, pp. 354–355. The priors of Florence, like the priors of Perugia and the Elders of Lucca, were the chief governing council of the city.

[73] Sercambi, *Croniche*, pp. 356–357.

[74] Sercambi, *Croniche*, pp. 360–367.

Farneta near Lucca, the Badia di San Donnino in Pisa, the Badia di Guamo—where they left large wax candles as gifts. They carried similar candles in a torchlight parade to San Martino on the evening of September 2, when they returned to Lucca. Their final act, before dispersing to their homes, was to return their crucifix to San Frediano.

A third group of Lucchesi Bianchi set out the very next day, carrying the crucifix from San Pietro Somaldi.[75] Their circuit took them to Florence; they returned to Lucca on September 13, the eve of the festival of the Holy Cross. Like the second group, they went in formal procession to San Martino, returned their crucifix to its resting place in San Pietro Somaldi, and dispersed. This marked the end of the unusually protracted Bianchi devotions in Lucca, which lasted over a month as group after group took its turn to don the white robes.

By the middle of September, when life in Lucca finally returned to normal, the Bianchi devotion had spread all over central Italy and even reached Rome. In Pistoia, the devotion was adopted immediately after the visit of the Lucchesi Bianchi on August 13.[76] The next day, the town council met and decided to allocate money for the reception of visiting Bianchi, to release prisoners as the Lucchesi had requested, and to encourage the people of Pistoia to go out in procession. The following days were spent in preparation: the bishop preached the devotion, parties went about making peace in the city and contado, the council repatriated exiles, and the podestà bent to the general will and freed prisoners. The procession set out on Sunday, August 17, the same day that the Bianchi processions began in Bergamo. The Pistoiese Bianchi moved at a more leisurely pace than the Lucchesi and covered less ground. Their circuit took them to Quarrata, Carmignano, Signa, Brozzi, and Fiesole. They waited for a day at Fiesole. Florence was engrossed in the celebrations marking King Ladislaus's occupation of Naples, and it was impossible to get to the shrine of Santa Maria Impruneta, with its miracle-working image of the Madonna, without passing through Florence. They entered Florence on August 22, accompanied by the bishop of Fiesole; after visiting the principal churches of the city—the cathedral, the baptistry, Or San Michele, the Santissima Annunziata, Santa Maria No-

[75] Sercambi, *Croniche*, p. 367.
[76] Dominici, *Cronaca*, pp. 73–86, 93–101, 105–108.

vella, and Santa Croce—they crossed the Arno to spend the night at San Miniato al Monte. They were better received in Florence than the Lucchesi had been, and in the general enthusiasm, the crucifix they carried performed a number of miraculous cures.[77] The next morning they began their homeward journey by parading through the Oltrarno section of Florence, stopping at a church they had missed on the previous day, Santo Spirito. They visited Peretola, Campi, and Prato, before returning to Pistoia on August 28.

While this party was making its rounds, other processions were held in Pistoia for those, like Luca Dominici, who were unable to leave home. Luca regarded this internal procession as a poor second-best, and lamented that he had not been able to take part in the external one: "I thought I would go along, but because my father and my mother went, I could not go, so as not to leave the house and my wife all alone. Nothing I said would persuade my mother to stay home and let me go."[78] The internal processions visited each of the major churches in turn, and their visits, like those at Padua, were sometimes arranged to conform with the ecclesiastical calendar. The bishop of Pistoia, Andrea Franchi, stayed home and preached to the internal processions; he was an old man, and perhaps did not feel up to even the moderate rigors of the excursion.[79] On Saturday, the Bianchi in Pistoia fasted on bread and water and the usual market was not held. Most stores were closed, too, on August 26, the last of the nine days of devotion, when the internal procession marched forth to greet and welcome home the party returning from Prato.

In addition to hosting the group from Pistoia, Prato had welcomed the Bianchi from Lucca on August 14 or 15.[80] The people of Prato prepared to adopt the devotion in their turn, and on August 20 they set out under threatening skies. The weather then cleared suddenly,

---

[77] For an analysis of these miracles, see Chapter 4.

[78] "Io vi credetti ire, ma perchè mio padre e mia madre v'andorno, non vi potetti andare, per non lassare la casa sola e la donna e mai non potetti fare che mia madre volesse rimanere e lassarmi andare." Dominici, *Cronaca*, p. 81.

[79] I. Taurisano, *Il Beato Andrea Franchi* (Arezzo: n.p., 1922). Franchi resigned his bishopric on February 25, 1400, in favor of his nephew, Matteo Diamanti; he died May 26, 1401, after a long illness. See Dominici, *Cronaca*, pp. 289–290.

[80] "La Cronaca di Sandro Marcovaldi," ed. Ruggero Nuti, *Archivio storico pratese*, 18 (1940): 61–64; *Miscellanea* of Michelangelo Martini, in ser Lapo Mazzei, *Lettere di un notaro a un mercante del secolo XIV*, ed. Cesare Guasti (Florence: Le Monnier, 1880), vol. 2, p. 359, note.

and this sign of divine approval persuaded those who had hesitated to join the procession. Their route took them first to Sesto and then to Florence, which they seem to have skirted: they approached the Porta San Gallo but did not enter it, instead making a clockwise circuit of the walls to Rovezzano. From here they followed the course of the Arno upstream to Castello Sant'Angelo in Val di Sieve, Incisa, Figline, San Giovanni Valdarno, and Montevarchi; they returned via San Donato in Collina to Florence and then home to Prato. In contrast to the usual nine-day Bianchi devotions, the Bianchi of Prato spent eleven days in procession; they set out on August 20 and returned home on August 30.[81]

Starting around August 15, Florence had received parties of Bianchi from Lucca, Pistoia, Prato, and Pisa.[82] The Florentines were widely reported to be skeptical at first, but the repeated stimulus of these visits eventually moved them to participate also. Nor were all of the Florentines so reluctant. Some, in fact, joined the Bianchi from Lucca; they passed by Pistoia on August 25, on their way home.[83] But this was a relatively small and unusually impulsive group. On August 25 most Florentines were still preparing to adopt the devotion, parading through the streets, rousing their neighbors, and making peace.[84]

The main Florentine processions did not leave until August 28. The priors took care that everything was properly arranged and in good order; they organized the great external processions by quarters and announced internal processions for those who could not leave the city. The bishop of Florence led these internal processions, which looped out from the city each day and returned home each night. The whole city was swept up in the devotion. Coluccio Salutati may have been indulging in hyperbole when he exclaimed that "our whole city is in white," but he was not far from the truth.[85] Because of the Bianchi celebrations, the banks remained closed and all currency transactions were suspended; the only other time that this happened be-

[81] Dominici, *Cronaca*, p. 111.

[82] *Cronica volgare di Anonimo Fiorentino dall'anno 1385 al 1409, già attribuita a Piero di Giovanni Minerbetti*, ed. Elina Bellondi, in *RIS²*, 27, part 2, pp. 240–242; Biblioteca Riccardiana, Firenze, ms. 1808, *Priorista Fiorentina*, fol. 72r.

[83] Dominici, *Cronaca*, p. 104.

[84] Coluccio Salutati, *Epistolario*, ed. Francesco Novati (Rome: Istituto Storico Italiano, 1891–1911), vol. 3, pp. 357–358; Dominici, *Cronaca*, p. 109.

[85] "Tota nostra civitas est in albis." Salutati, *Epistolario*, vol. 3, p. 361.

tween 1389 and 1432 was in midsummer of 1400, at the height of the worst epidemic of plague since the Black Death of 1348.[86]

The main external procession was apparently drawn from the quarters of Santa Croce and Santa Maria Novella.[87] Led by the bishop of Fiesole, it set out from Porta San Niccolò and from Ripoli cut through the hills to San Donato in Collina, to avoid following a wide bend in the Arno. It returned to the river valley at Incisa, and then headed upstream through Figline, San Giovanni Valdarno, Montevarchi, and Quarata to Arezzo, which the group reached on September 2.[88] On their way back to Florence they followed the other bank of the Arno, passing through Laterina, Terranuova, Castelfranco, and Ponte a Sieve. This group included Francesco di Marco Datini, the well-known and very wealthy merchant of Prato, who reported that the small party of friends and business associates with which he performed the devotion returned home on Saturday, September 6. However, they did not take off their robes or sleep in a bed until Sunday, after they had escorted the bishop and the crucifix back to Fiesole and received the episcopal blessing.[89]

The quarter of San Giovanni took a different route to the same goal: these Bianchi followed the Val di Sieve, traversed the divide to

[86] Anthony Molho, *Florentine Public Finances in the Early Renaissance, 1400–1433* (Cambridge: Harvard University Press, 1971), p. 213, note a, cites an entry in a notebook recording daily exchange rates between the gold florin and the silver currency: "The exchange rate was unavailable because the banks were closed for the feast of the Bianchi, when everyone donned white" [translation mine].

[87] There is some confusion about the pairing of the urban quarters in these processions. The memoirs of Florentine Niccolò del Buono di Besi Busini report the pairing given here: Archivio di Stato di Firenze, Carte Strozziane, IV, 563, "Ricordanze di Niccolò del Buono di Bese Busini," hereafter abbreviated as ASF, "Ricordanze di Niccolò del Buono di Bese Busini," fol. 8or (I am grateful to Susannah Foster Baxendale, who brought this passage to my attention). However, a letter of messer Rosso di Andreozzo degli Orlandi to Piero di Bernardo Chiarini suggests that the quarter of San Giovanni, not Santa Maria Novella, accompanied Santa Croce to Arezzo: Archivio di Stato di Firenze, Corporazioni religiose soppresse, Badia di Firenze, 78, filza 315, lett. 212, 28 September 1399. Perhaps the organization of the processions was less rigid than was claimed. But since the "Ricordanze" of Niccolò del Buono Busini are supported by those of Francesco di Marco Datini, in Mazzei, *Lettere di un notaro*, p. xcix, I have chosen to follow that version of events. My thanks go to Elaine Rosenthal for sharing her knowledge of the Orlandi family.

[88] Mazzei, *Lettere di un notaro*, pp. xcix–ciii; Bellondi, *Cronica volgare di Anonimo Fiorentino*, pp. 241–242.

[89] Mazzei, *Lettere di un notaro*, p. ciii. On Datini, see Iris Origo, *The Merchant of Prato, Francesco di Marco Datini, 1335–1410* (New York: Knopf, 1957).

the upper reaches of the Arno, and then followed the Arno down-stream through the Casentino to Arezzo.[90] Their arrival apparently coincided with that of the party led by the bishop of Fiesole; Luca Dominici says that on September 2 three quarters of Florence were in Arezzo.[91] The fourth quarter, that of Santo Spirito, had gone south through the Valdelsa.[92]

The progress of the Bianchi after Arezzo has left no clear image, partly because the sources are few and laconic, partly because the processions tended to fragment and go in several directions. Luca Dominici heard in Pistoia that the Aretine Bianchi had set out for Perugia on September 7.[93] This date is plausible; the Florentine Bianchi had arrived at Arezzo on September 2, and most towns spent several days in preparation before setting out. This direction, more-over, would have led them past Cortona, which adopted the devotion at some unspecified date.[94] But according to Perugian records, the Bianchi who arrived in Perugia came from Siena, not Arezzo; on the other hand, a large number of Bianchi from Arezzo were reported in Città di Castello in September.[95] Perhaps the Aretine Bianchi set out in two distinct groups like those of Cortona, some of whom headed south to Chiusi while others went north to Città di Castello.[96] In addition to the parties from Arezzo and Cortona, smaller groups of Bianchi came to Città di Castello from Castiglion Fiorentino, Mon-tone, and the Casentino. The people of Città di Castello, however, were engaged in an intermittent war with the Ubaldini clan, and so did not dare to go far from the safety of their walls.[97] Perhaps in-spired by the Bianchi, Città di Castello agreed to a truce with the

[90] ASF, "Ricordanze di Niccolò del Buono di Bese Busini," fol. 8or.

[91] Dominici, Cronaca, p. 178. This joining of the two processions may explain part of the confusion over which quarter went where.

[92] ASF, "Ricordanze di Niccolò del Buono di Bese Busini," fol. 8or. One of the members of this group was Valorino di Barna di Valorino Ciurianni, who recorded that he was out of town, "essendo io tra Bianchi in Val d'Elsa," when one of his relatives was ill and drawing up his will in late August. Archivio di Stato di Firenze, Manoscritti, 77, "Ricordanze di Valorino di Barna di Valorino Ciurianni," fol. 32r.

[93] Dominici, Cronaca, p. 153.

[94] Sercambi, Croniche, pp. 369–370.

[95] Cronaca latina, edited in Giovanni Magherini Graziani, Storia di Città di Castello (Città di Castello: S. Lapi, 1890–1910), vol. 3, p. 201, n. 2.

[96] Biblioteca del Comune e dell'Accademia Etrusca di Cortona, ms. 532, p. 76; Girolamo Mancini, Cortona nel Medio Evo (Florence, 1897; rpt. Rome: Multigrafica, 1969), pp. 252–253.

[97] Magherini Graziani, Storia di Città di Castello, vol. 3, p. 202, n. 1.

Ubaldini on September 25. But by then the processions were over, and the movement of the Bianchi was not transmitted any further. The spread of the Bianchi devotion in this direction ended at Città di Castello, as it had at Como and Bergamo, in a flurry of local processions.[98]

Pisa is another city for which we have disappointingly little information about the Bianchi. The major fourteenth-century chronicler, Ranieri Sardo, died at about this time, and the patchy archival records for 1399 and 1400 do little to fill this gap in the chronicle record.[99] The lack of Pisan documentation is particularly frustrating, since this city was the starting point of a chain of processions which led eventually to Rome.

The party of Bianchi from Sarzana that first brought the devotion to Lucca on August 8 also introduced it to Pisa a few days later.[100] By August 18 small groups of Pisan Bianchi had started to appear in Lucca, and one party reportedly went to Florence.[101] Even in the general climate of reconciliation, this was perhaps too provocative. Gherardo d'Appiano had sold Pisa to Florence's great enemy, Giangaleazzo Visconti, in February 1399, and the Florentines were so disturbed by this that in July they were still trying to put the blame for their failed foreign policy on those universal scapegoats, the Venetians.[102] The main body of Pisan Bianchi accordingly chose to avoid

[98] There is the odd story of how letters from Florence brought the Bianchi devotion to Fermo: Antonio di Niccolò, *Cronaca Fermana*, in *Cronache della città di Fermo*, ed. Gaetano De Minicis and Marco Tabarrini, *Documenti di storia italiana*, 4 (Florence, 1870), pp. 27–28. Antonio di Niccolò's account is rather confused—perhaps understandably so, since he wrote this portion of his chronicle well after the events he describes—and it is possible that the Bianchi came to Fermo along the Adriatic coast, from Ancona. But the only information we have on events in Ancona, aside from a miracle reported by Luca Dominici (*Cronaca*, p. 215), is the bald statement by the local antiquarian that "Ancona welcomed them: so it is written." Agostino Peruzzi, *Storia d'Ancona dalla sua fondazione all'anno MDXXXII* (Pesaro: Tipografia Nobili, 1835), vol. 2, p. 208.

[99] Ranieri Sardo, *Cronaca di Pisa*, ed. Ottavio Banti (Rome: Istituto Storico Italiano, 1963).

[100] Sercambi, *Croniche*, pp. 316–318; Domenico da Peccioli, *Chronica antiqua*, pp. 577–578.

[101] Sercambi, *Croniche*, pp. 356–357; Dominici, *Cronaca*, p. 93; Bellondi, *Cronaca volgare di Anonimo Fiorentino*, p. 241.

[102] Gene Brucker, *The Civic World of Early Renaissance Florence* (Princeton: Princeton University Press, 1977), p. 168. Brucker errs in identifying the ruler of Pisa as Jacopo d'Appiano, who had died in August 1398.

Florence and go instead to Siena, probably by way of the Val d'Era and Volterra.[103]

We can not be sure exactly when they set out, but the Pisan Bianchi were evidently before the gates of Siena on August 22, for on that date the Sienese town council, or *concistoro*, granted them permission to enter the city, allowed them to celebrate mass at the public chapel in the Piazza del Campo, and even loaned them the altar furnishings of the communal sacristy.[104] The next day, when the Bianchi entered to celebrate mass before the Palazzo Pubblico, the concistoro had everything placed in readiness to receive the Bianchi, "who for the most part are Pisans," and instructed the official in charge of the grain supply to distribute bread at public expense.[105] Nothing in the public record confirms the rumors of Sienese mistrust and reluctance that reached Luca Dominici's ears.[106]

Two days later, on August 25, the concistoro met again, this time to see to the Sienese performance of the Bianchi devotions. The members of this council granted the request of the bishop of Siena that everyone be allowed to do penance and don white "for the honor and reverence of omnipotent God and his mother, the glorious Virgin Mary."[107] They proclaimed a holiday, suspended all civil cases, and declared that no one could be seized for any monetary debt, whether owed to the commune or to a private individual, before the middle of September.[108] They instructed the official in charge of the grain supply to prepare bread for the expedition.[109] On August 28, they extended the suspension of civil cases to include criminal cases.[110] Two days later, they responded affirmatively to letters from Volterra requesting permission to come to Siena.[111] This Volterran request must have been

---

[103] Dominici, *Cronaca*, p. 112.

[104] Archivio di Stato di Siena, Concistoro, 210 (1 luglio 1399–31 agosto 1399), fol. 40v. Giovanni Sercambi (*Croniche*, p. 361) mentions that when the Bianchi from Lucca entered Pisa on August 25, they encountered the Pisan Bianchi who were just then returning home. This would put their departure on August 17, which fits with the arrival of the Bianchi from Sarzana sometime around August 12 or 13, and with the appearance of the Pisan Bianchi at Siena on August 22.

[105] "Qui pro maiori parte sunt Pisani." Archivio di Stato di Siena, Concistoro, 210, fol. 41r.

[106] Dominici, *Cronaca*, pp. 113–114.

[107] "ad honorem et reverentiam omnipotentis Dei et gloriose Marie Verginis matris eius." Archivio di Stato di Siena, Concistoro, 210, fol. 41v.

[108] Archivio di Stato di Siena, Concistoro, 210, fol. 41v.

[109] Archivio di Stato di Siena, Concistoro, 210, fol. 41v.

[110] Archivio di Stato di Siena, Concistoro, 210, fol. 42r.

[111] Archivio di Stato di Siena, Concistoro, 210, fol. 43r.

sparked by the passage of the Pisan Bianchi, and as soon as they had won Sienese permission, the Bianchi of Volterra set out on a circuit that blithely ignored political tensions: after visiting Siena, they proceeded to Florence, where 2,000 of them were reported on September 6.[112]

The Sienese Bianchi, meanwhile, had gone to Perugia. On their way there, they sparked the conversion of the notoriously dissolute lord of Cortona, Uguccio da Casale, who abandoned his vices, dropped his initial opposition to the Bianchi, and personally donned the white robes and led his people to Città di Castello.[113] Some of the Sienese Bianchi may have reached Perugia at the end of August or on September 1; their main body was there on September 2, when the populace of Perugia joined the Sienese in clamoring for the release of prisoners.[114] On September 3, the Perugian priors decreed unanimously that a properly honorable reception be given to the "most holy and devout company of Bianchi dressed in white robes, for the honor and reverence of the Holy Trinity and the most glorious Virgin Mary."[115] Bread, wine, wax, and every other necessity were to be provided for these Bianchi, who for the most part were from Siena.[116]

Over the following days, while the populace of Perugia joined enthusiastically in the Bianchi devotions, the priors attended to the ordinary business of governance: making themselves available to hear complaints, arranging to garrison a fortified town, and so on.[117] For some who joined the processions, the government hewed too closely to business as usual. On September 20, the priors had to declare a retroactive holiday, from September 2 to September 14; this official

---

[112] Luca Dominici, *Cronaca*, p. 112, says the Volterrans set out on August 31; he reports their presence in Florence on p. 135.

[113] Dominici, *Cronaca*, p. 153; *Cronaca latina*, in Magherini Graziani, *Storia di Città di Castello*, vol. 3, p. 201, n. 1; Sercambi, *Croniche*, pp. 369–370. This startling transformation apparently proved lasting; Uguccio died the following year, on October 11, 1400, while tending the plague-stricken in the hospital of Santa Maria Nuova in Florence. Girolamo Mancini, *Cortona nel Medio Evo*, pp. 252–253.

[114] Archivio di Stato di Perugia, Consigli e riformanze, 44, fol. 133v. The arrival of an advance party in late August would help to explain the extremely rapid transmission of the devotion to Orvieto.

[115] ". . . sanctissimam et devotissimam sotietatem Blancorum, veste alba indutorum, ad honorem et reverentiam sanctissime trinitatis et gloriosissime Virginis Marie." Archivio di Stato di Perugia, Consigli e riformanze, 44, fol. 130r.

[116] "In magno numero civitatis Senarum." Archivio di Stato di Perugia, Consigli e riformanze, 44, fol. 130r.

[117] Archivio di Stato di Perugia, Consigli e riformanze, 44, fols. 130v–131v.

declaration preserved those who had taken part in the Bianchi devotions from harassment by zealous Perugian officials, who had taken this opportunity to seize contumacious individuals against whom cases were pending.[118]

From September 6 to 14, the Bianchi of Perugia made a circuit through the towns of Umbria: Assisi, Spello, Foligno, Spoleto, and Todi.[119] The main body of the procession passed through Spoleto on September 10, though smaller parties had begun to arrive two days earlier. An offshoot of this procession reached L'Aquila on September 12; as the Bianchi penetrated deeper into the Umbrian hill country, the procession apparently splintered.[120] The group that visited Vallo di Nera, whether the main body of Perugian Bianchi or a smaller fragment, was memorialized in a fresco painted there in July 1401.[121]

Some Bianchi from Perugia did not dawdle in this regional circuit, and instead raced south toward Rome. As the movement approached Rome, its passage from city to city accelerated. The Sienese Bianchi entered Perugia around September 1 and their main party was there on September 2, but on that date some Perugians were already introducing the devotion to Orvieto.

The rapid spread of the Bianchi devotion to Orvieto was due in part to the fortuitous presence of some prominent Orvietans in Perugia when the Sienese Bianchi arrived there. Count Francesco di Montemarte reports that his son Ranuccio, who was in Perugia at the

---

[118] Archivio de Stato di Perugia, Consigli e riformanze, 44, fol. 134r.

[119] I have based these dates on the holiday decreed by the priors, which covers the period from the entrance of the main party of Bianchi in Perugia to the end of the Perugian celebrations. The narrative sources for Perugia are stingy with dates; see *Memorie di Perugia dall'anno 1351 al 1438*, in *Cronache della città di Perugia*, ed. Ariodante Fabretti (Turin: Tipi privati dell'editore, 1887–1892), vol. 1, pp. 206–207, and Pompeo Pellini, *Dell'historia di Perugia* (Venice, 1664; rpt. Bologna: Forni, 1968), *Parte seconda*, pp. 112–114. There are also some brief mentions in other Umbrian chronicles: "Le cronache di Spello degli Olorini," reconstructed by D. M. Faloci Pulignani, in *Bollettino della R. Deputazione di storia patria per l'Umbria*, 23 (1918): 278; Parruccio Zampolini, *Frammenti degli annali di Spoleto dal 1304 al 1424*, in *Documenti storici inediti in sussidio delle memorie umbre*, ed. Achille Sansi (Foligno: P. Sgariglia, 1879), p. 135; Guerriero da Gubbio, *Cronaca*, ed. Giuseppe Mazzatinti, in *RIS²*, 21, part 4, p. 33.

[120] Alessandro de Ritiis, *Chronica civitatis Aquilae*, ed. Leopoldo Cassese, in *Archivio storico per le provincie napoletane*, n.s., 27 (1941): 173–174; Niccolò di Borbona, *Cronaca delle cose dell'Aquila, dall'anno 1363 all'anno 1424*, in Ludovico Antonio Muratori, *Antiquitates Italicae Medii Aevi*, vol. 6, col. 861.

[121] Pietro Pirri, "Una pittura storica di Cola di Pietro da Camerino in S. Maria di Vallo di Nera," *Archivio per la storia ecclesiastica dell'Umbria*, 4 (1917–1919): 275–285.

time, donned the white robes on the spot and just as quickly set off for home.[122] Ranuccio was the first of the Bianchi to come to Orvieto, arriving on September 2 together with many others from Perugia and Città della Pieve. On September 6 the Orvietans, men and women, dressed themselves in white, and on September 7 they set out for Rome. Once again, Ranuccio blazed the trail: he had left Orvieto on September 4, bound for Montefiascone, Viterbo, and Vetralla, all on the route to Rome.

On the road to Rome, at the town of Sutri, a striking miracle was recorded on September 6.[123] The Bianchi there, as in so many other places, were trying to make peace, though this time they were engaged in the rather uncommon task of settling a domestic disagreement between Matteo Trovari and his wife. Matteo proved obdurate, and so the leader of this group, a German knight named Henricus, turned to the crucifix and pleaded for help. In response to his plea, the image of Christ changed color and trembled; the wound in Christ's side opened and blood ran down his chest, leg, and shin and dripped from his big toe onto the marble floor in front of the altar. At the sight of this miracle, the crowd cried out. The bishop of Sutri sent one of his servants to see what the uproar was about, and when he learned, he charged a notary public with recording what had happened and collecting depositions from witnesses to the event.

The miracle in Sutri did more than just restore domestic harmony between Matteo Trovari and his wife—though considering Matteo's stubbornness, that task alone would have been enough for any one miracle. The bleeding crucifix of Sutri also helped persuade the entire city of Rome to adopt the Bianchi devotion.

When a small group of Bianchi arrived at Rome late in August, they were mocked by many Romans and honored by a few, but imitated by no one.[124] Things were different on September 7, when Count Niccola d'Anguillara entered Rome at the head of a large party of Bianchi, including many women; the count himself was barefoot

---

[122] Montemarte, *Cronaca*, pp. 266–268. His brother Ridolfo, irked and envious at the way Ranuccio had made this devotion his own, refused to have anything to do with it: p. 268.

[123] Vincenzo Federici, "Il miracolo del crocefisso della compagnia dei Bianchi a Sutri," in *Scritti di storia, di filologia, e d'arte per le nozze Fedele-De Fabritiis* (Naples: Riccardo Ricciardi, 1908), pp. 107–118.

[124] Dominici, *Cronaca*, p. 147.

and carried a crucifix. He was received by the pope, to whom he explained that he too had initially made fun of the Bianchi. But at Sutri, said Niccola, "I saw this crucifix which I hold in my hands shed real blood from its side; moved by this, and for no other reason, I and my followers have acted thus."[125] The following day, the feast of the Nativity of the Virgin, Niccola was joined in Rome by his brother Francesco and by Count Niccolò Gentile di Monterano; the sight of these three great lords barefoot and carrying crosses moved the Roman populace, sensitive as always to status, and reports of it spread far and wide.[126] The lay prisons were emptied on September 8; the ecclesiastical one, the following day. On September 9, too, the pope blessed the crowd of Bianchi, now swelled by fresh arrivals from Montefiascone. The Veronica was displayed, and word went around that the Holy Door would be opened and the heads of St. Peter and St. Paul placed on the altar of St. Peter's. Rare and wonderful spiritual benefits were promised, and the Bianchi continued to flow into Rome to profit from them; the main party of Orvietans, which had set out on September 7, arrived on September 10.[127]

Meanwhile, the Romans had begun preparing to join the devotions. During the week of September 7–15, Rome swarmed with Bianchi, both Romans and those who had streamed to Rome from other cities. But the Roman devotions, unlike those elsewhere, preserved the divisions of the city; they formed around discrete bonds of national identity or clientage, rather than merging in a single undifferentiated procession. The Florentine community, for instance, planned to assemble in Sant'Orsola on September 11 and take part in the devotions as a group; as the factor of Gabriello di messer Bartolomeo Panciatichi wrote from Rome on September 10, one of his friends was busy preparing the group's robes.[128] The noble clans, too, played a leading part. Francesco d'Anguillara brought his farm laborers to Rome; Giordano Colonna headed another large group; and

[125] "Io vidi al crocifisso che io porto in mano gittare vero sangue per lo costato, di che compunto io e i miei abbiamo per questo fatto così e altra cagione non m'indusse." Dominici, Cronaca, p. 148.

[126] Dominici, Cronaca, p. 193.

[127] Dominici, Cronaca, p. 149.

[128] Dominici, Cronaca, p. 149. Much of Luca Dominici's information about events in Rome came from this letter, which he transcribed into his chronicle. On the foreign communities in Rome, see Egmont Lee, "Foreigners in Quattrocento Rome," Renaissance and Reformation/Renaissance et Réforme, n.s., 7 (1983): 135–146.

Niccola Orsini led 1,500 Romans toward Tagliacozzo, one of the Orsini family fiefs.[129]

The segmented nature of the Roman processions may have been due in part to lingering official mistrust. Boniface IX was widely reported to be apprehensive about this confluence of foreigners.[130] Zaccaria Trevisan, the senator of Rome, received from Coluccio Salutati a glowing description of the Bianchi devotions in Florence, but he showed himself considerably less enthusiastic about the Bianchi in Rome.[131] He took it upon himself to investigate someone who displayed a bleeding crucifix and claimed to be John the Baptist reborn. Carpenters who examined the crucifix at his behest quickly discovered the mechanism by which the charlatan called forth mock blood.[132] Boniface and Trevisan had good reason to be watchful, for in this time of religious excitement, the people of Rome were all too ready to believe in this self-proclaimed John the Baptist and his wonderful bleeding crucifix, or in any other reported miracle. When a rumor of miracles at Santa Maria in Campo di Fiori and at Castel Sant'Angelo flew through the city one night, the streets suddenly filled with torch-carrying Romans, flagellating themselves and crying for divine mercy.[133] In such circumstances, the authorities evidently thought it best not to sponsor a general procession.

---

[129] Dominici, *Cronica*, pp. 148, 193, 150.

[130] Montemarte, *Cronaca*, p. 268: "the pope was very suspicious that the gathering of such a multitude might spark an uprising against him, either at Rome or elsewhere." Archivio Datini di Prato, no. 897, lett. Montpellier-Barcelona, comp. Datini a Baldo Villanuzzi; October 17, 1399: "It seems that in Rome the pope was very frightened of these Bianchi."

[131] Salutati, *Epistolario*, pp. 355–359. On Trevisan, see Percy Gothein, *Zaccaria Trevisan il Vecchio: La vita e l'ambiente*, Miscellanea di studi e memorie a cura della R. Deputazione di Storia patria per le Venezie, 4 (Venice, 1942); Francesco Antonio Vitale, *Storia diplomatica de' Senatori di Roma dalla decadenza dell'impero romano fino a nostri tempi*, 2 vols. (Rome, 1791), vol. 2, pp. 356–358.

[132] Dominici, *Cronaca*, pp. 204–206, who says he heard this story from the general of the Franciscans. But such stories were circulating in many places: Dietrich von Niem, *De scismate libri tres*, ed. G. Erler (Leipzig: Veit, 1890), p. 169, places the arrest of a "pseudopropheta" in Acquapendente; Montemarte, *Cronaca*, pp. 267–268, tells of the unmasking of a charlatan at Orvieto. However, the last part of Francesco di Montemarte's chronicle, including this passage, has suffered some mutilations; a comparison with Luca di Domenico Manenti, *Cronaca*, ed. Luigi Fumi, in *RIS²*, 15, part 5, p. 407, raises some doubt about whether this charlatan in Orvieto was connected in any way with the Bianchi, since Manenti places this incident in March, well before the advent of the Bianchi.

[133] Dominici, *Cronaca*, p. 150.

Those processions that were staged, such as the one to Tagliacozzo led by Niccola Orsini, stayed within the immediate area of Rome. Even in the disrupted world of the Great Schism, Rome remained the seat of the apostles and the capital city of Christendom.[134] It exerted a powerful gravitational pull on the Bianchi; although only a few individual Bianchi made the long journey to Rome, the movement as a whole was drawn in that direction and moved increasingly swiftly as it got closer. Once Rome was reached, the spread of the devotion ceased. There was no comparable center, no goal sufficiently attractive to lure the Romans out of Rome.

Rural, Private, and Secondary Devotions

When described like this, the movement of the Bianchi appears to be a sharply defined urban phenomenon: great processions move from city to city through a rural void.[135] But the countryside through which they moved was far from void. Even in the remarkably urbanized areas of northern and central Italy, the majority of people still lived in the market towns, hamlets, and scattered homesteads of the contado. These people, too, participated in the Bianchi devotions, though their participation is harder to trace.

Sometimes the *contadini* simply swelled the ranks of an urban procession, which grew by accretion as it progressed through the countryside. This is what happened at Bergamo: when the Bianchi set out on August 27, they were thought to number 6,000; by the next day, that estimate had increased to 10,000.[136] Estimates of their numbers continued to grow, to 16,000 on August 31 and finally to 20,000 by the last day of the devotions. These figures are not based on any exact count and are undoubtedly exaggerated; nonetheless, they suggest the steady growth of the procession, which by this count tripled

[134] A large share of the pilgrims who flocked to Rome for the jubilee of 1400 came from areas belonging to the Avignon obedience. Federigo Melis, "Movimento di popoli e motivi economici nel giubileo del 1400," in *Miscellanea Gilles Gérard Meersseman* (Padua: Antenore, 1970), pp. 343–367.

[135] The only work dedicated to the Bianchi in the countryside is an essay by Diana M. Webb, "Penitence and Peace-Making in City and Contado: The Bianchi of 1399," in *The Church in Town and Countryside*, ed. Derek Baker, Studies in Church History, 16 (Oxford: Basil Blackwell, 1979), pp. 243–256.

[136] Capasso, *Chronicon Bergomense*, pp. 95–97.

in size as it followed its course. Similarly, when the Pistoiese Bianchi set out on August 17, 1,550 men and 1,350 women were counted; when they entered Florence five days later, they numbered 7,500.[137] The Lucchese Bianchi, who numbered more than a thousand when they first set out, were steadily augmented by the addition of other groups until their procession had doubled in size.[138]

But the *contadini* also staged separate processions of their own. The inhabitants of Lucignano, a small town overlooking the Valdichiana, participated in "this Bianchi penance" by forming their own procession, apart from any urban one.[139] Many such village processions were reported by Luca Dominici. On August 28, 800 Bianchi from the contado of Lucca lodged at Brandeglio, in the contado of Pistoia.[140] Bianchi from Sambuca in the mountains above Pistoia were responsible for a miracle in the Bolognese hill country—one of the rare instances of contact across the Apennines.[141] On one day, September 8, Luca recorded the passage through Pistoia of 600 Bianchi from Montecatini, 1,000 from Montelupo and Capraia, 150 in three brigades from the contado of Pisa, 300 from the Val di Pesa, 100 from Bientina, 100 from Monte Carlo in the contado of Lucca, 300 from Signa and La Lastra, 40 from Usigliano and Bagni di Casciana near Pisa, 200 from Monte Scudaio and other *castelle* in the Pisan Maremma, 150 from Borgo di San Marco di Pisa, 50 from Ponte ad Ena, 25 from Marti in the contado of Pisa, 50 from Calcinaia in the contado of Pisa, and 30 from Lucca.[142] And so it went: "nearly every day groups of these Bianchi from various places arrive in the contado, some large groups and

---

[137] Dominici, *Cronaca*, pp. 80, 94.

[138] Sercambi, *Croniche*, p. 349. Sercambi says their numbers increased from the initial thousand (p. 348) to 1,500 (p. 349) and finally 2,000 (p. 350).

[139] Archivio di Stato di Siena, Concistoro, Carteggio, 1845 (25 marzo 1399–25 ottobre 1399), fol. 72r: lett. of Dino di Giovanni dei Marzi, Sienese vicar in Lucignano, September 14, 1399.

[140] Dominici, *Cronaca*, pp. 110–111.

[141] Dominici, *Cronaca*, p. 134. The other instances of contact across the Apennines are also cases of capillary action by small groups: the 220 Bianchi from Tizzana who stopped at Pistoia on their way back from Lombardy, having "followed many obscure trails" (p. 162); the 300 Bianchi from Stagno and Granaione and other towns in the contado of Bologna who visited Piteccio, Brandeglio, and other towns in the contado of Pistoia (pp. 173, 175, 176); and the 120 Bianchi from Bagno alla Porretta, in the contado of Bologna, who visited Pistoia on October 10 (p. 189). And Bagno alla Porretta, the modern Porretta Terme, is actually in the middle of the Apennines, no farther from Pistoia than it is from Bologna; the same is true of the other towns.

[142] Dominici, *Cronaca*, pp. 133–134.

some little ones; and they make processions like the rest."[143] Nor did the residents of the Pistoiese contado merely receive these visitors: "Our whole contado likewise went on procession; they had dressed themselves like us in white with their priests and their cross; each commune by itself and two communes or parishes together went in good order from town to town all singing the usual song."[144]

For those who worked the land, to go about here and there visiting cities and towns meant a major risk. In the cities, shopkeepers could close their stores for a few days and just lose a little business; bankers could go on holiday with no fear that their money would spoil. But even in the cities there were many agricultural laborers; these people were taking a terrible chance when they left their crops in the fields, and their concerns became more pressing as harvest time approached. On September 10, as a new procession was about to set out from Pistoia, "it was unanimously decided in council that the vintage be put off until September 22, out of affection for those who are going in our processions."[145] In the smaller towns and villages scattered throughout the countryside, a larger share of the populace was engaged directly in agriculture, and the inflexible routine of tending the ripening crops sometimes took precedence over these voluntary devotions. Near Rimini the people of Verucchio, Montescudo, Santarcangelo, and other towns adopted a course of action opposite to that of Pistoia: rather than put off the vintage, they put off the procession.[146] Once the grapes were gathered, on October 14, they set off to make their devotions; they headed toward Cesena, moving in a direction opposite to that taken by the main Bianchi procession a couple of weeks earlier.

Circulating with these small groups of rural Bianchi were other groups, equally small but of a very different character. One of them

[143] "Per lo contado quasi ogni dì capitavano brigate di questi Bianchi di diversi paesi, quando grandi e quando piccole e fanno le processioni come li altri." Dominici, *Cronaca*, p. 118.

[144] "Tutto il nostro contado similmente faceva processione; quelli eran rimasi come noi vestiti di bianco con loro preti e con la loro croce; ogni comune per sè e due comuni o cappelle insieme ordinatamente di villa in villa cantando tutti la laude usata." Dominici, *Cronaca*, p. 101.

[145] "In consiglio si vinse unitamente per amore di quelli che vanno e delle nostre processioni non si faccia la vendemmia fino a dì 22 di settembre." Dominici, *Cronaca*, pp. 138–139.

[146] Cesare Clementini, *Raccolto istorico della fondazione di Rimino e dell'origine e vite de' Malatesti* (Rimini, 1617–1627; rpt. Bologna: Forni, 1969), vol. 2, p. 251. Note the comparatively late date of this account.

appears in Luca Dominici's list of the many parties of Bianchi that passed through Pistoia on September 8: the group of thirty Bianchi from Lucca. These were clearly not *contadini*; Luca specifies that they were from "Lucca di dentro," inside the city walls.[147] But they were just as clearly not part of any of the major processions of Bianchi from Lucca. They were people who had decided to perform a more personal devotion.

Some of these groups evidently formed along neighborhood lines; Luca Dominici mentions one group of thirty Bianchi from the quarter of Santa Croce in Florence.[148] What caught Luca's eye more often, however, was the social status of these small parties. Occasionally they were composed of ordinary folks, "persone mezzane," like the fifty men and women who arrived from Florence on September 25; the many parties not assigned any particular social classification probably fall into this category too.[149] But often they were composed of the rich, the prominent, or the powerful—"persone molto da bene" like the ten Pisans who arrived in Pistoia on the same day as those ordinary Florentines, the thirty well-born Florentines who came on the next day, and the many other such groups mentioned by ser Luca.[150]

We are fortunate in being able to penetrate within one of these groups and see beyond the chronicler's superficial characterization. Messer Rosso di Andreozzo degli Orlandi was a prominent Florentine lawyer with very good political connections.[151] He took part in the main Florentine procession to Arezzo, but apparently that was not enough for him. On September 14, he and a group of equally prominent citizens, including some of his political contacts who had just left office, set out on a private devotional journey modelled on the Bianchi celebrations. He described this pilgrimage in a letter to a friend in Venice:

> On the 13th of this month, in a letter which I sent you through the bank of Giacomino di Goccio (through which I will send you this and almost all of my letters), I wrote you about the procession of the

---

[147] Dominici, *Cronaca*, p. 134.

[148] Dominici, *Cronaca*, p. 180.

[149] Dominici, *Cronaca*, p. 176.

[150] Dominici, *Cronaca*, pp. 155, 159–160, 176–178, 181, 189–190, 198, 200, 210–211, and 213.

[151] Martines, *Lawyers and Statecraft in Renaissance Florence*, pp. 107, 159, and 483.

Bianchi and how our quarter and that of San Giovanni, myself included, went through the contado as far as Arezzo, etc. And then part of the old *signori* and members of the councils, that is, those who left office, together with a certain group which included me went on the aforesaid or a similar procession to Vallombrosa and La Verna, where there was remission of sin and penance. From there they went to Arezzo and returned to Florence, whence they had set out on September 14; they returned and entered Florence on the 23rd. We received the greatest consolation from that journey and procession. God grant that it be beneficial to us.[152]

Messer Rosso's phrase "the aforesaid or a similar procession" reveals that this pilgrimage and the Bianchi devotions were closely linked but not exactly the same: his first impulse was to identify the two, but then he admitted the distinction.

Much more than in the regular Bianchi processions, these visits by parties of distinguished pilgrims served as the occasion for ceremonial receptions and the exchange of honors.[153] On October 10, Pistoia welcomed a particularly striking group—200 aristocratic Florentines, both men and women, who were escorted to their lodgings by

[152] "A dì XIII del presente mese per una lettera la quale ti mandai per lo bancho di Giachomino di Ghoccio (per la quale ti manderò questa et mando quasi tutte le mie lettere), ti scrissi de la processioni de Bianchi et chome al nostro quartiere et quello di San Giovanni tra quali io fui andarono per lo chontado fino ad Arezzo, ecc. Et di poi parte de signori et collegi vecchi, cioè usciti d'uficio, chon certa brighata tra quali fu io andarono a la detta o simile processione a Valenbrosa et a La Vernia ove era perdono di cholpa et di pena, et indi andarono ad Arezzo, et tornarono a Firenze onde partirono a dì XIIII et tornarono et in Firenze rientrarono a dì XXIII, nel quale viaggio et processione avemmo grandissima chonsolatione. Dio ce l'abbia fatto et faccia valevole." Archivio di Stato di Firenze, Corporazioni religiose soppresse, Badia di Firenze, 78, filza 315, lett. 212: Rosso di Andreozzo degli Orlandi to Piero di Bernardo Chiarini; September 28, 1399. This letter was brought to my attention by Elaine Rosenthal.

[153] Of course, the main processions also involved the exchange of honors. The Bianchi from Lucca were particularly well received in Pistoia, and when the Pistoiese Bianchi visited Lucca, they were lavished with attention. "They received from the city of Lucca and from many individual citizens more things than I can recount. The Lucchesi never seemed to have their fill of honoring them, repeating constantly: 'We are forever indebted to the Pistoiese for the honor we received from them.'" Dominici, *Cronaca*, p. 140. The Pistoiese Bianchi also received especially honorable treatment in Florence from Nofri di Andrea Vittori, whose father was then *capitano* in Pistoia, and from Vanni Castellani, who was about to go to Pistoia as podestà; these people had a personal obligation to fulfill. Dominici, *Cronaca*, p. 91.

a great number of the well-born Pistoiese ladies.[154] The next day they went in procession to the cathedral, where they heard mass and listened to a sermon. The ceremonies were especially elaborate: the main altar was uncovered in their honor, the organs were played, and they were shown the altar of San Jacopo and the treasure of Sant'Atto. On their departure, as on their arrival, they were honorably accompanied by the fine ladies of Pistoia, who saw them to the city gates and beyond.

Such exchanges of honors were pleasant, but they were not the essence of these private devotions. That essence is exposed by messer Rosso's interest in "perdono di cholpa et di pena," remission of sins. Far more than the main Bianchi processions, the private devotions were attuned to offers of specific spiritual benefits, and so were directed towards the sacred places of the region. Messer Rosso and his companions went to Vallombrosa and La Verna to collect the indulgences available to pilgrims there. But the less isolated shrines drew the largest crowds and brought the apparently haphazard passage of small groups into an ordered pattern. September 6 and 7 were especially busy days in Pistoia; Luca Dominici recorded the passage of dozens of groups, generally from the lower Arno: Pisa and its contado, Lucca, Pescia, Camaiore, the Garfagnana, and so on. "And in addition to this, on that day there came many more Bianchi from various places, without a crucifix, and all of these and more were going to Prato."[155] These small groups of Bianchi were not making just any circuit; they were gathering at Prato for the feast of the Nativity of the Virgin, when the Holy Girdle preserved there is displayed. Luca himself went there to see the Holy Girdle, and found the whole road from Pistoia to Prato jammed with pilgrims.

> And we entered Prato. Prato was so crammed that you could not walk through the streets; the whole piazza was full. There were certainly more than fifty crucifixes and crosses there, of the Bianchi from various places; and the church, too, was filled with many other people. The Holy Girdle was then displayed in the usual fashion that first time, after which many people left; we did so, after we had looked around Prato and eaten. And then it was shown many more

[154] Dominici, *Cronaca*, pp. 189–190.

[155] "E oltre a questo ne venneno detto dì moltissimi ancora di diversi luoghi, Bianchi senza crocifisso e andavano tutti questi e altri a Prato." Dominici, *Cronaca*, p. 124; see also p. 130.

times that day. The whole way back we found the road swarming with great numbers of people, going and coming, and the vast majority were Bianchi.[156]

A few days later, the groups of pilgrims were heading in the other direction, towards the west. Parties from Prato, Castello Fiorentino, Santa Croce di Valdarno, San Casciano, and Magnone in the Florentine contado passed through Pistoia. "And likewise many more groups are going now, with very many citizens, men, women, and others, and the aforesaid groups are going to Lucca to the feast of the Holy Cross."[157] On September 14, when these groups massed in Lucca to see the Volto Santo, they formed an imposing assemblage. "Today at Lucca there was such a crowd of Bianchi that no one would believe it or think it possible, all making orderly procession with their crucifixes and singing steadily the usual song. There wasn't a person who did not weep and cry out of piety and tenderness, and it is certain that in more than fifty years there have not been so many people in Lucca on a single day."[158] The Lucchese chronicler Giovanni Sercambi estimated that in all the crowd numbered 25,000.[159]

The small groups of Bianchi, whether rural parties or those engaged in personal devotions, formed great waves of pilgrims which sloshed back and forth in the lower Arno basin between Prato and Lucca. In Prato, the Holy Girdle was displayed every Sunday to crowds that only gradually dwindled. Forty parties of Bianchi, each with its own crucifix, were there to see it on September 21; 3,000 Florentines and many others from Lucca and the Valdinievole were

---

[156] "E entramo in Prato: in Prato era pieno per modo non si poteva ire per via, su la piazza era pieno: cio chè vi era che di certo vi erano più di cinquanta fra crocifissi e croci di Bianchi di diversi paesi e moltissimamente altra gente è piena anco la pieve. Mostrossi allora la Cintola al modo usato la prima volta, poi molti si partirono; e simile, noi veduto che avemo per Prato e desinato avemo; e poi il dì si mostrò moltissime volte: venendone noi tuttavolta la strada trovamo piena di gente andava e veniva in gran numero e tutti i più Bianchi." Dominici, *Cronaca*, p. 132.

[157] "E così più altre brigate vanno testeso moltissimi cittadini, uomini, donne e altri e le soprascritte brigate vanno a Lucca alla festa di S. Croce." Dominici, *Cronaca*, p. 154.

[158] "Oggi a Lucca è stata tanta gente di Bianchi che non si potrebbe credere, nè pensare, tutti facendo processione con crocifisso ordinatamente e cantando sempre la lalde usata: non era persona che non piangesse e non lagrimasse di pietà e di tenerezza che di certo più di cinquanta anni è che per un dì non fu in Lucca tanta gente." Dominici, *Cronaca*, p. 160.

[159] Sercambi, *Croniche*, p. 368.

there on September 28; thirty groups from various places on October 5; and "a great many people" on October 19.[160] In keeping with the primarily Marian orientation of the Bianchi devotion, this shrine of the Virgin was apparently more popular with the Bianchi than the image of Christ at Lucca. Still, Luca Dominici does mention groups of Bianchi returning from Lucca, and Giovanni Sercambi says that the Volto Santo was the first thing sought by the Bianchi, immediately upon their arrival.[161]

These established shrines in Prato and Lucca were being challenged by another: the shrine of the Virgin at Cigoli, near San Miniato. This shrine had once been prominent. Franco Sacchetti, writing in the 1380s about changing fashions in the cult of the Virgin Mary, said that everyone used to rush to the Virgin at Cigoli, before she was eclipsed by the fame of Santa Maria della Selva, who was in her turn supplanted by another, and so on through half a dozen shrines.[162] Evidently the Virgin of Cigoli still exercised a certain attraction in 1399, since the earliest parties of Bianchi in Tuscany made a point of visiting her shrine.[163] The guardians of this cult recognized an opportunity to restore its faded prestige, and once the devotion of the Bianchi had taken root in the region, they tried to take advantage of this outpouring of piety by manipulating a young visionary.[164] The visionary in question was a girl just ten or eleven years old, a shepherdess in the Valdelsa.[165] One day she saw the Virgin Mary, who

[160] Dominici, *Cronaca*, pp. 173, 177, 181, and 199.

[161] Dominici, *Cronaca*, p. 180; Sercambi, *Croniche*, pp. 317, 319.

[162] The full list of shrines includes Santa Maria a Cigoli, Santa Maria della Selva, Santa Maria Impruneta, Santa Maria Primerana in Fiesole, the Madonna at Or San Michele, the Santissima Annunziata, and finally Santa Maria delle Grazie on the Rubaconte bridge. Franco Sacchetti, *La Battaglia delle belle donne; Le Lettere; Le Sposizioni di Vangeli*, ed. Alberto Chiari (Bari: Laterza, 1938), p. 103.

[163] Sercambi, *Croniche*, pp. 317–318; Domenico da Peccioli, *Chronica antiqua*, p. 578.

[164] On this episode, see Daniel Bornstein, "The Shrine of Santa Maria a Cigoli: Female Visionaries and Clerical Promoters," *Mélanges de l'Ecole Française de Rome, Moyen Age–Temps Modernes*, 98 (1986): 219–228.

[165] Dominici, *Cronaca*, pp. 182–184. On the cults of a number of holy women from this region who started their careers as shepherdesses (Verdiana da Castelfiorentino, Giovanna da Signa, Giulia da Certaldo), see Anna Benvenuti Papi, "'Velut in sepulchro': Cellane e recluse nella tradizione agiografica italiana," in *Culto dei santi, istituzioni, e classi sociali in età preindustriale*, ed. Sofia Boesch Gajano and Lucia Sebastiani (L'Aquila and Rome: Japadre, 1984), pp. 365–455. On the contrast between this rural model of female sanctity and an urban one in which

commanded her to go sweep out the local church, sound the bell, and tell everyone "that whoever had not joined the Bianchi should do so, and everyone should perform the greatest penance, abstinence, fasts, charity, and other good deeds in order to placate God, and that everybody should go to Santa Maria at Cigoli holding a candle."[166] When the shepherdess was not believed, the Virgin appeared to her once more and told her to order the cross on the altar to spin three times as an authenticating sign. Her words were obeyed by the cross, and the people began to believe this child. Not only that, but she herself was transformed: "all at once this girl, who was rough, crude, and filthy, became delicate, beautiful, and angelic."[167] Luca Dominici was willing to believe this, although he had to take it pretty much on faith, since she always kept her face covered.[168]

This child was taken to Cigoli in a formal procession. First came some Bianchi carrying a crucifix, followed by the cross which had spun around as a sign. Then came the girl, dressed in white, veiled, and protected from the crowds by a square formed by four rods; inside the square with her were her mother and another girl to keep her company. She was surrounded by many friars, priests, and prelates, one of whom served as her spokesman: "and when she wants to say something or ask for silence, she says it to a preacher who accompanies them and he repeats it and preaches."[169] She was able to discover the hidden sins of those she met; of course, many of these revelations were delivered by her priestly mouthpiece, since the girl herself "speaks very little and eats almost nothing and performs great

---

the holy woman is typically a young widow from a good family, see Benvenuti Papi, "Frati mendicanti e pinzochere in Toscana: Dalla marginalità sociale a modello di santità," in *Temi e problemi nella mistica femminile trecentesca* (Todi: Accademia Tudertina, 1983), pp. 109–135.

[166] "Che chi non era fatto de' Bianchi si facesse e ciascuno facesse grandissima penitenzia, astinenzia, digiuni, limosine, e altri beni per placare Dio e che ogni persona vada a S. Maria a Cievoli con un lume in mano." Dominici, *Cronaca*, p. 182. Note the emphasis on formal obligations.

[167] "Allora subito questa fanciulla che era grossolana rozza e sozza, si diventò delicata bella e angelica." Dominici, *Cronaca*, p. 183.

[168] "Porta coperto il volto e non si scopre." Dominici, *Cronaca*, p. 183. See also pp. 201 ("she kept her face covered") and 203 ("she almost never shows herself, she hardly shows her face at all: and she has become a very beautiful girl, whereas before she was very plain").

[169] "E quando vuole dire or che si dica nulla, il dice a uno predicatore che va con loro e elli lo ridice e predica." Dominici, *Cronaca*, p. 183.

abstinence."[170] Luca Dominici, impressed by all this, exclaimed "blessed is he who can touch and see her!"[171] But it was difficult to do either, as she was kept veiled and sheltered from the crowd, and when she stayed in Florence, she was cloistered in a monastery. Unable to approach her, people touched her from a distance with olive branches.

The extent of clerical control over this child was evident in her visit to Pistoia, on October 22.[172] She was paraded through the streets, accompanied by her mother and surrounded by friars, priests, and prelates. This escort deposited the girl and her mother in a convent and bolted the doors against the crowd. Once the child was hidden away, the crowd was allowed to enter the church, "and there the men who were with her spoke and said many things about her and the miracles she had said and done and predicted."[173] These men also told of the horrible fates suffered by those who had mocked this girl—how one young man fell dead, and a priest fell ill, and so on. And they announced that new devotions of varying lengths were required: eleven days for the eleven apostles left after the crucifixion, and five days for the five wounds of Christ. These devotions could not be performed just anywhere; people were to go to such places as Santa Maria Impruneta, Fiesole, and—first on the list—Cigoli.[174]

This visionary child was seconded by another seer, a woman of thirty-six from the Valdesa di Pisa.[175] She was warned by the Virgin that the divine sentence of doom had been revoked only in part, and that a great epidemic threatened—something which by then was obvious to all. To ward off this doom, everyone was to fast and to go with candles to Santa Maria a Cigoli. Luca Dominici was more reserved in his account of this woman, referring what he reported to third parties and concluding: "When I know about this, I will tell you. May Christ help us all."[176] He showed no such hesitation in accepting the statements of the girl, who during her visit to Pistoia

---

[170] "Parla molto poco e mangia quasi niente e fa grande astinenzia." Luca Dominici, *Cronaca*, p. 203.

[171] "Beato chi la può toccare e vedere." Dominici, *Cronaca*, p. 184.

[172] Dominici, *Cronaca*, pp. 201–203; here she is referred to as "the aforesaid girl from Florence" (p. 201), apparently because she had just come from her stay there.

[173] "E ivi li uomini, che erano con lei dissono e dicevano di lei moltissime cose e miracoli aveva detti e fatti e predetti." Dominici, *Cronaca*, p. 203.

[174] Santa Maria Impruneta and Santa Maria Primerana at Fiesole also appear in Franco Sacchetti's list of competing Marian shrines, cited in note 162.

[175] Dominici, *Cronaca*, pp. 184–185.

[176] "Quando ne saperò tel dirò. Cristo ci aiuti tutti." Luca Dominici, *Cronaca*, p. 185.

announced that the divine sentence had already been revoked and many other fine things which, alas, turned out to be untrue, as the long lists of plague victims in his own chronicle attest.[177]

For the moment, at least, the vigorous promotion of the shrine through these visionaries, especially the girl, had its desired effect. A steady flow of small parties visited the shrine at Cigoli, and at times large crowds of Bianchi were reported to have gathered there. On September 28, 2,000 Bianchi from around Florence and Prato were on their way there, and another 2,000 had just set out from Florence.[178] On October 18 and 19, a total of 4,000 Bianchi were reported at Cigoli, made up of small groups such as the parties of 20 or 30 Bianchi from Pistoia and 150 from the *contado* who went there on this occasion.[179] Gatherings at Cigoli may have partially eclipsed the Volto Santo in Lucca, as this Marian shrine took its place as a regional focus of pilgrimage in western Tuscany.

But the success of the shrine at Cigoli proved fleeting; it is now entirely forgotten, while the Holy Girdle at Prato and the Volto Santo at Lucca continue to attract throngs of devotees on their annual feast days. The girl, and her mother, disappeared, perhaps into some convent. But their brief moment of glory allows us to see more clearly the distinctive character of the Bianchi devotion. This girl was clearly the puppet of those around her—perhaps of her mother, certainly of the clerical promoters of the shrine at Cigoli.[180] It was they who selected a child who was easy to dupe or otherwise control. It was they who doubtless turned the crank that turned the cross, and so created the miracle that validated her vision. It was they who kept the crowds from her, who covered her up and locked her away. And it was they who spoke for her in self-serving prophecies and pronouncements. The Bianchi devotion, in contrast, was lay in inspiration and direction. Priests and prelates and friars joined in, and were even welcomed to prominent roles, but they did not invent and control the movement. They could, and did, try to take advantage of this erup-

---

[177] Dominici, *Cronaca*, p. 192. The lists of plague victims cover pp. 238–285; the total given at the end is 2,301 dead.

[178] Dominici, *Cronaca*, pp. 177–178.

[179] Dominici, *Cronaca*, pp. 198–199.

[180] Webb, "Penitence and Peace-Making," pp. 248–249, considers this an instance of "temporary social reversal in operation, with the humble inspired to take spiritual initiatives." It is hard to see that any initiative was left to this child.

tion of popular fervor, but no one tried to exploit it quite as crassly as the promoters of the shrine at Cigoli.

A clerical hand is also apparent in the revival of the Bianchi devotion, this time as a seven-day instead of a nine-day affair, which spread from Genoa starting late in August. Like the peasant of the origin legend and the shepherd girl of the shrine at Cigoli, the visionary in Genoa was from the lower classes: an emancipated slave girl in the service of Federico Vivaldi. The Virgin Mary appeared to her in a dream, bearing a message very much like that delivered to the second of the Cigoli visionaries: the Genoese had not sufficiently purified themselves to allay Christ's wrath, and so they should undertake a second procession. She was examined by theologians and other prudent men, and after this investigation Archbishop Jacopo Fieschi declared that everyone should fast for three days and then perform seven days of processional visits to the churches of Genoa. These processions began on August 28, but they did not receive the mass support and participation of the Bianchi devotions. Fewer people joined the processions, and they sang softly, in contrast to the hearty singing of the original Bianchi. Some people did not even bother to leave work.[181]

This seven-day revival, like the original devotion, spread from Genoa into Tuscany.[182] This time, however, the means of transmission differed. Instead of being spread by example, by crowds of visiting Bianchi who inspired their neighbors, it was spread by proclamation, by letters from prelate to prelate who in turn exhorted their flocks to adopt it. In Pistoia, "the lord bishop preached very well, and among other things he told of a miracle which happened in Genoa this past July; the archbishop of Genoa wrote of this miracle to the bishop of Luni, and the bishop of Luni wrote to our bishop and to the bishops of Florence and Prato and Lucca and other places."[183] And by the time this vision was preached by bishop Andrea Franchi in Pistoia, it had been transformed. The servant girl had received a

---

[181] Stella, *Annales Genuenses*, p. 241.

[182] It could not spread north into Lombardy, where travel had already been restricted because of the plague. Quarantine restrictions in the Po valley effectively prevented the sort of secondary developments that sprang up south of the Apennines.

[183] "Messer lo Vescovo predicò molto bene e fra l'altre cose notificò un miracolo intervenuto a Genova il mese di luglio passato, il quale l'arcivescovo di Genova scrisse al vescovo di Luni e quello di Luni al vescovo nostro e a quello di Firenze e a Prato e a Lucca e in altri luoghi." Dominici, *Cronaca*, p. 125.

name, Melica; her dream had been changed into a miraculous visitation while she prayed in Santa Maria del Monte (where the Bianchi had first preached in Genoa); this apparition, which incorporated elements of the origin story of the Bianchi, had been repeated for her master Federico Vivaldi, his wife, and a certain Roberto degli Imperiali of Genoa.[184] Like the shepherd girl, this servant was quickly encased in layer upon layer of ecclesiastical and secular authority.

When the new round of processions started in Pistoia on September 14, the reaction was very much like that in Genoa. Along with the 4,000 marchers dressed in white, there were another 400 who did not bother to put on robes.[185] By the third day of these processions, Bishop Andrea Franchi felt compelled to add an extra incentive—an offer of forty days of indulgence for all who participated. This emphasis on formal obligations and privileges typified these processions: as Luca Dominici said, "for these seven days we did not eat meat and we observed a good deal of abstinence and penitence, by the grace of God."[186] And in return for these formal sacrifices, participants received the formal privileges of pardons and indulgences.

Like the groups engaging in personal devotions, these processions were also less inclusive and less cohesive than the original Bianchi processions. Instead of uniting in a single great procession in which all differences were submerged, people circulated in distinct groups corresponding to precise social categories. The ordinary folk followed the bishop in the morning; but in the afternoon, the members of an elite group "went like us where we did this morning."[187] This select group included such local luminaries as messer Bonifazio dei Gambacorti, messer Piero della Vacca Odaldi, Niccolao di Bartolomeo Lapi, ser Niccolò di ser Andrea, and messer Agnolo Panciatichi.[188] Other groups were age-specific, like the children who dressed like their elders in white and went from church to church singing piously.[189] Still others were neighborhood-based, like the 120 people from the

---

[184] Dominici, *Cronaca*, pp. 125–127.

[185] Dominici, *Cronaca*, pp. 157–158.

[186] "Questi setti dì non mangiammo carne e facemmo assai astignienza e penitenzia, grazia di Dio." Dominici, *Cronaca*, p. 158; the offer of indulgences is on p. 162.

[187] "Andorno dove e come noi stamane." Dominici, *Cronaca*, p. 162. This group, in keeping with its elite social character, was rather small, numbering between 50 and perhaps 100 persons.

[188] Dominici, *Cronaca*, pp. 160, 164.

[189] Dominici, *Cronaca*, pp. 159–160.

parish of Santa Maria del Bambino, from Santa Maria Maggiore, from Sant'Ilario, and from San Salvatore and their neighbors.[190]

The full extent to which these formal processions replicated social categories can be discerned in the great procession of September 7, in which the Pistoiese returned to Santa Maria a Ripalta the crucifix they had carried in the Bianchi devotions, and at which the bishop announced the new seven-day devotion.[191] First came three parade masters, "great citizens" dressed in white, followed by the giant candles of the flagellant confraternities, fourteen pairs in all. The rector of Santa Maria carried the crucifix, which, like the shepherdess, was protected from the crowd by a square of four rods. A musician played the viola and sang the "Stabat Mater." Then came priests, friars, and canons; abbots; masters of sacred theology; the general of the Augustinian friars; and the lord bishop, all of them dressed for the occasion in their full clerical regalia of surplices and amices, stoles and maniples. After the clergy came the secular officials, along with some people not dressed in white; these were probably holders of lesser offices. Next followed the lay religious groups: some Gesuates, Apostoli and the like; then the flagellants, almost all bare-chested and barefoot, each of the fourteen confraternities in turn.[192] After them came the people without any corporate identity: men in white, then women, more men in white, and, last of all, men not dressed in white. Here, visibly enacted for all to see, were the significant religious categories of Pistoiese society.

To be sure, the original Bianchi processions had contained distinct groups formed on the basis of social ties. When the Bianchi first came to Genoa, nobles and prominent citizens of the rural areas came "cum eorum familiis," with their followers; when they came to Rome, count Francesco d'Anguillara entered with his wife and children and with his *terrazzani*, the peasants who worked his lands.[193] Francesco di Marco Datini went on the Florentine procession with a group which included relatives, neighbors, friends, employees, and servants.[194] If

---

[190] Dominici, *Cronaca*, pp. 158–159.

[191] Dominici, *Cronaca*, pp. 129–130.

[192] Ser Luca names the fourteen confraternities in order. Dominici, *Cronaca*, pp. 129–130.

[193] Stella, *Annales Genuenses*, p. 239; Dominici, *Cronaca*, p. 148.

[194] Mazzei, *Lettere di un notaro*, pp. c–ci: "First of all, Niccolò dell'Ammannato Tecchini, my brother-in-law; Stoldo di Lorenzo di ser Berizzo, my partner; Cristofano Pantaleoni, my friend and neighbor; Giovanni di Domenico di Cambio, my

we were able to penetrate the plain white surface of those processions, we would doubtless find many more such networks uniting specific groups of Bianchi. But it is significant that we are not usually allowed to penetrate that uniform surface. Those who described the Bianchi processions perceived them as undifferentiated wholes, in which all social distinctions were subsumed in a fundamental unity. This unity could not last; the white robes that concealed distinctions of person and place had to be removed, and the preexisting social categories once more acknowledged. This was not a liminal ritual, marking the betwixt-and-between stage of the transition from one rank or status to another; it was a voluntary ritual performance, at the end of which people returned to their former places.[195] But the sense of solidarity, of oneness, of *communitas* that they had experienced in these liminoid devotions was treasured by the participants, and its potential for reducing social tensions was prized by participants and observers alike.

It was precisely this sense of *communitas* that was missing from the seven-day revival. Participants sensed the difference; they were slightly defensive about the value of what they were doing, and they suspected that other people, elsewhere, would not appreciate it. In Genoa, Giorgio Stella said that the Pisans, upon hearing of the woman's dream, wanted to perform the second round of processions like the Genoese, but their ruler would not allow them.[196] In Pistoia, Luca Dominici told of how a parish priest tried to promote the seven-day devotion in Florence, but "the priors had him detained, thinking that this thing was done maliciously."[197] To condemn this devotion as something "fatta a malizia" was excessively harsh, though we have

---

factor; Filippo di Giovanni Benci, my factor; Piero d'Antonio Zampini, my factor; Franciesco di Ghinozzo Amidei, my factor; Guido di Sandro, my factor; Giovanni di Martino, my servant; Simone di Giovanni, Maso di Bartolo dell Starna, workers for Ghinozzo Amidei; Nastagio di Berizzo di Bonanno."

[195] Arnold van Gennep, *The Rites of Passage*, trans. Monika B. Vizedom and Gabrielle L. Caffee (Chicago: University of Chicago Press, 1960); Victor W. Turner, *The Ritual Process* (Chicago: Aldine, 1969), pp. 94–130. For the distinction between liminal and liminoid, see Turner, *From Ritual to Theatre: The Human Seriousness of Play* (New York: Performing Arts Journal Publications, 1982), pp. 20–60, esp. pp. 52–55. For a discussion of pilgrimage as a liminoid phenomenon, see Victor Turner and Edith Turner, *Image and Pilgrimage in Christian Culture* (Oxford: Basil Blackwell, 1978), pp. 1–39.

[196] Stella, *Annales Genuenses*, p. 241.

[197] "I priori l'hanno fatto ritenere pensando sia cosa fatta a malizia." Dominici, *Cronaca*, pp. 154–155.

seen that it was deliberately propagated and promoted by highly placed members of the ecclesiastical hierarchy. And it seems odd, at first sight, that a devotion so attuned to the structure of society should have been received with such suspicion. But precisely because it so carefully replicated and reinforced social categories, it did not hold out the promise of erasing those categories in a moment, however fleeting, of amicable unity and brotherhood. That was the promise of the Bianchi, and it was the hope that this promise might be fulfilled that won them the support of even those who did not join their ranks—of skeptics like Count Francesco di Montemarte and cautious officials like the priors of Florence.

CHAPTER FOUR

SONGS AND SIGNS:

THE SPIRITUALITY OF THE BIANCHI

Praying Jesus Christ and you, Maria,
that to the Bianchi and others the gift of grace be given:
as their dress is pure and their speech is just,
so may every holy result follow from it.
And as the world for so many long years
has suffered in wars and travail and trouble,
so may it rest in the fifteenth century
with all good things, both seen and unseen,
each person acknowledging the Eternal Father,
forever praying to the merciful Mother;
and like the prayer at the end of history,
may we all receive the glory of paradise.
— from a poem by Franco Sacchetti
about the Bianchi movement

SPIRITUALITY IS NOT A MEDIEVAL WORD. It was coined in the nine-teenth century to describe the interior dimension of religious life, a dimension studied through the analysis of such systematic texts as biblical commentaries and ascetic treatises. It thus was applied primarily to the small groups of people—monks, mystics, religious elites of one sort or another—who produced those theological texts. More recently, historians have recognized that the mass of the faith-ful, too, had an interior religious life that is worthy of attention. But since ordinary believers did not codify their beliefs in theological trea-

Epigraph: Franco Sacchetti, *Il Libro delle Rime*, ed. Alberto Chiari (Bari: Laterza, 1936), pp. 362–363.

tises, their spirituality must be approached through other, less systematic texts: songs, prayers, descriptions of cultic behavior, devotional images, and so on.[1] From such sources we can assemble the materials needed for studying spirituality in the broader sense defined by André Vauchez: the dynamic unity of the content of a faith and the manner in which the faith is lived by people in their historical context.[2]

We are fortunate in having sufficient, and sufficiently varied, documentation to study the spirituality of the Bianchi, to penetrate behind the described actions of the Bianchi and gain some insight into the beliefs that inspired their actions and the state of mind in which they performed them. The descriptions themselves offer a varied picture, since they present the Bianchi as viewed by sympathizers and opponents, skeptics and participants. In addition, we have contemporary depictions of the Bianchi in frescoes and in manuscript illuminations, and spontaneous reactions to them in private correspondence and in diaries. We have the texts of songs sung by the Bianchi, both those written expressly by or for them and those they adopted. We have accounts of miracles and prophecies associated with them. Though it is always hard to decipher past states of mind, the mass and variety of this documentation permit reasonably sound conclusions about the general spirituality of the Bianchi and even suggest local and personal variations.

In sifting this material, it is essential to keep what is "normative" for the Bianchi firmly in mind, and not give undue weight to any single document from any one place. Excessive reliance on a limited

---

[1] Giuseppe De Luca founded the *Archivio italiano per la storia della pietà* in order to make available texts from outside the canon of spiritual writings. De Luca's *Introduzione alla storia della pietà* (Rome: Edizioni di storia e letteratura, 1962) offers both a programmatic call for widening the history of spirituality to include a more eclectic selection of texts and a passionate defense of ascribing spiritual value to vernacular and popular writings.

[2] André Vauchez, *La spiritualité du Moyen Age occidental, VIIIe-XIIe siècles* (Paris: P.U.F., 1975), pp. 5–8. See also Caroline Walker Bynum, *Jesus as Mother: Studies in the Spirituality of the High Middle Ages* (Berkeley and Los Angeles: University of California Press, 1982), pp. 3–8, and the reflections of Ovidio Capitani, Claudio Leonardi, Franco Cardini, Giuseppe Cremascoli, Grado G. Merlo, Massimo Oldoni, Adriano Peroni, and Cesare Vasoli on "La spiritualità medievale: Metodi, bilanci, prospettive," in *Studi Medievali*, ser. 3, 28 (1987): 1–65. For an overview of Italian spirituality during the period of the Bianchi, see Giorgio Cracco, "La spiritualità italiana del Tre-Quattrocento: Linee interpretative," *Studia Patavina*, 18 (1971): 74–116.

set of sources has been partially responsible for the sharply contrasting interpretations historians have offered of the spirituality of the Bianchi. For example, Arsenio Frugoni based his suggestion that the Bianchi processions were a kind of giant holiday excursion largely on the diary of Francesco di Marco Datini. This source does seem to confirm Frugoni's contention that joining the Bianchi was more a safe little adventure than a serious act of penitence; the banners, songs, and sermons broke the daily routine; a picnic provided by their hosts awaited the Bianchi at the end of each day; and the nine days of devotion were over before the demands on the participants could become arduous or boring.[3] Benjamin Kedar ignored the evidence of Datini's diary and instead used the Genoese chronicle of Giorgio Stella to support the diametrically opposed conclusion that the Bianchi were representatives of a spirituality far more frenzied than that of the flagellants of 1260. According to Kedar, the Genoese, who had preserved their equanimity when the flagellants appeared, were easily excited by the advent of the Bianchi: skepticism vanished, miracles were seen everywhere, and "fear of God's wrath nourished an almost insatiable need for acts of penitence."[4]

But reliance on limited samples of the available evidence only partly explains these contrasting interpretations. More important are the assumptions that guide these historians in reading and selecting from the documentation. Frugoni sees the spirituality of the late Middle Ages as feeble, attenuated, and debased by comparison with the impassioned belief that had inspired the great movements of reform—both orthodox and heterodox—of the twelfth and thirteenth centuries. He accordingly seeks out those aspects of the Bianchi devotions that tend to support his assumptions, and ignores the considerable evidence of profound religious enthusiasm. Kedar believes that the troubles of the fourteenth century—demographic collapse, economic dislocation, political instability—fed a spirituality that was intense, fevered, almost hysterical, in contrast to the optimistic and measured religious outlook of the centuries of medieval expansion. This belief leads him to see flagellation where there was none. A

---

[3] Arsenio Frugoni, "La devozione dei Bianchi del 1399," in *L'attesa dell'età nuova nella spiritualità della fine del medioevo*, Convegni del Centro di Studi sulla Spiritualità Medievale, 3 (Todi: Accademia Tudertina, 1962), pp. 232–248.

[4] Benjamin Z. Kedar, *Merchants in Crisis: Genoese and Venetian Men of Affairs and the Fourteenth-Century Depression* (New Haven: Yale University Press, 1976), pp. 113–117.

letter from Genoa states explicitly that the Bianchi there wore closed garments and did not beat themselves; and the chronicle of Giorgio Stella, which is the foundation for Kedar's account, notes that the one day of flagellant processions was organized by the flagellant confraternities and did not count among the nine days of Bianchi devotions.[5]

In essaying a sounder definition of the spiritual outlook of the Bianchi, I shall draw principally on two kinds of material: the *laude*, or vernacular devotional lyrics sung by the Bianchi, and the accounts of miracles performed by the Bianchi. These two sources have the merit of surviving in substantial quantities. We have thousands of lines of religious poetry linked with the Bianchi movement, and reports of hundreds of their miracles. Moreover, these songs and signs were recorded in widely scattered locales, and so our analysis will not be tethered to any one place or text. Finally, since the songs were the common property of groups of Bianchi and gave voice to their shared sentiments, while the miracles were by definition extraordinary and singular occurrences, their variations will establish the bounds and their intersection will define the core of Bianchi spirituality.

Devoutly Making Melody

The Bianchi laude are an ideal index to religious attitudes, for they were truly popular lyrics that appealed to broad sectors of the populace. Some were performed by skilled musicians: Luca Dominici heard a singer dressed in white who played the viola beautifully and admired what apparently was a traveling balladeer, who on this occasion donned white and sang the story of the Bianchi's origins "molto bene."[6] But it was not just professional balladeers who sang these laude: in the general enthusiasm for the Bianchi devotion, the Bianchi laude replaced other popular songs. Even at work, it was the Bianchi songs that people sang: "Everyone—men and women, great and small, Bianchi and the rest—was always singing the "Stabat Mater"

[5] The letter, quoted in Dominici, *Cronaca*, p. 220, says that the Bianchi robes were "chiusi senza battere" closed, *without beating*; flagellants wore robes with open backs, exposing their shoulders to the blows of the whip. Stella, *Annales Genuenses*, pp. 239–240.

[6] Dominici, *Cronaca*, pp. 117, 139, 203.

and other laude, even while working; and all the other songs have been forgotten and set aside."[7]

Vernacular devotional songs had been common in Italy from the thirteenth century; laude formed a regular part of many paraliturgical devotions, and they were sung by confraternities that took their name—the *laudesi*—from this practice, as the confraternities of *battuti* or *disciplinati* took their name from the regular practice of self-flagellation.[8] Laude varied greatly in sophistication of form and acuity of content, according to the talent of their authors. Some were written by well-known poets such as Jacopone da Todi; many others are anonymous. They generally followed popular verse forms such as the *ballata*, which had simple rhyme schemes and regular metrical patterns and so lent themselves to being sung.[9] My concern, however, is not with their formal characteristics, but with their content.

It is, of course, always hazardous to read poetry in search of devotional attitudes or states of mind. Poems are literary constructs, and as such they represent the poet's response to a literary tradition, as well as giving voice to the thoughts or emotions that he or she wished to express. Under these circumstances, it is hard—sometimes impossible—to distinguish between traditional topoi and immediate convictions. For these reasons I have chosen not to consider the sonnet Francesco da Fiano wrote on setting aside his white robes when the processions ended: even though we know from other sources that the Bianchi cherished their identifying robes, Francesco's poem

---

[7] "Ciascuno, uomini e donne, grandi e piccoli, Bianchi e altri, sempre cantando la lalda 'Stabat Mater' e altre lalde, eziandio lavorando: e tutte l'altre canzone e canti sono dimenticati e lassansi stare." Dominici, *Cronaca*, p. 173. See also p. 197: "All the songs have disappeared and everybody is singing laude."

[8] On the distinction between *laudesi* and *disciplinati* confraternities, see Ronald F. E. Weissman, *Ritual Brotherhood in Renaissance Florence* (New York: Academic Press, 1982), pp. 43–58. The distinction between the two groups was not always as firm as Weissman makes it seem; *disciplinati* also sang laude. See, for example, Ignazio Baldelli, "La lauda e i disciplinati," *Il Movimento dei Disciplinati*, pp. 338–367.

[9] In addition to Cyrilla Barr, *The Monophonic Lauda and the Lay Religious Confraternities of Tuscany and Umbria in the Late Middle Ages*, Early Drama, Art, and Music Monograph Series, 10 (Kalamazoo: Medieval Institute Publications, 1988), see Fernando Liuzzi, *La lauda e i primordi della melodia italiana* (Rome: Librerio dello stato, 1935); and, on the Bianchi laude in particular, Bernard Toscani, "Contributi alla storia musicale delle laude dei Bianchi," *Studi musicali* 9 (1980): 161–170. Some excellent editions of laude have appeared in recent years: see, for instance, *Laude cortonesi dal secolo XIII al XV*, ed. Giorgio Varanini, Luigi Banfi, Anna Ceruti Burgio, and Giulio Cattin (Florence: Olschki, 1981–1985), and *Laude di Borgo San Sepolcro*, ed. Ermanno Cappelletti (Florence: Olschki, 1986).

seems both too self-consciously Petrarchan and too carefully individual in the emotion it expresses to be of much help in understanding
the more general devotion of the Bianchi.[10]

In considering the laude themselves as a possible source of insight,
we must query not only their authors' attitudes but also the response
the songs evoked in the Bianchi who sang them. Their lyrics, whether
in Italian or Latin, are sometimes well-crafted poems which depend
for part of their effect on resonance with other texts; such sophisti-
cated literary play was clearly beyond the compositional abilities of
most of the Bianchi.[11] Though most of these lyrics are anonymous, in
some cases we know the names of the authors—and this information, rather than clarifying our understanding, can exacerbate the
problem before us. We know, for instance, that Jacopo di messer
Bertoldo da Montepulciano wrote the *ballata* "Misericordia, o Redentore" for the Bianchi.[12] We also know that Jacopo could not have participated in the Bianchi processions, since at that time he was confined in the Stinche, the prison of Florence.[13] He might have hoped
for some personal benefit from the Bianchi devotions, for one of the
acts of mercy commonly urged by the Bianchi was the release of prisoners. But he could also have composed this lyric on commission, for
a purely economic reward: Jacopo supported himself in prison not
just by copying manuscripts, but by writing poetry to order. Was
Jacopo expressing his own sincere religious feelings, earning his
keep, or inciting a group of religious enthusiasts in the hope of winning his freedom? And did the Bianchi sing his lyric—if in fact they
did sing it—because it caught *their* own religious feelings, because it

[10] "Poesie religiose di Francesco da Fiano," ed. Roberto Weiss, *Archivio italiano
per la storia della pietà*, 2 (Rome, 1959): 206.

[11] Obviously, this does not mean that the bulk of the Bianchi were unable to
appreciate the laude. Luca Dominici, who transcribed only a single lauda in his
long and detailed chronicle of the Bianchi, nonetheless wrote repeatedly and ap-
preciatively of "a beautiful new lauda" (p. 198), "a new lauda" (p. 199), "an extremely beautiful new lauda" (p. 206), and so on.

[12] *Le laude dei Bianchi*, ed. Bernard Toscani (Florence: Libreria Editrice Fiorentina,
1979), pp. 115–132. I am grateful to the publisher for permission to quote the
material from this volume that appears in this chapter.

[13] Guido Zaccagnini, "Iacopo da Montepulciano," *Giornale storico della letteratura
italiana*, 86 (1925): 225–288. The Stinche hosted a number of important writers:
Giovanni Villani, Giovanni Cavalcanti, Cennino Cennini, Francesco Berni, Niccolò
Machiavelli, and Benvenuti Cellini were all remanded there at one time or an-
other, for crimes ranging from nonpayment of debt to sodomy or treason. See
Marvin E. Wolfgang, "A Florentine Prison: Le Carceri delle Stinche," *Studies in the
Renaissance*, 7 (1960): 149–152.

had a pretty tune (lost, as are all of the Bianchi melodies) and words, or because someone told them to sing along?

Finally, there are the textual problems. Religious poetry of this sort was prized—was copied and collected—for its devotional content, not for its artistry and perceived aesthetic value. Copyists accordingly felt free to make whatever alterations, deletions, additions, or substitutions they desired. Since the metrical patterns and rhyme schemes were conventional, it was easy for a copyist to lift entire stanzas from one poem and insert them in another.[14] This propensity for scribal change would lead one to suppose that the best and most accurate text would be the oldest; that is, the one most nearly contemporaneous with the movement. But the nature of the texts that contain most of the Bianchi laude suggests a contrary argument.

The source nearest to the movement is the chronicle of Giovanni Sercambi.[15] Sercambi was an eyewitness of the Bianchi in Lucca, and his extensive description of their activities there and elsewhere is roughly contemporaneous with the movement. He included in his description six Italian laude and two Latin hymns; he probably wrote these down after hearing them sung, rather than taking them from some written text.[16] When recording what he thought he remembered hearing, he sometimes flattened the lyrics, smoothing odd details into more standard fare. And since the main technical device used by the authors of these laude was the repetition of key words—the first thirty-one lines of "Pace, pace, Signor mio" contain the word "pace" twenty-one times[17]—he had ample stimulus to do the same in his transcriptions.

[14] All of this can be illustrated from the tangled textual history of the most widely documented of the Bianchi laude, "Misericordia, eterno Dio," which is found in at least twenty-four manuscripts. See Toscani, Le laude, pp. 51–54.

[15] Giovanni Sercambi, Croniche, vol. 2, pp. 290–371. Furio Possenti, La poesia nelle Croniche di Giovanni Sercambi (Lucca: Accademia Lucchese di Scienze, Lettere e Arti, 1974), does little more than paraphrase the poems.

[16] On the other hand, Sercambi inserted in his description a poem labelled "Canzone morale ad exemplo" which has nothing to do with the Bianchi (pp. 309–312); he must have had a text of this poem lying around and thought this an opportune time to make use of it. Such use of previously collected material was common practice among chroniclers; to cite just one example, Leone Cobelli inserted in his late quattrocento chronicle of Forlì over 200 lines of verse drawn from a book of prophecies. Ottavia Niccoli, Prophecy and People in Renaissance Italy, trans. Lydia G. Cochrane (Princeton: Princeton University Press, 1990), p. 11.

[17] Toscani, Le laude, pp. 86–87.

The other main source is a collection of religious poetry dating from the middle of the fifteenth century. This manuscript, Vatican Chigiano L.VII.266, represents the personal collection of Filippo di Lorenzo Benci: an imposing mass of more than 700 laude, of which 16 are connected with the Bianchi.[18] As a collector of this sort of poetry, Benci made special efforts to preserve the distinctive features (rare enough in any case) which distinguished one of these lyrics from all the rest, and his versions often preserve readings more difficult than those of Sercambi.[19] We cannot, therefore, simply assume that his versions, though collected half a century after the movement of the Bianchi, are any less reliable than Giovanni Sercambi's. They may be more so.

A third source poses another textual problem, one that, fortunately, admits of a plausible (if not definitive) solution. A mid-fifteenth century manuscript in Rome, Biblioteca Casanatense 4061, is a *laudario*, or collection of laude, containing twenty-six Italian laude as well as thirteen Latin lyrics. In 1920, twenty-three laude from this manuscript were published by Gennaro Maria Monti as a collection of Bianchi laude.[20] It is doubtful, however, that this collection has any direct connection with the Bianchi movement. The Bianchi laude in Sercambi's chronicle and Benci's collection are closely related. Of the eight lyrics transcribed by Sercambi, five appear also in Benci's collection, and one of the three that do not is explicitly extraneous to the Bianchi.[21] In contrast, just two of the twenty-three laude in Monti's edition appear in these other sources. Moreover, only three of the rest speak of the Bianchi; they tell the legend of the movement's ori-

---

[18] These are the laude edited by Toscani. Benci's father and brother were also skilled copyists: see the entry on Lorenzo Benci by Eugenio Ragni in the *Dizionario biografico degli italiani*, vol. 8 (Rome: Istituto della Enciclopedia Italiana, 1966), pp. 196–197.

[19] Compare, for example, "Vergine Maria beata" (Toscani, *Le laude*, pp. 159–161; Sercambi, *Croniche*, pp. 332–334), lines 14 and 46, and "Peccatori, tutti piangete" (Toscani, pp. 170–172; Sercambi, pp. 342–343), where line 30 in Toscani's text corresponds to line 33 in Sercambi's; in each of these cases Toscani has preferred Sercambi's reading over the more obscure one found in Benci's manuscript.

[20] Gennaro Maria Monti, *Un laudario umbro quattrocentista dei Bianchi* (Todi: Atanòr, 1920).

[21] "Misericordia, eterno Iddio," "Del segno ch'è aparito," "Questo legno della croce," "Vergine Maria beata," and "Peccatori, tutti piangete" appear in both Sercambi and Toscani. "Nuova lucie è aparita" and "Signor nostro omnipotente" appear only in Sercambi. "Dato che fu a questo mondo il lume" is a didactic canzone which has no connection to the Bianchi.

gin, but in a form that is both less complete and less specific than other versions, and framed in a general context of judgment and salvation.[22] Most of these laude have nothing specifically to do with the Bianchi, and instead treat common devotional themes. Some even describe events that quite clearly occurred *after* the movement of the Bianchi.

It is these laude that offer a clue to the nature of this collection. The first song in Monti's edition, "Ihesu, figliolo de Maria," describes a miracle that took place in the church of Santa Chiara, presumably in Assisi.[23] Mary appears, gleaming and dressed in white; she vanishes and then reappears, giving a benediction with her hand. The crown of thorns on the crucified Jesus also starts to glow. These signs are repeated several times. Another apparition of the Virgin is the subject of "Apparve la Vergen gloriosa."[24] In the fields outside Assisi, Mary appears to a boy who is free of sin; the boy's father, a sinner, cannot see or hear her. She explains to the boy that the nine days of the Bianchi devotion did not suffice. Everyone must put on white robes for a further six days of devotion, make peace, forgive one another, and restore their ill-gotten wealth to its rightful owners. Those who fail to follow these instructions will suffer immediate death and eternal damnation.

This apparition of the Virgin clearly belongs to the period of religious excitement that followed the passage of the Bianchi, and in its heightened sense of doom it may also reflect the fear of the spreading epidemic of plague.[25] The apparition in Santa Chiara, too, fits this later context. These local visionary experiences apparently led to the foundation in Assisi of a confraternity which produced or collected

---

[22] "Misericordia, etterno Padre" appears in both Monti and Toscani; "Peccatori, tutti piangete" appears in all three sources. "Matre, non ci abandonare," "Misericordia, pecchaturi," and "Se, pecchatore, te vol salvare" are the three versions of the origin legend in Monti, *Un laudario*, pp. 113–117, 117–121, and 124–127.

[23] Monti, *Un laudario*, pp. 69–71. The song appears third in the manuscript laudario from which Monti's edition is taken.

[24] Monti, *Un laudario*, pp. 92–96. A discussion of the miracle in Assisi, based on this lauda, can be found in Arnaldo Fortini, *La Madonna dell'Oliva* (Venezia: Nuova editoriale, 1956). It was also mentioned by a doctor from Prato named Bettino, who planned to assemble a book on the Bianchi miracles. He admitted, however, that this one puzzled him: "I have that one from Assisi, but it is not entirely clear in my mind." Mazzei, *Lettere di un notaro*, vol. 2, p. 360.

[25] On the relation between the Bianchi and the plague, see Alfonso Corradi, "Del movimento de' Bianchi e della peste del 1399 e 1400," *Rendiconti del Reale Istituto Lombardo di scienze e lettere*, ser. 2, 24 (1891): 1055–1058; see also Chapter 3.

the songs that fill the fifteenth-century laudario. Many of these songs refer to "this fraternity," "dear brethren," "my fraternity," or even "white fraternity."[26] Several of the laude are clearly related to the sort of dramatic performances staged by confraternities, performances that differed markedly from the simpler Bianchi devotions.[27] Since there is no mention of flagellation, and since many of the songs refer to the act of singing, this was presumably a confraternity of *laudesi*. Indeed, the last lauda in Monti's edition, "Laudiam Jhesu, el figliol de Maria," contains two lines that can be taken as a summary statement of the confraternity's purpose: "humbly but with lofty song, let us devoutly make melody."[28] In short, the laudario ascribed by Monti to the Bianchi belonged instead to a confraternity of white-robed *laudesi*, who took their inspiration from an apparition which occurred in the wake of the Bianchi.[29]

This new ascription reduces markedly the amount of material we can consider as truly representative of the Bianchi laude. But at the same time, the Monti edition now gives us a body of material that is especially useful for purposes of comparison, since it is so closely related to the movement of the Bianchi: if the proximate origin of this confraternity was a post-Bianchi vision, its only slightly more distant origin was the Bianchi movement itself. The compiler (or compilers) of the laudario evidently felt a bond with the Bianchi, for he (or they) included in the collection *three* versions of the origin legend of the Bianchi.[30] By comparing the laude definitely connected to the Bianchi with

---

[26] Monti, *Un laudario*: "Questa compagnia" (p. 131), "cari fratelli" (p. 71), "mia compagnia" (p. 73), and "biancha compagnia" (pp. 80 and 120).

[27] Especially "Con humilità laudare" and "Cum grande devotione;" Monti, *Un laudario*, pp. 128–132. On confraternal theater, see Mario Sensi, "Fraternite disciplinate e sacre rappresentazioni a Foligno nel secolo XV," *Quaderni del Centro di Documentazione sul Movimento dei Disciplinati*, 18 (Perugia: Centro di Documentazione sul Movimento dei Disciplinati, 1974), pp. 39–117, and two contributions to *Il Movimento dei Disciplinati*: Mario Appollonio, "Lauda drammatica umbra e metodi per l'indagine critica delle forme drammaturgiche," pp. 395–433, and Angela Maria Terruggia, "In quale momento i disciplinati hanno dato origine al loro teatro?" pp. 434–459.

[28] "Cum summo canto e humilemente,/devotamente facciam melodia;" Monti, *Un laudario*, p. 137.

[29] This miracle is dated to October, about one month after the Bianchi passed through the area of Assisi, in the *Cronaca latina* cited in Giovanni Magherini Graziani, *Storia di Città di Castello* (Città di Castello: S. Lapi, 1890–1910), vol. 3, p. 202, n. 1.

[30] Monti, *Un laudario*, pp. 113–117, 117–121, and 124–127. These laude, how-

this collection which is very close to, yet distinct from the movement, we can grasp more easily the distinctive religiosity of the Bianchi.

The laude of the Bianchi are couched in a language that is remarkably simple and concrete. Theological terms appear very rarely, and biblical references are generally to the most familiar material, such as the birth and the Passion of Jesus. Simple words of great power—peace, mercy, prayer—carry these songs; they are repeated in a steady iteration throughout most of the laude of the Bianchi. Those laude written in dialogue form keep the dramatic structure very simple: there are never more than three interlocutors; only two interlocutors converse at a time; and they speak a straightforward and colloquial language.

The laude in Monti's edition, by contrast, are more complex. Some of them have well-developed dramatic structures: the sixteen-line fragment "Cum grande devotione" looks like part of a representation of the martyrdom of St. Stephen.[31] Scene directions are given in Latin, and the characters—two Hebrews, two widows, and the apostles, all in just sixteen lines—are identified. The lauda that precedes this one in the collection, "Con humilità laudare," is appropriate for a Christmas pageant of the birth of Jesus. It recounts the prophecies of his birth, the annunciation to the shepherds and their adoration of the child, praise of Mary, prophecies of John the Baptist, the birth in the manger, and the journey and gifts of the Magi.[32] The language, too, is more elaborate, with many biblical references and theological and ecclesiastical terms. "Vergine, o del cielo regina" mentions Gabriel, Lucifer, and Longinus, and fills out the Passion story with the names of Pilate, Caiaphas, Anna, and Herod.[33] "Io Maria, matre de Dio" includes references to sin, damnation, baptism, the perfection of divine love, concupiscence, crucifixion, confession, communion, and simony.[34] In "Nuy te pregamo, o matre sancta," Mary recommends confession three times a year—an unusually high number for a pe-

---

ever, appear late in the collection, whereas in Sercambi's chronicle and Benci's collection the song recounting the origin story appears at the start, where one would logically expect to find it.

[31] Monti, *Un laudario*, p. 132.

[32] Monti, *Un laudario*, pp. 128–132. The sequence of these two laude suggests the possibility that the entire laudario was arranged in accordance with a calendrical cycle of performances; however, most of the laude are too general to be assigned convincingly to particular dates.

[33] Monti, *Un laudario*, pp. 96–99.

[34] Monti, *Un laudario*, pp. 87–92. There are ten occurrences of "peccato" and its variants in this lauda.

riod in which the clergy was struggling to make annual confession a
regular practice for ordinary believers, but in line with the greater
frequency of sacramental observance commonly stipulated in confraternity statutes.[35]

Since confraternities generally had to receive episcopal approval
and often met under direct clerical supervision, it is hardly surprising
that these laude, and several others in the same collection, suggest
the touch of a cleric. The language of a few of the Bianchi laude
points to a similar influence—and these are also the laude ascribed to
a cleric or other learned person. Jacopo da Montepulciano's "Misericordia, o Redentore" is a text woven from biblical references.[36] In
this lauda, Mary intercedes with Jesus on behalf of sinning humankind and reinforces her plea with appeals to sacred history: if you
could draw water from the rock, you can bring sinners to tears; if you
could create light, you can illuminate them. You cured the leprous,
resurrected Lazarus, protected Daniel in the lions' den and the three
Hebrews in the fiery furnace, freed David from Goliath, drew your
people from Pharaoh's grasp, saved Peter from the sea and from
prison, forgave Mary Magdalen and the adulteress, even promised
paradise to the thief crucified with you: if you could do all these
things, you can save humankind now. "Vede, o peccatori," ascribed
to the Augustinian maestro Grazia di Santo Spirito, also stands out
from the rest of the Bianchi laude: it is written in a more elaborate
metrical scheme, and it expresses different concerns.[37] It stresses pain
and sorrow ("lagrimare," "pianga," "dolori," "pene," "punisce"),
urges flagellation, and, in lines that apply the traditional topos of the
coming of spring to the dawning of the end of time, hails the advent
of the millennium:

> Il mondo si rinnuova. . . .
> L'ultima età del mondo
> fiorisce e fassi bella.
> (lines 2, 5–6)

> The world is made anew. . . .
> The last age of the world
> blooms and adorns itself.

---

[35] Monti, Un laudario, pp. 111–113.
[36] Toscani, Le laude, pp. 115–132.
[37] Toscani, Le laude, pp. 82–85.

In short, this lauda seems less a song of the Bianchi than a response to them, voiced by a friar with an apocalyptic bent.[38]

The typical Bianchi laude share with these more individual lyrics, and also with much of the religious literature of the later Middle Ages, a fascination with divine wrath. In nearly all of these songs, Jesus appears as an angry god, intent on destroying a sinful world. He is "forte adirato," greatly enraged against humankind—as he has been many times in the past.[39] He has forgiven human sin before, but his mercy has not been properly acknowledged: people keep on sinning, and they honor God with hypocritical words:

> Voi gridate colla bocca,
> ma dentro al cuor non vi tocca:
> siete pien' di crudeltà. . . .

> "Misericordia" gridate,
> l'uno all'altro no lla fate:
> siete pien' di falsità.
> > (Toscani, pp. 154, 155)

> You cry with your mouths,
> but it doesn't touch your heart:
> you are full of cruelty. . . .

> You cry "mercy,"
> but don't give any to one another:
> you are full of deceit.

His sentence of doom is now fixed; he is sending "death, pestilence, and war" on humanity.[40] The origin legend expressed this graphically: on the pilgrim's instructions, the peasant throws one of the three pieces of bread into the spring, a symbolic enactment of the destruction which awaits one-third of humankind. The lauda that tells this story is even more graphic: the bread dipped in the spring suddenly becomes full of blood and worms, and the peasant is afraid to touch it.[41]

---

[38] The apocalyptic tenor of maestro Grazia's response to the Bianchi is also evident in his preaching; see Dominici, *Cronaca*, pp. 168–170. His excessive enthusiasm troubled the Florentine government; see below, Chapter 5.

[39] Toscani, *Le laude*, p. 114.

[40] "Morte, pistolenza e guerra"; Toscani, *Le laude*, p. 100.

[41] Toscani, *Le laude*, p. 75.

The Jesus of the Bianchi laude is not simply offended by human sinfulness: he seems to be embittered against humanity for the physical pain and humiliation he suffered. When Mary tries to plead for humankind, he replies:

> Felli pecatori, or mi guardate,
> mani e piè mi fur chiovate,
> e alla colonna le sferzate,
> sostenni per loro gran dolore.
>
> E lla corona delle spine
> portai in capo con gran martìre;
> aceto e fiele mi dieron bere,
> e di', madre, ch'io perdoni al pecatore?
>
> (Toscani, p. 166)

> Wicked sinners, now look at me,
> my hands and feet were nailed,
> and in the scourging at the column,
> I bore great suffering for them.
>
> And I wore the crown of thorns
> on my head with great agony;
> they gave me vinegar and gall to drink,
> and you tell me, mother, to forgive the sinner?

Speaking directly to humankind, he says:

> Per voi sostenni ria morte;
> del ciel v'apersi le porte,
> che godessi tal degnità.
>
> Voi ne siete sconoscenti
> e ingrati e nigrigenti
> a sseguir nulla bontà.
>
> Furmi confitti piè e mani
> per voi perfidi cristiani,
> pien' d'ogni malvagità.
>
> (Toscani, p. 155)

> For you I bore a cruel death;
> the gates of heaven I opened for you,
> so that you might enjoy that honor.

You are oblivious to this
and ungrateful and negligent
about doing any good.

I was fastened hand and foot
for you perfidious Christians,
full of every wickedness.

In Jacopo da Montepulciano's poem, Jesus describes in grim detail all of
the agonies and indignities he suffered at his crucifixion. But his pains
were wasted: people today strive to outdo one another in wicked
deeds. They commit usury, murder, theft, and blasphemy; they plun-
der churches and the poor; they would willingly see him crucified again:

> Stanno ognor col cor più fisso
> a voler me crocifisso.
>   (Toscani, p. 128)

Each moment they set their hearts ever more
on wanting me crucified.

The same image occurs in a sermon preached to the Bianchi by the
author of "Vedete, o peccatori," maestro Grazia di Santo Spirito:
God, speaking to Mary of their Son, says that "the Jews crucified him
once, but Christians crucify him a thousand times a day."[42]

Jesus' intimate fury at the pain and humiliation of his Passion
might seem an entirely appropriate response, and one with particular
resonance for people as sensitive to questions of honor as the Italians
of the late Middle Ages.[43] It was not, however, part of the standard
interpretation of the crucifixion. Late medieval teaching on the crucifixion was dominated by Anselm of Canterbury's formulation of the
doctrine of redemption and the plan of salvation. According to Anselm, humanity dishonored God by refusing to obey him, a sin that
had been transmitted by Adam to all succeeding generations. Jesus's
acceptance of crucifixion and death had given God a satisfaction

---

[42] "I giudei il crocifisseno una volta, ma i cristiani il crocifiggono ogni dì mille
volte." Dominici, *Cronaca*, p. 169.

[43] For a brief definition of the complex concept of honor, see Julius Kirshner,
Pursuing Honor While Avoiding Sin: The Monte delle Doti of Florence, Quaderni dei
"Studi Senesi," 41 (Milan: Giuffre, 1978), pp. 5–6.

greater than the honor taken away by Adam's sin.[44] The orthodox teaching, then, deemed dishonorable not Jesus's crucifixion, but
Adam's disobedience; the crucifixion, while full of suffering, was also
full of glory. In this respect the Bianchi image of a God angered and
offended by humankind's treatment of his Son differs from the domi-
nant orthodox image of a God so gracious that he freely sacrificed his
only Son in order to offer sinful humanity the possibility of redemption.

While the textual uncertainties of the laude make me hesitate to
place too much weight on individual words, some variations in the
text of "Peccatori, tutti piangete" command attention. This lauda is
the only one that appears in Benci's collection, Sercambi's chronicle,
and the laudario edited by Monti.[45] But where Benci's text speaks of
the "croce lacrimosa," the tearful cross, Monti's reads "croce gloriosa," the glorious cross; where Benci's text laments the "morte ob-
robriosa," the shameful death of Jesus, Monti's text has "morte do-
lorosa," painful death.[46] In short, the text in the confraternity laudario
follows a more conventional interpretation of the crucifixion than the
Bianchi lauda, one in which the crucifixion is glorious and painful
rather than tearful and opprobrious, a triumph won through the willing acceptance of suffering rather than a shame inflicted. It is this
stress on shame and anguish in the Bianchi lauda that adds a special
edge to the wrath of Jesus.[47]

The only hope for escape from the destruction willed by this angry
god is the Virgin Mary. The Bianchi poets rarely call on other saints,
who—through an elaborate iconographic tradition—had come to be

[44] Anselm of Canterbury, *Cur Deus homo*, bk. I, ch. 11, in his *Opera omnia*, ed. F.
S. Schmitt (Stuttgart: Friedrich Frommann Verlag, 1968), vol. 2, pp. 68–69. See
also Jaroslav Pelikan, *The Christian Tradition: A History of the Development of Doctrine*,
vol. 3, *The Growth of Medieval Theology (600–1300)* (Chicago: University of Chicago
Press, 1978), pp. 106–118; vol. 4, *The Reformation of Church and Dogma (1300–1700)*
(Chicago: University of Chicago Press, 1984), pp. 22–38.

[45] Toscani, *Le laude*, pp. 170–172; Sercambi, *Chroniche*, pp. 342–343; Monti, *Un
laudario*, pp. 85–87.

[46] Sercambi's text falls between the other two: it has "crocie gloriosa" like
Monti's, but "morte obobriosa" like the one edited by Toscani.

[47] I do not wish to suggest that the "opprobrious death" of the Bianchi laude
was in any way heterodox. In fact, it recurs in perfectly orthodox writers ranging
from John of Salisbury to Catherine of Siena. See John of Salisbury, *Policraticus: Of
the Frivolities of Courtiers and the Footprints of Philosophers*, ed. and trans. Cary J.
Nederman (Cambridge: Cambridge University Press, 1990), pp. 59–60; Catherine
of Siena, *The Dialogue*, trans. Suzanne Noffke (New York: Paulist Press, 1980), pp.
47, 52, 76, and 156.

recognized as patrons of specific cities, organizations, occupational groups, or persons. Such distinctions dissolved under the impact of the Bianchi movement, or at least disappeared under the white robes of the Bianchi, leaving an undifferentiated mass of people. And who was better suited to speak for this generalized humankind than Mary, the mother of God and hence of us all?

> A voi, madre santa Maria,
> ricorriàn, c'avocata sia
> oggi, sempre e tuttavia
> dinanzi al Padre Salvatore.
> (Toscani, p. 163)

> To you, holy mother Mary,
> we resort, so that you may be our advocate
> today, always, and in every way
> before our Father Savior.

As in the origin legend, it is she who instructs sinners on how to approach their Lord properly and who offers to intercede personally on their behalf. The laude in dialogue form generally depict sinners appealing to Mary for aid or Mary carrying their appeal to God. "Alto Iddio, Signor verace" opens with an appeal for divine mercy (lines 1–23), but the sinners quickly turn to Mary (lines 24–87); she then presents their case before God (lines 88–127) and delivers to her eager supplicants the favorable decision she has won for them (lines 128–159).[48] "Misericordia, eterno Iddio" opens with an appeal to God, but ends with thanks to the Virgin.[49] The most outstanding example of Mary's advocacy is "Signor nostro omnipotente;" this lauda is a direct exchange between sinning humankind and their angry God, but the sinners' pleas for mercy are said to be granted because of Mary's intercession—even though she never appears in this poem. As her son admits,

> E' non è la prima volta
> che mia madre, o gente stolta,
> la sentenza m'à rivolta,
> tanto mi sa ben pregare.
> (Sercambi, p. 332)

---

[48] Toscani, Le laude, pp. 162–169.
[49] Toscani, Le laude, pp. 96–101.

And this is not the first time
that my mother, o foolish people,
has averted my judgment,
so well does she know how to plead with me.

This approach to God through an intermediary is typical of Mediterranean society, in which relationships with patron saints and human patrons follow the same pattern.[50] But there is a tension inherent in this system of relations. It can seem as if the supplicant is giving honor and deference not to the ultimate dispenser of favors, but to the intermediary who arranges them. Why not approach the source of power directly? This tension is voiced explicitly in "Venne Gesù a colui," when Jesus asks the peasant:

> Or mi di', se t'è in piacere,
> chi tti induce ad ubidire
> quella donna più che mene,
> che non mi vuoi contentare?
> (Toscani, p. 72)

> Now tell me, if you please,
> who is leading you to obey
> that woman rather than me,
> so that you do not wish to gratify me?

The answer is a surprising one: "that woman" was so menacing, so resplendent and obviously supernatural, that the peasant was terrified and did not know what to do. Here the awesome quality of the Virgin, usually hidden behind a humble appearance, shines forth and appalls the witness; she displays just the sort of terrifying grandeur that more often characterizes Jesus. When her sacredness is revealed, Mary is hardly more approachable than Jesus himself; when her sacredness is hidden but still known, Mary is the perfect intermediary between the sinner and God.

Mary is the supreme point of contact between human and divine, for she was the means through which the Word became flesh. Her

[50]See Ronald Weissman, "Taking Patronage Seriously: Mediterranean Values and Renaissance Society," in *Patronage, Art, and Society in Renaissance Italy,* ed. F. W. Kent and Patricia Simons with J. C. Eade (Oxford: Clarendon Press, 1987), pp. 25–45; and, for the modern period, William A. Christian, Jr., *Person and God in a Spanish Valley* (New York: Academic Press, 1972).

intimate bonds with the God who is at once her father, her spouse, and above all her son are the basis for her efficacy as advocate. She is able to press her pleas, as she does in "Misericordia, o Redentore," not only in terms of generalized sacred history, but also in the personal terms of her relationship with her son: she begs in the name of his birth, of the seven joys she had in him, of the milk with which she nursed him, and so on.[51] When her initial pleas are rejected in "Alto Iddio, Signor verace," she suddenly rephrases her request "by the milk which you sucked from my breast," and it is immediately granted.[52] This shift of discourse from the general to the intimately personal transforms the Virgin into Mary and the Christ into Jesus, and when the mother speaks to her son, she cannot be refused:

> Misericordia mi fa' fare
> per lo tuo dolce pregare;
> madre, non tel vo' negare,
> dolce vergine Maria.
> (Toscani, p. 104)

> You make me be merciful
> with your sweet praying;
> mother, I would not withhold it from you,
> sweet virgin Mary.

In her prayers, Mary offers a model of how to approach God. When sinners address God directly, as in "Signor nostro omnipotente," and find all of their pleas for mercy rejected, they make one final plea by Jesus's birth, by the three Magi and the gifts they bore: they do what Mary does, and transform Christ the threatening God into Jesus the accessible man. Beyond this particular ploy, though, Mary is generally the one who knows how to pray and can teach this skill to humankind. In the Bianchi laude, "pregare" and its variants normally appear in connection with Mary. Of the eight instances of forms of "pregare" in "Madre di pietà fontana," for example, seven are connected with Mary.[53] When people pray, they usually pray Mary to pray for them:

> O dolce vergine Maria,
> di noi guardia e compagnia,

---

[51] Toscani, *Le laude*, pp. 129–131.
[52] "Per lo latte che del mio petto poppasti." Toscani, *Le laude*, p. 167.
[53] Toscani, *Le laude*, pp. 112–114.

preghiànti che 'n piacer ti sia
che prieghi il nostro Salvatore.
                    (Toscani, p. 97)

O sweet virgin Mary,
our guardian and companion,
we pray you that you may be willing
to pray to our Savior.

Preghiamo la vergine madre
prieghi Gesù etterno Padre
che cci conduchi a gloria.
                    (Toscani, p. 95)

We pray the virgin mother
that she pray Jesus the eternal Father
that he may lead us to glory.

But people turn to Mary not just because she is a proven expert at
prayer, and not necessarily because she is the person most intimately
connected to God; they seek her guidance because she can understand and empathize with their sinful condition. She knows that people sin, but she is more willing to forgive than Jesus. This is why
appeals for divine mercy are quickly redirected from God to Mary.
The change is marked in the language of the laude. "Misericordia,
eterno Iddio" opens as a cry to God for mercy: "misericordia" occurs
nine times in the first eleven lines. The speaker then turns to Mary,
and instead of "misericordia" we find "pregare" and its variants—
eight times in lines 12–63—as he implores Mary to intercede for him.[54]
"Pace, pace, Signor mio" is also divided into two halves. The first
half is an appeal to God for peace and mercy, with twenty-one occurrences of "pace" and six of "misericordia" in the first thirty-one lines.
In lines 31–63, however, "misericordia" is not mentioned and "pace"
appears only twice; instead, we find "preghiànti," "pregate," "pri-
ega," and so on—seven instances, in contrast with none in the first
half—and "peccatore," "peccato," and other variants—five instances,
in contrast with a single appearance in the first half. The core of the

[54] Toscani, Le laude, pp. 96–101.

second half is summed up in the plea: "pregate pel peccatore," pray for the sinner.[55]

Not only does Mary understand and forgive sin and sinners; she knows and expresses the proper emotional response to the drama of salvation. Several of the Bianchi laude treat the Passion, but generally from Mary's point of view. In "Misericordia, Creatore" she actually tells the story of the Passion herself, revealing again and again her suffering heart:

> Poco Cristo meco stato
> era, a me fu profetato
> che 'l mio cor saria passato
> d'un coltello, o dolorosa. . . .
>
> tutto 'l cor sotto al mio petto
> facea l'anima angosciosa.
>
> Oimè! sempre il guatava
> quando al populo predicava;
> tutto 'l cor mi si schiantava,
> ch'a sua morte era pensosa.
> (Toscani, p. 135)

> Christ had been with me just a little while
> when it was foretold to me
> that my heart would be transfixed
> by a knife, o sorrowful woman. . . .
>
> The whole heart in my breast
> filled my soul with anguish.
>
> Alas! it always gazed longingly
> when he preached to the people;
> my whole heart burst,
> for it was mindful of his death.

---

[55] Toscani, *Le laude*, pp. 86–87. Carlo Ginzburg has noted a similar quality in the image of Mary in Jacopo Passavanti's *Specchio della vera penitenza*: "Mary, therefore, not Christ, is close to humankind, to their sufferings and their misery; and Mary can accomplish everything, because her prayers are irresistible" (my translation). Ginzburg also notes the use of Mary as an easily accessible focal point for the emotions of the worshipper. Carlo Ginzburg, "Folklore, magia, religione," in *Storia d'Italia*, vol. 1: *I caratteri originali* (Turin: Einaudi, 1972), pp. 619–620.

More often, we are asked to contemplate Mary at the foot of the cross and to apprehend the meaning and emotional charge of the crucifixion as she does. This appears most clearly in the two laude "Peccatori, tutti piangete."[56] One of them directs our attention immediately to Mary, who is not at the center of the scene on Calvary, but the means of comprehending the central drama:

> Peccatori, tutti piangete
> con Maria, la qual vedete
> tanta afflitta e dolorosa.
>
> A piè della santa croce
> Maria sta con umil voce,
> colla faccia lagrimosa.
> (Toscani, p. 170)
>
> Sinners, weep together
> with Mary, whom you see
> so afflicted and sorrowful.
>
> At the foot of the holy cross
> Mary stands with humble voice,
> with her tear-streaked face.

The other is presented under a caption that explicitly directs our empathy: "How out of compassion we should lament the Passion of Christ, seeing it makes his mother weep."[57] The attitude adopted here is that expressed in the Latin hymn "Stabat Mater," and indeed that lyric was associated especially closely with the Bianchi. Giovanni Sercambi included the text of the "Stabat Mater" in his account of the Bianchi in Lucca; Giorgio Stella gave one of the best early texts of the "Stabat Mater" in his description of the Bianchi in Genoa; and other chroniclers mentioned the Bianchi's use of this lyric all over northern and central Italy.[58] The Bianchi played a major part in diffusing and

---

[56] Here is just one example of the textual confusions that plague anyone who wants to study this sort of poetry. Though laude are usually identified by their first line, these two distinct lyrics share identical first stanzas.

[57] "Come per compassione dobbiamo piangere la Passione di Cristo, vedendola piangere alla madre." Toscani, Le laude, p. 150.

[58] Sercambi, Chroniche, pp. 321–324; Stella, Annales Genuenses, pp. 237–238.

popularizing the "Stabat Mater," as they adopted it as their theme song and rendered it freely into the vernacular in *laude* such as "Peccatori, tutti piangete" and "Misericordia, Creatore." These songs all express a highly emotional, almost pathetic piety, though none does so more blatantly than the literal tearjerker "Peccatori, tutti piangete."

> Piangi, piangi, peccatore,
> piangi, piangi il tuo errore,
> piangi sanz'aver mai posa.
> > (Toscani, p. 151)

> Weep, weep, sinner,
> weep, weep for your wrongdoing,
> weep without ever pausing.

According to this lyric, the emotional release of tears will actually cleanse the sinner's soul; a purely physical action will result in spiritual redemption:

> Con le lacrime lavate
> i peccati che vvoi fate
> e l'opera viziosa.
> > (Toscani, p. 151)

> With tears you wash away
> the sins which you commit
> and wicked behavior.

The Bianchi laude do not just wallow in emotion; they urge once more the traditional Christian program of social justice, based on the works of mercy enumerated in the Last Judgment in Matthew 25:31–46. There the blessed are received into eternal life because they fed, clothed, and sheltered Christ as embodied in the poor, while those who failed in their charitable duties are condemned to everlasting punishment. Jacopo da Montepulciano echoes this gospel passage when he has Jesus detail the failings of sinful humankind:

> Veggion me iscalzo e nudo,
> non mi fan di panni scudo,

e più tosto al triste ludo
volion lor sustanze dare.

Sete porto e affamato,
niun ben da llor m'è dato,
e essendo incarcerato,
niun me vuol visitare.

Sono infermo, e non mi aiuta
già niuno, ma me rifiuta,
e apena mi saluta
né mi vuol carità fare.

Quando giungo al loro albergo,
ciaschedun vi volge il tergo;
contra mme pigliano sbergo
per volermi fuor cacciare.
                    (Toscani, pp. 128–129)

They see me barefoot and naked,
but do not cover me with clothes,
and they would rather give their goods
to miserable gambling.

I suffer thirst and hunger,
but they give me nothing,
and as I lie in prison,
no one wants to visit me.

I am ill, and yet no one
helps me, but refuses,
and hardly greets me
nor wishes to give me charity.

When I arrive at their hostel,
each one there turns his back;
they arm themselves against me
in their desire to throw me out.

The reference to lying neglected in prison has a personal bite, for
Jacopo himself had been imprisoned since 1390. But this statement
cannot be reduced to a purely personal reference. For one thing, it

expresses a deeply rooted tradition of Christian charity based on treating "the least of these my brethren" as an incarnation of Jesus.[59] It is a tradition with biblical sources that are deliberately echoed by Jacopo, and it also appears in Bianchi laude that have no apparent personal reference. It is placed in Mary's mouth in "Misericordia, Creatore," where it adheres less closely to the scriptural original:

> Le limosine non fate
> e 'l prigion non scarcerate;
> l'affamato non atate
> nella sua fame penosa.
>
> E lo 'ngnudo non vestite,
> né llo infermo non udite;
> colla lingua ognun ferite
> d'ogni fama ingiuriosa.
> (Toscani, p. 142)
>
> You do not give alms
> nor do you release the prisoner;
> you do not help the hungry
> in his aching hunger.
>
> And you do not clothe the naked,
> nor do you heed the sick;
> with your tongue you wound everyone
> with every harmful slander.

And it can be discerned in generalized form in the action of "Venne Gesù a colui" and "Del segno ch'è aparito," the lyrics that recount the origin story: the peasant is expected to provide bread for the hungry stranger who accosts him, a stranger who in this case turns out to actually be Jesus.

Moreover, this teaching was enacted in the Bianchi movement, as its participants tried to institute it as a social program.[60] Although they received charity in the form of food and lodging on their travels, the Bianchi were not especially involved in dispensing it. Instead,

---

[59] See in general Michel Mollat, *The Poor in the Middle Ages: An Essay in Social History*, trans. Arthur Goldhammer (New Haven: Yale University Press, 1986).
[60] On these efforts, see Chapter 5.

they concentrated on a program of pacification. They insisted that everyone forgive their enemies and make peace with them before joining the processions. And they tried to convince individuals in the cities they visited to lay down their weapons and make peace, while urging the governments to repatriate exiles and release prisoners.

So far, I have considered general themes in the corpus of Bianchi laude. At this point, I would like to suggest some tentative distinctions and try to place a few of the laude at specific stages in the unfolding of the movement. It is possible that the general devotional statements of certain laude were associated with specific actions of the Bianchi, actions performed at various stages of the nine-day cycle. "Misericordia, eterno Iddio" could well have served as the lauda which introduced the devotion to a new town. It opens with a cry for divine mercy, then goes on to request Mary's intercession, admonish sinners, and exhort them to reform, before ending with an offer of thanks.[61] The two laude which recount the origin legend, and especially "Venne Gesù a colui," are clearly meant to be instructive: they explain the origin and meaning of the movement, and tell their listeners how to behave as Bianchi.

In addition to reflecting stages in the internal development of the movement in any one town, the Bianchi laude reveal reactions to external events, most notably to the spreading epidemic of the plague. As we have seen, the epidemic of 1399 and 1400 had a complex relationship to the movement of the Bianchi. In Lombardy, where the epidemic was already well under way at the time of the first Bianchi devotions, the exigencies of public health hampered the spread of the devotion. In Tuscany, on the other hand, people looked with horror on the ravages north of the Apennines and hoped that participation in the Bianchi devotions would protect them from the dreaded disease.[62] This is the promise implied by Mary, after she instructs the peasant in the new devotion which he is to preach:

> Se faranno tutto questo,
> figliuol mio, i' t'imprometto,

---

[61] Toscani, Le laude, pp. 96–101.

[62] One Tuscan author remarked on the spread of the epidemic and then said: "So that God might bestow his grace upon us, the shops here have been closed for nine days and the whole city and the contado have gone in procession, all dressed in white." Archivio Datini di Prato, no. 864, lett. Firenze-Barcellona, Associazione "ai veli" Francesco Datini e Domenico di Cambio, September 27, 1399.

per lo padre Gesù Cristo
gli farà tutti salvare.
                    (Toscani, p. 78)

If they do all this,
my son, I promise you,
Jesus Christ will have the Father
save them all.

But as the plague began to make inroads south of the mountains, this hope was replaced by a more intense and immediate fear. This change is reflected in the differences between the two versions of "Del segno ch'è aparito." The version in Sercambi's chronicle, placed at the start of his account of the Bianchi devotions in Lucca, has one stanza that is not in Benci's version:

Gridando fortemente:
Misericordia, Idio, misericordia,
Pace con gran concordia;
Ognun gridava di bianco vestita.
                    (lines 103–106)

Crying loudly:
Mercy, God, mercy,
peace with great concord;
each white-robed person cried.

This is mainline Bianchi devotion: divine mercy and peace are linked with human concord. But Benci's version, too, has one stanza that is not found in the other:

e pregando umilemente
il Signore nostro che cci liberasse
e lla sentenza voltasse,
stando il paese tutto isbaledito.
                    (Toscani, p. 110)

and humbly praying
our Lord to release us
and turn aside his judgment,
the whole land being terrified.

Here, the general terror and dismay make imperative the hopeless wish that God might liberate humankind from a sentence already in execution. Finally, fear changed to resignation as the plague definitely arrived. "Venne Gesù a colui" contains a passage that must be a later addition, since it requests an additional seven days of devotions, reviving and repeating the basic nine-day procession (lines 237–252). This passage could have been interpolated no earlier than late summer or early autumn, when such abbreviated revivals of the devotion began to appear at Genoa, Assisi, and elsewhere, and the lapse of a few months is reflected in a changed apprehension of death. There is no longer any hope of escape; one-third of humankind must perish. But if everyone repents, confesses, and follows the prescribed devotions, at least their souls will not perish with their bodies:

"Ognun sia bene avvisato
e pentuto e confessato,
pensando essere di quel lato
che vorrà a sse chiamare.

Peccatore, ista' avisato
se non vuogli esser dannato
ché Cristo è diliberato
di vo' 'l terzo a ssé chiamare."

"Poi che non ci val pregare,
che non possiamo iscampare,
fà del corpo che tti pare;
fà ttu l'anima salvare."
(Toscani, pp. 80–81)

"Let each one be well advised
and penitent and confessed,
if he is thinking of being on that side
which He will want to gather to Himself.

Sinner, be advised,
if you do not want to be damned,
that Christ has decided
to gather one third of you to himself."

"Since prayer will not help us,
for we cannot escape,
do what you wish with the body;
save the soul.

Here is no frantic cry to turn aside death, but only a resigned prayer
that the soul not go the way of the doomed flesh.

Some of the Bianchi laude thus record attitudes that shifted in response to changing circumstances, becoming first more apprehensive
and then resigned as the epidemic approached and struck central
Italy. A few laude, especially those written by clerics, testify to a fascination with an impending apocalypse. But the majority of the Bianchi lyrics are less extravagant. They treat such themes as divine dis-
pleasure at sin and willingness to forgive transgression, the role of
Mary as mediatrix between God and humanity, the necessity of penitence in the work of redemption, the sacred obligation to succor the
needy and downtrodden, and so on. And maestro Grazia's apocalyptic "Vedete, o peccatori," too, was a perfectly orthodox statement of a
common concern of late medieval spirituality. Even the most distinctive of the Bianchi laude treat subjects that were part of the common
stock of late medieval spirituality, and do so in terms that are hardly
distinguishable from other religious texts of the time. They are, in
short, expressions of ordinary religious sentiments, couched in very
ordinary verse.

Many Fine Miracles

Despite the frequency with which they occurred in the Middle
Ages, miracles were nonetheless considered to be outside the normal
run of events.[63] Augustine had propounded an all-inclusive theory of
miracles: since God had created both the world and the people that
inhabit it, every event, whatever the immediate cause, was ultimately
traceable to the action of God. But by the twelfth century, the definition of miracles had narrowed. For the most part, miracles were con-

---

[63] For what follows, see Benedicta Ward, *Miracles and the Medieval Mind: Theory,
Record and Event, 1000–1215* (Philadelphia: University of Pennsylvania Press, 1982).

sidered to be only those events produced by the hand of God acting directly, rather than by God acting through the course of nature or human will. Accordingly, miracles were the clearest possible certification of divine approval, and their occurrence confirmed the holiness of saints—or of movements such as the Bianchi.[64]

To be sure, there were people who were skeptical about miracles. Even a cleric like the canon messer Justo di Filippo di Gaio, writing from Genoa (where, he said, a boy had been resurrected and wondrous lights had appeared above a statue of the Virgin during mass), remarked: "The only miracle I want to see is peace made between warring parties, without anyone else meddling."[65] Count Francesco di Montemarte was more emphatic:

> Many people said that many miracles were seen, though God knows if that were true. I myself saw nothing which seemed miraculous, other than seeing all Italy stirred up in one moment, so that there was hardly anyone of any condition, great or small, men or women, who did not dress in that fashion and perform the aforesaid things and confess and receive communion with great devotion and make peace and forgive any person for any injury, even a mortal one, however great the injury had been. And this truly seemed and seems to me to be something miraculous, for no lord however great, neither pope nor emperor nor king, could ever have so stirred people, if not for the will of God.[66]

Any abrupt transformation of behavior could easily be considered a miracle; in the movement of the Bianchi, as Francesco di Montemarte noted, such transformation most commonly took the form of sudden

---

[64] The importance of miracles in the canonization process is stressed throughout André Vauchez's *La Sainteté en occident aux derniers siècles du Moyen Age d'après les procès de canonisation et les documents hagiographiques* (Rome: Ecole Française de Rome, 1981).

[65] "Non vo vedere altro miracolo se non che delle paci si fanno fra chi ha guerra, senza che altri vi si frametta." Quoted in Dominici, *Cronaca*, p. 203.

[66] "Fu detto da molti essersi visti molti miracoli, quali Dio sa se fosse vero. Io niuna cosa viddi che mi paresse miracolosa, salvo che vedere in un punto tutta Italia commossa, e questo che di niuna conditione, grandi, nè piccoli, maschi e femmine fe che quasi non si vestissero in quel modo et osservasse le cose dette et che con gran divotione si confessassero et communicassero, et far pace e perdonare, per qualsisia ingiuria a qualunque persona, quantunque di morte, per grande che fosse stata ingiuriosa, e questo veramente mi è paruto cosa miracolosa e mi pare, perchè niun signore per grande, nè papa, nè imperatore, nè re haverìa potuto far questa commotione, salvo il voler di Dio." Montemarte, *Cronaca*, p. 267.

amity between long-standing enemies, though it was also manifested by prostitutes who married or entered convents and by usurers who restored their illicit gains.[67] In one case, a man's entire way of life was transformed by his encounter with the Bianchi. Piero di Niccola Baronti of Pistoia was in Lucca when the Bianchi arrived there. He had never been noted for his devoutness; indeed, Luca Dominici says he was a rather dissolute young man. But when he saw the Bianchi and the wonders they performed, his life changed. He was the one who carried the cross at the head of the Bianchi from Lucca when they entered his native city. Nor did he abandon his robes at the end of nine days of devotion like everyone else. He remained white-robed and barefoot, and would not leave the crucifix he had carried in procession. He lived like a hermit, which greatly impressed the people of Lucca: they believed him to be a holy man ("santo uomo") and supported him, even going so far as to purchase a house for him and his followers. He became, in effect, a permanent living testimonial to the transformative power of the Bianchi.[68]

Andrea Franchi, the saintly bishop of Pistoia, took the occasion of the Bianchi to urge *all* of his people to reform their lives. In a sermon that brought to a close the Bianchi devotions in that city, he admonished everyone "to do good and to keep on God's good side and to make peace and to remain all united and in concord with one another."[69] At the same time, he tried to dissuade them from seeking after other sorts of miracles, by telling the story of a man, blind in

---

[67] Dominici, *Cronaca*, p. 203.

[68] Dominici, *Cronaca*, pp. 58–59, 156–157, and 210. Baronti eventually entered the priesthood; see Luca Dominici, *Cronaca seconda*, ed. Giovan Carlo Gigliotti, Pubblicazioni della Società pistoiese di storia patria, Rerum Pistoriensium Scriptores, 3 (Pistoia: Alberto Pacinotti, 1939), p. 31. Medieval cities supported large numbers of urban hermits, often with public funds: see Mario Sensi, "Incarcerate e recluse in Umbria nei secoli XIII e XIV: Un bizzocaggio centro-italiano," in *Il movimento religioso femminile in Umbria nei secoli XIII-XIV*, ed. Roberto Rusconi (Florence: La Nuova Italia, 1984), pp. 105–106; and Giovanna Casagrande, "Note su manifestazioni di vita comunitaria nel movimento penitenziale in Umbria nei secoli XIII, XIV, XV," in *Prime manifestazioni di vita comunitaria maschile e femminile nel movimento francescano della penitenza (1215–1447)*, Atti del Convegno di Studi Francescani, Assisi, 30 giugno-2 luglio 1981, ed. Raffaele Pazzelli and Lino Temperini (Rome: Commissione Storica Internazionale T.O.R., 1982), pp. 463–464. For a study of similar figures in modern Europe, see William A. Christian, Jr., "Holy People in Peasant Europe," *Comparative Studies in Society and History*, 15 (1973): 106–114.

[69] "Di far bene e di star bene con messer Dominedio e di far le paci e di stare tutti uniti e in concordia insieme." Dominici, *Cronaca*, p. 171.

one eye, who had prayed to have his sight restored and ended up blind in both eyes.

However, the chronicler who recorded this cautionary tale, Luca Dominici, also recorded more than 150 miracles: cures, apparitions, signs and wonders, even a couple of resurrections. What are we to make of these? First of all, Luca was generally a reliable observer and careful writer: his references to actions taken by the government of Pistoia have been checked in the town archives, and have been confirmed in precise detail.[70] For this reason alone, his descriptions of miracles would deserve to be taken seriously.

But this is not the only reason to place faith in Luca Dominici's account, for it quickly becomes apparent that none of the truly fantastic miracles he mentions took place in Pistoia, where he was writing. In Genoa, a boy was resurrected. In Siena, the sun loomed larger than usual and was surrounded by a corona of flames, the bishop was stricken dumb, and a woman dreamed a revelation that the city would be swallowed in the earth if the Bianchi were not allowed to enter. In Lucca, a floating stone identified a blasphemer. In the area of Bologna, a man was carried aloft by devils and then rescued by angels. A man in Ancona who had mocked the Bianchi was less lucky: devils there swept him to a great height, dropped him, and left him on the point of death. In another town near Bologna a fiery cross and the Virgin Mary appeared to the Bianchi, but not to the rest of the people—until they too put on white clothes. Near Rome, a crowd of devils on horseback plunged into the Tiber. In Rome, another devil carried off a boy, but in response to prayers he released the boy and devoured some beasts instead. Several of the more extravagant miracle stories came to Luca's ears from churchmen. Bishop Andrea Franchi of Pistoia preached about a procession of devils that had plunged into the Arno at Pisa. The bishop of Volterra sent a letter describing a cloud of Bianchi, who turned out to be souls released from purgatory by the Virgin Mary. And maestro Grazia di Santo Spirito, always willing to put an extreme interpretation on things, told how at Passignano a carved Christ had tried to climb down from his cross.[71]

Luca Dominici took these stories with a grain of salt. He appreciated maestro Grazia's sermon more for its eloquence than for its ve-

---

[70] Dominici, *Cronaca*, notes by Gigliotti, passim.
[71] Dominici, *Cronaca*, pp. 55 and 221–222 (Genoa), 113–114 (Siena), 120–121 (Lucca), 127 and 137 (region of Bologna), 215 (Ancona), 194 and 215 (Rome), 93 (Andrea Franchi), 191–192 (bishop of Volterra), and 164 (maestro Grazia).

racity, commenting that "he said many other things and many images and many very charming examples, for he is one of the greatest
scholars in this region."[72] He reserved his judgment on what the
bishop of Volterra had to say, remarking that "this was *considered to be*
a very great miracle."[73] When a report came from the Chianti that a
boy had been resurrected, Luca recorded this as just another unconfirmed report—"si dice che. . ."—and promised to confirm this
rumor if and when he learned something more certain.[74]

In contrast with these faraway and fantastic miracles are some
seemingly ordinary events, which Luca interpreted as revealing the
direct intervention of God. Some lilies flowered suddenly; a rose
bloomed out of season; rain cleared in time for the Bianchi to start
their procession.[75] In Rome, a boy was unjustly convicted on the basis
of a confession extracted through torture, but when he was being led
to execution, fifteen voices from the crowd proclaimed his innocence.
A barrel of wine thought to have been emptied by the Bianchi proved
to be full, and the wine it contained was exceptionally good.[76] Niccolao d'Agnolo Metti suddenly decided to take into his house the
wife to whom he had been sworn for over three years.[77] Piero del
Botte's lost donkey returned home with its harness intact.[78]

This last miracle might strike us as almost ludicrously commonplace: what could be more ordinary than a lost animal finding its way
home? Yet this sort of event could be subsumed in Augustine's wider
definition of miracles as an instance of God acting through the course
of nature. This wider definition remained a part of the traditional
understanding of miracles, available when needed. And it was called
on to justify the perception of miraculous intervention in a case very
much like that of Piero del Botte's donkey. In his collection of the
miracles of Thomas Becket, William of Canterbury told of a knight
who recovered his lost horse through the intervention of St. Thomas,
and asserted the miraculous character of this event against those who

[72] "Molte altre cose e molte figure disse, e molti bellissimi esempli, per ciò che
elli è de' più valenti maestri di questi paesi." Dominici, *Cronaca*, p. 165.
[73] "Questo fu *reputato* grandissimo miracolo." Dominici, *Cronaca*, p. 192; my emphasis.
[74] "Se il saprò di certo il dirò." Dominici, *Cronaca*, p. 181.
[75] Dominici, *Cronaca*, pp. 144, 191, and 145.
[76] Dominici, *Cronaca*, pp. 118–119.
[77] Dominici, *Cronaca*, p. 105.
[78] Dominici, *Cronaca*, p. 87.

doubted it by pointing out that nothing happens except through God's will.[79]

For the most part, however, the miracles Luca Dominici attributed to the Bianchi are neither wildly extravagant nor ordinary events seen sub specie aeternitatis. The core of them is comprised by some sixty miraculous cures cited in precise detail—disease, victim, date, and place of cure—as opposed to a generic reference to the "many and varied miracles" performed by the Bianchi in such-and-such a place. In reporting these cures, too, Luca avoided making claims for events to which he could not personally attest: "Many fine miracles happened at Pisa and similarly at Lucca, but since I cannot report everything, and also because I do not know everything for certain, I will leave off speaking of them."[80] He also noted carefully that not all of these cures were perfectly successful. The mother of Taddeo Bracciolini, for example, came to the crucifix on crutches, left them there, and went away "more or less freely on her own feet."[81] The wife of Mazzeo Cinchi, who had been totally blind ("non vedea punto lume"), "recovered her sight somewhat, and even though she could not see fully, at least she saw somewhat."[82] Finally, there is the case of a cripple well known to the chronicler: "A certain Antonio di Lucardo of the commune of Santa Maria in Torre sold bread in our market and walked with crutches and could hardly get around; on the day that the group from San Miniato was here, they led him to their crucifix and had him kiss it, and now, even though he is not totally cured, still he gets around without crutches and is half cured."[83]

Luca's caution, his unwillingness to subscribe wholeheartedly to reports of fantastic events or to record cures which he could not verify, and his scrupulousness in noting imperfect recoveries all attest to

---

[79] William of Canterbury, *Vita et passio S. Thomae*, in *Materials for the History of Thomas Becket, Archbishop of Canterbury*, ed. James Craigie Robertson (Rolls Series, vol. 67), vol. 1, pp. 282–283.

[80] "A Pisa sono intervenuti bellissimi miracoli e molti e similmente a Lucca, ma perché non potrei dire ogni cosa, e anco perché ogni cosa non so di certo, lasso stare il dire di quelli." Dominici, *Cronaca*, p. 131.

[81] "Quasi libera pe' suoi piedi." Dominici, *Cronaca*, p. 108.

[82] "Alquanto si ralluminò, e benchè non vedesse a pieno, pure vedeva in parte." Dominici, *Cronaca*, p. 108.

[83] "Uno Antonio di Lucardo, comune di S. Maria in Torre, che vendeva il pane alla nostra Sala e andava a griccie e a fatica poteva ire la brigata di S. Miniato lo dì che e' ci fu lo menarono al loro crocifisso e fecilelo baciare, e testeso, benché non sia in tutto guarito, pure va senza griccie e è mezzo guarito." Dominici, *Cronaca*, p. 145.

his honesty and reliability as a witness. The cures that he reported in detail and without reservation were those he was convinced were genuine.

According to Luca Dominici, eleven people were cured of insanity or demonic possession. The striking characteristic of this group is gender: all eleven were women.[84] One man, Nanni di Berto Comandi, went suddenly mad on November 10, when the Bianchi devotions were gradually winding to a close; he was seized, whipped, and thrown into prison—where he apparently recovered, since in 1401 he served on one of the communal councils.[85] The women, in contrast, were cured by contact with a Bianchi crucifix. To give but one example, when the Bianchi from Pistoia were at San Miniato al Monte, just outside of Florence, a woman "afflicted by Satan, who would not leave her for anything," was brought to them. She struggled against the crowd, shouting that "I will go to hell and threaten all the souls there, if you make me leave here." But she was gripped firmly by the hair and forced to kiss the cross. Upon this, the devil left her; she knelt before the crucifix, thanking it and adoring it.[86] The other examples, though less dramatic, follow the same pattern.

Twenty-eight cripples or paralytics were cured. These were predominantly males: ten boys and twelve men, but only four women and two girls.[87] Some had useless arms; others hobbled on crutches; a few could not walk at all. The cripples, like the madwomen, were cured by kissing the crucifix. A boy who had been born with his fists closed so that he could not use his hands kissed the cross, opened his fists, and embraced the crucifix. In Florence, the crippled sons of two poor women, one about twelve years old and the other about six, embraced and kissed the cross; they were cured on the spot, left their crutches, and ran off. Another cure happened less abruptly. A man approached the cross, confessed, and kissed it. Nothing seemed to happen—the cross could not work its wonders every time—and he turned to leave. He had not gone fifteen steps when his crutches fell

[84] Dominici, *Cronaca*, pp. 62 (three examples), 63, 82, 89, 97–98, 108, 141, 152, and 165. This gender-linked pattern of possession suggests a possible connection with the later gender-linked pattern of witchcraft accusations. Systematic study of shrine records of miraculous cures would be needed to confirm this pattern.

[85] Dominici, *Cronaca*, pp. 209–210.

[86] "Che aveva satan' a dosso, e per nessun modo ne voleva uscire." "Io me n'andrò in inferno e pericolerò tutte l'anime, se voi me fate uscire quinci." Dominici, *Cronaca*, pp. 97–98.

[87] Dominici, *Cronaca*, pp. 61–63, 83, 93–94, 96–98, 108, 141, 145, 165, and 167.

away and he walked without them. He gave the Bianchi his crutches and left, cured, to tell the priors of Florence his story. A man who had the use of his arm restored to him gave the only statement we have of what one of these cures felt like:

> Another man with a withered and useless arm crossed the Arno and went up there to San Miniato and there devoutly presented himself to the crucifix; and when he had touched the crucifix with his arm and kissed it, at once he was freed and healed in the presence of many people, and he fainted. And when he revived, he said that he felt the entire arm tingle, which was the blood returning to the veins, and he extended it and used it just like the other.[88]

Eight people were cured of assorted illnesses. A boy was cured of fever, and three women and one man of unspecified "illness."[89] A girl was relieved of pain in her breast, a man was cured of "cancer," and a German whose lips were split in a cruciform shape found his harelip miraculously healed.[90]

A few people were cured of disorders affecting their sense organs. A girl was cured of deafness, and three men were cured of muteness.[91] Two women and three men had their sight restored.[92] For one of the men, it was a touch-and-go cure. He was an old man, over sixty years old, and it took more than five hours of prayer at the foot of the cross to cure his blindness. This great success was crowned with other signs: flowers appeared above the cross and two white doves nearly alighted on it. The Bianchi who had mediated this miracle wanted to take the old man with them, but he refused to make peace with someone who had burned his house and so would not join their procession. When he had gone perhaps a hundred paces, he once again lost his sight; not until he had made peace, joined the Bianchi,

---

[88] "Un altro uomo guasto e rattratto d'un braccio entrò per Arno e andò lassù a S. Miniato e ivi divotamente si raccomandò al Crocifisso, tocco che ebbe il Crocifisso col braccio, e baciatolo, subito presente molta gente fu libero e guarito e tramortì: e quando fu risentito, disse che sentìa per tutto il braccio formicolare, chè erano le vene che riavevano il sangue e destendevalo e menavalo come l'altro." Dominici, *Cronaca*, p. 98. The other cures mentioned are found on pp. 63 (closed fists), 98 (the two boys), and 93–94 (the Florentine cripple).

[89] Dominici, *Cronaca*, pp. 215 (boy); 96, 97, and 108 (women); 97 (man).

[90] Dominici, *Cronaca*, pp. 98 (breast), 82 (cancer), 193 (harelip).

[91] Dominici, *Cronaca*, pp. 63 (deaf girl); 94, 112, and 154 (mute men).

[92] Dominici, *Cronaca*, pp. 62 and 108 (women); 63, 157, and 168 (men).

and said many more prayers was the use of his eyes restored to him more permanently.[93]

Four people were relieved of multiple afflictions. A twelve-year-old girl in Florence was deaf, mute, and blind in her right eye; the cross of the Bianchi from Pistoia cured her. In Prato, a woman named Anna Unghera had a bad arm, was blind in one eye, and saw little with the other; she kissed the crucifix "very devoutly" and was cured. Antone di Paolo Fenzi had an uncle (Luca Dominici didn't know his name) who was blind and mute, with two useless arms and "malignant spirits upon him"; this is the only man who was cured of possession, and that was but one of his many problems. He was led to Santa Croce in Florence, where the Bianchi from Pistoia were resting with their crucifix, and after he had kissed it three times, he was cured. Also in Florence, at the hospital of San Gallo, this same crucifix cured a man who was blind, deaf, and mute, with two useless arms: "you never saw anything more deformed."[94]

These healing miracles all fit into the common categories of cures made familiar by the biblical miracles of Jesus and the apostles and by the subsequent miracles of innumerable saints: the blind see, the deaf hear, the mute speak, the lame walk, the possessed are restored to their proper selves. Such miracles were part of a complex belief system, within which they could convey multiple meanings. They were signs of divine power, of God's triumph over the forces of evil. They were portents of the course of history, and as such documented God's ability to shape events. They were instances in the continuing revelation of God's purpose, "an avenue to deeper or inward meaning, a symbolic vehicle by which timeless truth could be perceived behind outward event."[95] They were a testimony to the sanctity of those who performed them, a divine validation of their spiritual authority.

In order for miracles to convey these meanings convincingly, they had to be reliably attested. To that end, registers of miracles were kept at pilgrimage shrines, and in the later Middle Ages, approximately 90 percent of the miracles recorded in these registers were

---

[93] Dominici, *Cronaca*, p. 157.

[94] "Non si vide mai più deforme cosa." Dominici, *Cronaca*, p. 63. The other cures are described on pp. 96 (girl in Florence), 105 (Anna Unghera), and 63 (uncle of Antone di Paolo Fenzi).

[95] Howard Clark Kee, *Miracle in the Early Christian World: A Study in Sociohistorical Method* (New Haven: Yale University Press, 1983), p. 221.

cures.[96] A fourteenth-century fresco in the church of Santa Margherita in Cortona showed one of these registers being created: a crowd of cripples swarms around the exposed body of St. Margherita, while in a corner a notary records the responses to their prayers.[97] The keepers of these registers were hardly impartial, since they stood to profit from a widespread belief in the thaumaturgical powers of their shrines. But they were also worried about the disrepute into which they might fall if they advertised cures that proved fraudulent, and so they often insisted on collecting testimony from witnesses and sometimes rejected unsupported claims. No doubt a number of fraudulent cures went undetected, and the keepers of the registers were only too willing to promote the reputations of their shrines by compiling thick dossiers of uninvestigated cures. But a growing number of historians have taken the position that fraud played a minor part in healing miracles, and that some other explanation for these cures must be sought.

Following the lead of anthropologists who have studied folk medicine and faith healing, recent historians have accepted the phenomenal reality of miraculous cures and identified a number of illnesses that might respond, or seem to respond, to an appeal for divine help.[98] Some illnesses are of brief duration; when their end coincides with an appeal to a saintly healer, that "cure," which would have happened in any case, is attributed to the intervention of the saint. Other illnesses, such as malaria and rheumatoid arthritis, are chronic but subject to remission; when a temporary improvement coincides with an appeal to a saint, that "cure" too is attributed to the saint. Still other illnesses are psychogenic; when the sufferer is convinced that a saintly healer has the power and willingness to cure his affliction, his

[96] Ronald C. Finucane, *Miracles and Pilgrims: Popular Beliefs in Medieval England* (London: J. M. Dent & Sons, 1977), pp. 59–60.

[97] Daniel Bornstein, "Pittori sconosciuti e pitture perdute nella Cortona tardomedioevale," *Rivista d'Arte*, 42 (1990): 228, fig. 1.

[98] Finucane, for instance, follows the studies of Una Maclean, *Magical Medicine: A Nigerian Case Study* (New York: Penguin Books, 1971), and "Sickness Behavior among the Yoruba," in *Witchcraft and Healing*, Proceedings of a Seminar held in the Centre of African Studies, University of Edinburgh, 14th and 15th February 1969 (Edinburgh: Centre of African Studies, University of Edinburgh, n.d.), pp. 29–40. See, however, the methodological observations of Ramsey MacMullen, *Christianizing the Roman Empire, A.D. 100–400* (New Haven: Yale University Press, 1984), pp. 22–24, with (on p. 7) some reservations about treating an anthropologizing approach as anything more than a heuristic device that can alert us to points in the historical record that might otherwise be missed.

appeal will often be granted. This last category can be a particularly tempting diagnosis, since one well-known psychological disorder, hysteria, can produce a wide variety of physical symptoms—paralysis and contractions, convulsive seizures, loss of speech and sensory disturbances—and responds readily to suggestion.[99]

The Bianchi healing miracles, like those recorded in the shrine registers, can all be plausibly placed in one or another of these categories, though there is not enough evidence to make any such diagnosis conclusive. Yet the substitution of a modern, nonmiraculous explanation of these cures for the explanation accepted by the Bianchi would make trivial or pathological that which was central to the Bianchi miracles: belief.[100] The miraculous cures happened because people believed that they could, and in the right circumstances would, happen. And because they happened, they reinforced the general belief system that allowed them to happen and confirmed the sacred authority of the particular mediators through whom they were enacted.[101]

These cures did not just benefit the persons whose afflictions were miraculously relieved; they also helped propagate the devotion of the Bianchi. When one person was cured because he or she believed in this devotion, others witnessed the cure and were moved to believe. A cripple healed in Florence told the priors of his cure; "the priors, having formally investigated this event, marveled greatly, and then the devotion gripped the Florentines more strongly than words could express."[102]

Sometimes the person afflicted and the person moved to believe were one and the same; mockery of or resistance to the Bianchi was

[99] Finucane, *Miracles and Pilgrims*, pp. 79–80. On the diagnosis and treatment of hysteria, see Alan Krohn, *Hysteria, the Elusive Neurosis* (New York: International Universities Press, 1978).

[100] Similarly, in their analysis of miracles in the first centuries of the Christian church, neither MacMullen, *Christianizing the Roman Empire*, nor Kee, *Miracles in the Early Christian World*, sees much point in trying to diagnose ailments and explain cures "scientifically." Instead, they accept that miracles were observed to occur and seek to explain how they functioned in a system of belief.

[101] The pioneering historical study of the operation of such a system is that of Marc Bloch, *Les rois thaumaturges: Etude sur le caractère surnaturel attribué à la puissance royale particulièrement en France et en Angleterre* (Strassbourg, 1924; rpt. Paris: Armand Colin, 1961).

[102] "I priori, fatto solenne esamine di questo fatto, molto si meravigliorno e allora la divozione entrò si forte a' Fiorentini, che non si potrèbbe dire." Dominici, *Cronaca*, p. 94.

followed by divine punishment, change of heart, and divine cure, in a pattern that lays bare one mechanism of conversion. Becarello da Larciano promised to go with the Bianchi and then failed to keep his word; he immediately fell ill and became numb, and was cured only when he decided to fulfill his original intention. The condottiere Broglia da Chieri tried to strike the leader of a troop of Bianchi, but his lance fell from his hand and he was unable to grip his sword; he kissed their cross and asked their pardon, regained the use of his hands, and joined their troop.[103] The painter Antone di Vita had promised to make peace with an enemy, but instead tried to kill him. All at once, "he was stricken very ill, and then on that day he made peace and was instantly much improved, and in particular when he came to San Lorenzo to hear the aforesaid mass his pains left him, especially one in his leg; these pains had appeared miraculously because he did not want to make that peace, and he went through the city and at once was healed."[104] An Augustinian friar who did not want to carry the crucifix in procession was struck dumb and beaten by black shadows; he was cured when he agreed to carry it. Domenico Lenzi da Cavarzano insisted on working in the fields despite the prohibition on labor; his oxen, more pious than their master, would not budge, so he beat them. Three bullocks appeared, pummeled him, and vanished, which terrified him and helped him to see the error of his ways. A mishap also befell a druggist who did not want to quit work to join the Bianchi: "That morning Vita the druggist, who works in the shop of Pavolo di Contolino, did not want to go in procession; walking in the shop, he caught his neck on a rope,

---

[103] Dominici, *Cronaca*, pp. 99 (Becarello) and 159 (Broglia). Broglia da Chieri's conversion resembles that of Uguccio da Casale, lord of Cortona; both men also perished in 1400 from the plague. On Uguccio, see Dominici, *Cronaca*, p. 153; *Cronaca latina*, in Magherini Graziani, *Storia di Città di Castello*, vol. 3, p. 201, n. 1; Sercambi, *Croniche*, pp. 369–370. There is no mention of Broglia's conversion, however, in a letter that mentions the threatening passage of the condottiere and his troops. "Two people from Marciano who arrived from Arezzo report that messer Broglia has raided Bartolomeo da Pietramala's [castle] Citerna and done a lot of damage, and that messer Broglia was headed toward Arezzo and coming in this direction." Archivio di Stato di Siena, Concistoro, Carteggio, 1845 (25 marzo 1399–25 ottobre 1399), fol. 72r: letter of Dino di Giovanni dei Marzi, Sienese vicar in Lucignano, September 14, 1399.

[104] "Li prese un gran male, poi la fece detto dì e subito migliorò molto e specialmente ché venne a S. Lorenzo a udire la detta messa assai doglie si li cessorno da dosso e specialmente della gamba, le quali li erano apparite miracolosamente per non voler fare la detta pace; e andò per la terra e subito fu libero." Dominici, *Cronaca*, p. 88.

and if he had not turned back he would have remained hung by the neck. When he saw this, he went devoutly in procession each morning like the others."[105]

Some of these miracles of affliction and conversion came very close to being miracles of vengeance, in which people are punished for injuring the divine dignity. On August 22, Papo di Rinaldo made fun of a friend who wanted him to join the Bianchi; he went home, fell ill with a fever, went mad, and died the next day—despite the prayers of the Bianchi, which seemed to help him a little at first.[106] In Lucca, two masons were working on a bridge. One wanted to go see the Bianchi; the other sneered and said "Go ahead, see the bestiality." He fell to his death.[107] Bano da Fossato, who had spoken ill of the Bianchi and blasphemed God, had his mouth twisted in an awful grimace; he wandered about seeking a cure, but without success. Lomo Cecchi dal Colle di Buggiano could not be persuaded to stop plowing and join the devotion; he told the Bianchi to go about their business and let him go about his. Heavenly fire consumed half his arm. A man who joined the Bianchi without reforming his way of life fell into a well and could not be pulled out. And so it went, time after time.[108] These ferocious displays of divine wrath complemented the miracles of divine mercy—a heavenly carrot-and-stick that urged on the devotion of the Bianchi. Luca Dominici noticed the general pattern: this new devotion "healed the sick, and he who did not believe or who mocked it fell sick, and this person had one mishap and that one another."[109]

The irruptions of divine wrath appeared from nowhere, like the consuming fire that struck Lomo Cecchi. The cures, on the other hand, were performed by means of specific, tangible objects: the crucifixes the Bianchi bore. Luca Dominici tended to see the miracles of

[105] "La detta mattina non volendo Vita speziale, che sta in bottega di Pavolo di Contolino, ire a pricissione e andando per bottega se li appiccò alla gola una fune, che se non è che tornò a rieto rimeneva appiccato per la gola e poi veduto questo vi andò ogni mattina divotamente come gli altri a procissione." Dominici, *Cronaca*, p. 167; see also pp. 63–64, 86–87, 112, 113, 122–123 (the Augustinian friar), 134, 144–145 (Domenico Lenzi), 153, and 156.

[106] Dominici, *Cronaca*, pp. 92–93, 100.

[107] "Va', vedi le bestialità." Dominici, *Cronaca*, p. 57.

[108] See, for example, Dominici, *Cronaca*, pp. 109–110, 123 (Lomo Cecchi), 133–134, 154, 188–189 (Bano da Fossato), 191 (the man who fell down the well), and 215.

[109] "Sanava infermi e chi non lo credeva o facevasene beffe infermava e chi aveva un accidente e chi un altro." Dominici, *Cronaca*, p. 55.

peacemaking as happening through the medium of the Bianchi themselves, and the miracles of healing as happening through their crucifixes: "It is true that these groups did a great deal of good, and Christ displayed many fine miracles by means of their crucifixes."[110] Though the Bianchi had the normal human power of persuasion, any peace compact that seemed beyond ordinary persuasion was attributed to a divinely inspired change of heart.[111] But the Bianchi and their crucifixes had no special innate power; they were simply the medium through which the divine power was made manifest. Like the relics of the saints or the living bodies of holy men and women, the crucifixes of the Bianchi were objects in which the sacred became tangible and accessible. Suppliants kissed the crucifix or embraced it as they begged for divine mercy, and they revered the wonder-working crucifixes as the instruments of God.

The Bianchi crucifixes frequently worked miracles not on the people around them, but on themselves. Luca Dominici filled his chronicle with stories of crucifixes that bled or cried or sweated; he also noted the tale used by maestro Grazia to embellish a sermon, in which a carved Christ tried to climb down from his cross.[112] Sometimes crucifixes which had shown themselves to be miraculous by shedding blood went on to perform cures, but not always: the miracle could be apparent either in the image alone, or in the person who was marvelously cured of affliction. Images of the Virgin, too, behaved in wondrous ways. Painted Virgins turned to face the crucified Son; they wept tears of crystal or shed a few drops of blood.[113] Occasionally these images were revealed to be the devices of charlatans, who rigged hollow crucifixes to ooze blood on command; occasionally, too, they were the objects of official inquests, in which depositions were collected from witnesses to attest to the verity of the wondrous event.[114] Most often, however, the simple testimony of

---

[110] "È vero che queste brigate faceano assai bene e assai belli miracoli mostrava Cristo per mezzo de' loro crocifissi." Dominici, *Cronaca*, p. 133.

[111] For instance, Dominici, *Cronaca*, p. 145: "Ser Filippo di ser Lazzaro di Giovanni Lazzerini made peace with some men from Lucca with whom he had a quarrel: by divine inspiration he went all the way to Lucca to make peace most admirably and with more humility than anyone could express."

[112] Dominici, *Cronaca*, p. 164.

[113] Dominici, *Cronaca*, pp. 109, 113, and 146 (weeping); 153 and 154 (bleeding); 176 and 193 (tears of blood). Sercambi, *Croniche*, p. 352 (turning head).

[114] Fraudulent miracles are exposed in Dominici, *Cronaca*, pp. 204–206, and

sight—and sometimes touch—was enough, as the visible effusion of liquid revealed the presence of the living god in the sacred image.

Those who had been healed through contact with these images sometimes responded with images, leaving wax figures as ex-voto offerings in recognition of their cures.[115] The use of wax ex-voto figures had been common practice for centuries, and the accumulation of huge numbers of these offerings could present grave problems for the more successful shrines. In Florence, they hung so heavily at the Santissima Annunziata that the walls had to be reinforced with a chain to prevent their collapse, and they fed the flames that swept Or San Michele in 1304, when a fire gutted the center of the city.[116] No such dramatic conflagration consumed the Bianchi ex-voto offerings, which gradually (so far as we know) went the way of all wax.[117] The spare descriptions that are all that survive of them do convey a tantalizing hint of the way images could correspond with other images— but only a hint. Nothing in the Bianchi documentation speaks to this issue with the clarity of the Spanish apparitions studied by William Christian.[118]

In the apparition stories collected by Christian (as elsewhere), paintings or statues of the Virgin were explicitly identified as the models for visions, which were then in turn depicted in new paintings or statues. The Bianchi founding story of Mary, Christ, and the

Montemarte, *Cronaca*, p. 267. The record of one episcopal inquest is published by Vincenzo Federici, "Il miracolo del crocifisso della compagnia dei Bianchi a Sutri," in *Scritti di storia, di filologia, e d'arte per le nozze Fedele-De Fabritiis* (Naples: Riccardo Ricciardi, 1908), pp. 107–118.

[115] Wax images are presented to Bianchi crucifixes in Dominici, *Cronaca*, pp. 105, 106, and 108–109; wax (not specified as being in the form of images) is given on pp. 117 and 143.

[116] Franco Sacchetti, *La Battaglia delle belle donne; Le Lettere; Le Sposizioni di Vangeli*, ed. Alberto Chiari (Bari: Laterza, 1938), p. 103; Dino Compagni, *Cronica* (Turin: Einaudi, 1968), p. 141.

[117] Because of the malleability of wax, few of these once-common offerings have survived. On one chance discovery, brought about by air raid damage, see U. M. Radford, "The Wax Images Found in Exeter Cathedral," *The Antiquities Journal*, 29 (1949): 164–168.

[118] William A. Christian, Jr., *Apparitions in Late Medieval and Renaissance Spain* (Princeton: Princeton University Press, 1981). On the cult of images, see Hans R. Hahnloser, "Du culte de l'image au Moyen Age," in *Cristianesimo e ragion di stato: L'umanesimo e il demoniaco nell'arte: Atti del II Congresso internazionale di studi umanistici*, ed. Enrico Castelli (Rome: Fratelli Bocca, 1953), pp. 225–233, and the provocative essay by Richard Trexler, "Florentine Religious Experience: The Sacred Image," *Studies in the Renaissance*, 19 (1972): 7–41.

peasant did serve as the basis for paintings, such as that which decorated a processional cross carried by a small party of Bianchi from Galluzzo; but there is no indication that an earlier painting lay behind that visionary encounter.[119] Similarly, when an unnamed woman from near Pisa was rewarded with a vision of Mary, St. Andrew, and St. John, all robed in white, after fifteen days of prayer in front of a painting of the Virgin, Luca Dominici does not say whether her vision corresponded to the painting.[120] Though we may suspect that her vision was inspired by a picture of Mary flanked by these two saints, our suspicions must remain unconfirmed. The descriptions of the Bianchi stop short of defining an iconocentric world in which individuals who receive cures from crucifixes and give wax figures as ex-voto offerings to these crucifixes are the medium through which image speaks to image.

Distancing ourselves, like Luca Dominici, from such extravagant fantasies, we may end this discussion with the sober words of an agent of Gabriello di messer Bartolomeo Panciatichi, who in Rome found himself tossed about by a crowd of people eager for miracles. The uproar was sufficiently unpleasant to make him wish he were anyplace but there. He had had more than enough of miracles: "I don't want to say anything more about these miracles, about which many people are talking here. For me it is enough to see and hear the whole world stirred to demand mercy and peace and to see peace follow and often mercy likewise, and these are marvelous things. May God help us all."[121]

Luca Dominici's reports of the Bianchi miracles, in the final analysis, confirm the impression given by the laude. There was nothing out of the ordinary in these miracles. They were the sorts of miracles—divine cures, divine protection, divine vengeance—commonly associated with shrines of saints, and they were understood, by those who witnessed them, as such events had commonly been understood since at least the twelfth century. The laude, too, were striking in their ordinariness. In both outlook and expression, they were very much of a piece with other expressions of the spirituality of this pe-

---

[119] Dominici, *Cronaca*, p. 161.

[120] Dominici, *Cronaca*, p. 184.

[121] "Di questi miracoli non vo' dire più oltra, molti ci se ne contano; a me basta vedere e udire il mondo commosso chiedendo *misericordia e pace* e vedere seguire la pace e così spesso seguire la misericordia e cose meravigliose sono. Iddio ci aiuti tutti." Quoted in Dominici, *Cronaca*, p. 150.

riod. Both sources show the Bianchi to have been as traditional in their devotional attitudes as they were indifferent to the subtleties of theological controversy. Theirs was a faith based largely on the physicality of the sacred image, the worldly pragmatism of relations with a saintly protector, the hope for occasional miracles, and a vivid sense of the human and material manifestations of the spiritual powers.[122] But it bears repeating that such attitudes were as likely to be found among educated clerics, rich merchants, and powerful lords as among woolworkers, stonecutters, and peasants. The spirituality of the Bianchi was part of the common currency of religious belief that circulated throughout all levels of late medieval society.

[122] Roberto Bizzocchi, "Clero e Chiesa nella società italiana alla fine del Medio Evo," in *Clero e società nell'Italia moderna*, ed. Mario Rosa (Rome and Bari: Laterza, 1992), p. 5.

CHAPTER FIVE

THE BIANCHI AND

THE AUTHORITIES

When the Elders of Lucca heard that many prominent citizens and a great number of women wanted to go on this pilgrimage, they had misgivings about this excursion and gave an order that no citizen or inhabitant, man or woman, should leave the city. And they planned to hold a meeting, to block this excursion. When it was learned that a meeting would be held on this subject, without much discussion, it suddenly seemed as if the word of God spoke in the ear of each man and woman who had thought of donning white and told them to go forth from Lucca without delay, so that more than a thousand men and women left Lucca at once, before the meeting could be held and the gates secured.

—from Giovanni Sercambi's description of the
Bianchi devotions in his native city of Lucca

IT IS EASY TO SEE why the religious authorities were generally delighted with the Bianchi. Representatives of the ecclesiastical hierarchy were accustomed to dealing with churchmen like Venturino da Bergamo and Manfredi da Vercelli, whose preaching contained radical challenges to the social and religious order. Venturino's assertion that the only true pope was a Roman one explicitly attacked the legitimacy of Benedict XII, resident in Avignon; the followers he attracted with this sort of preaching were, by his own admission, the dregs of

Epigraph: Sercambi, *Croniche*, p. 348.

society. Manfredi's conviction that the apocalypse was at hand led him to conclude that even the most fundamental social bonds, including marriage, were now dissolved. Though excommunicated by the archbishop of Florence and the master general of the Dominican order, Manfredi continued to preach and to attack his Franciscan rivals. People disturbed by the Schism longed for a definitive resolution to their religious uncertainties, and Manfredi seemed to offer one: prophecies circulated claiming that Manfredi would be the angelic pope and that he would restore the ancient dignity of the throne of St. Peter. Both Venturino and Manfredi were called to account, enjoined to silence, and then let loose to preach again when they agreed to follow papal directives. Venturino preached the crusade for Clement VI, and Manfredi became a fervent and effective foe of the Fraticelli.[1]

The Bianchi, in contrast, presented the ecclesiastical authorities with a promising opportunity rather than a challenge or threat. They were orthodox in their beliefs, traditional in their devotion, and orderly in their behavior. They promoted acceptable solutions to acknowledged problems; they voiced no threat to the established social and religious order. Above all, they had no charismatic leader who might proclaim radical teachings, and around whom apocalyptic fears and millenarian hopes could crystallize.

The absence of a charismatic leader made it easy for representatives of the ecclesiastical hierarchy to step in and assume leadership of the Bianchi devotions. We have seen how the archbishop of Genoa, Jacopo Fieschi, preached the novel devotion and placed himself at the head of the Bianchi processions, thereby giving the Bianchi the encouragement of official approval at a delicate early stage in the development of the movement. But throughout the course of that development, in city after city, other bishops did what Fieschi had done in Genoa. In Bologna, Ferrara, Fiesole, Florence, Modena, Padua,

---

[1] "Clara Gennaro, "Venturino da Bergamo e la 'peregrinatio' romana del 1335," in *Studi sul Medioevo cristiano offerti a Raffaello Morghen* (Rome: Istituto Storico Italiano per il Medio Evo, 1974), pp. 375–406; Raymond Creytens, O.P., "Manfred de Verceil O.P. et son traité contre les fraticelles," *Archivum Fratrum Praedicatorum*, 11 (1941): 173–208; Roberto Rusconi, "Fonti e documenti su Manfredi da Vercelli ed il suo movimento penitenziale," *Archivum Fratrum Praedicatorum*, 47 (1977): 51–107; and Rusconi, *L'attesa della fine: Crisi della società, profezia, ed Apocalisse in Italia al tempo del grande scisma d'Occidente (1378–1417)* (Rome: Istituto Storico Italiano per il Medio Evo, 1979). See also Chapter 1, above.

and Pistoia, the Bianchi processions were led by the local bishops.[2] The bishop of Modena did not simply lead his people to Bologna; he wandered as far afield as Ferrara, enthusiastically promoting the Bianchi devotion.[3] The bishop of Sutri set up a commission to collect testimony from witnesses to a miracle performed in his town by the Bianchi.[4] The bishop of Rome, Pope Boniface IX, displayed the major relics in his keeping to the Bianchi, and was moved to tears while listening to their laude. He was even reported to have granted a papal indulgence after the fact, for the benefit of all those who had performed the nine days of devotion.[5]

The crucial point is that Boniface issued this indulgence (if, indeed, he actually did issue it) *after the fact*: he and the other bishops were responding to an initiative that came from the mass of believers. They did their best to channel it, to direct it, and to turn it to their benefit, but they did not invent it. When clerics promoted a devotion of their own invention, such as the seven-day revival of the Bianchi processions or the cult of the Marian shrine at Cigoli, its emphasis was noticeably different from that of the Bianchi devotion. These clerically inspired rites were more elaborate and more specific in their symbolic references, more closely bound to ecclesiastical structures and doctrines, and more carefully mimetic of the existing social and political order. The Bianchi, for all their respect for orthodoxy and affection for tradition, were slightly aloof from these concerns.

This quality of respectful independence was also apparent in the Bianchi's relations with the mendicant orders. Of course, as the Bianchi made their rounds, they sought out the Dominican and Franciscan churches; after all, these were always among the major spiritual centers of any city.[6] And they delighted in sermons delivered by Dominicans, Franciscans, and Augustinians, the specialists in religious oratory. But nowhere were the Bianchi affiliated exclusively with any one order. In Florence, they visited the Franciscan basilica of Santa

---

[2] For a biography of the bishop of Pistoia, Andrea Franchi, see I. Taurisano, *Il Beato Andrea Franchi* (Arezzo: n.p., 1922).

[3] Jacopo Delaito, *Annales Estenses*, in *RIS*, 18, col. 957.

[4] Vincenzo Federici, "Il miracolo del crocifisso della compagnia dei Bianchi a Sutri," in *Scritti di storia, di filologia, e d'arte per le nozze Fedele-De Fabritiis* (Naples: Riccardo Ricciardi, 1908), pp. 107–118.

[5] Dominici, *Cronaca*, p. 178.

[6] See in general the papers of the round table "Les Ordres Mendiants et la Ville en Italie centrale (v. 1220–v. 1350)," published in *Mélanges de l'Ecole Française de Rome, Moyen Age–Temps Modernes*, 89 (1977): 557–773.

Croce and the Dominican church of Santa Maria Novella; in Lucca, they called at both the Dominicans' San Romano and the Franciscans' San Francesco. In Padua, they first visited the Dominican church of Sant'Agostino and then the Franciscan church of Sant'Antonio (a visit repeated on October 4, the feast of St. Francis), followed by the churches of the Augustinians and the Carmelites, as well as various monasteries and nunneries.[7] In Bergamo, two Dominicans and a Franciscan preached the sermons urging people to participate in the devotions, and an Augustinian preached the sermon initiating the processions.[8] The Bianchi paid their respects to all these orders, but clung to none of them. The mendicants, for their part, welcomed the attentions of the Bianchi and joined avidly—at times too avidly—in the devotions.

Preserving Public Order

If the ecclesiastical authorities felt no hesitation in welcoming this orthodox and traditional movement, the secular authorities were less sanguine about the problems the Bianchi posed. Indeed, one of those problems was how to rein in overly enthusiastic churchmen. In Venice, where the Council of Ten had banned the Bianchi processions, the Dominican reformer Giovanni Dominici was moved to defy this ban; he was arrested and exiled.[9] In Florence, maestro Grazia de' Castellani, an Augustinian of Santo Spirito, was swept up in the enthusiasm for the Bianchi. Just after the end of the Bianchi processions in Florence, he approached the priors with a double request: that he be released from the obligation to conduct an embassy on behalf of the republic, and that he be allowed to form a "congregatio."[10] In a meeting on September 9, the representative of the Standard-bearer of

[7] Giovanni Conversini da Ravenna, *La processione dei Bianchi nella città di Padova (1399)*, ed. and trans. Libia Cortese and Dino Cortese (Padua: Centro Studi Antoniani, 1978).

[8] *Chronicon Bergomense guelpho-ghibellinum*, ed. Carlo Capasso, in RIS², 16, part 2, pp. 94–95.

[9] I shall discuss this incident in detail later in this chapter.

[10] Archivio di Stato di Firenze, Consulte e pratiche, 34, fol. 14v. On maestro Grazia, who on several other occasions did perform diplomatic missions on behalf of Florence, see Domenico Guerri, *Il commento del Boccaccio a Dante* (Bari: Laterza, 1926), pp. 166–175.

Justice recommended against granting these requests, and added that if maestro Grazia did not wish to go on this diplomatic mission, he should stay put in his cell. Another civic official was a little more complaisant. He argued that maestro Grazia should be allowed to travel as he wished, though he should still be forbidden to form a new "societas": the Florentine government, suspicious as ever of the political entanglements of religious organizations, was united in its opposition to the founding of a new confraternity. Words were evidently less troubling than institutional innovations, for on September 17 maestro Grazia was preaching to the Bianchi in Pistoia, and soon after that date in Pacciana.[11] His sermons, like the song he wrote about the Bianchi, were laced with bloody and foreboding miracles and with calls to penitence.[12]

The Florentine priors were also concerned about the many reports of miracles that were circulating, reports spread by preachers like maestro Grazia or by simple word of mouth. On the day after they decided against allowing maestro Grazia to form a "congregatio," they adopted measures to prevent the spread of false accounts of miracles.[13] On September 12 they ordered an investigation of a particular miracle, possibly one of the bleeding crucifixes encountered so often in the Bianchi devotions.[14]

Authorities elsewhere shared this concern. In Rome, Zaccaria Trevisan arrested a charlatan who had a hollow cross rigged to ooze fake blood on command.[15] In Orvieto, according to Francesco di Montemarte, a Spaniard was arrested for working fraudulent miracles with a bleeding crucifix—a trick he said he had learned from a priest—and sent to Rome for punishment.[16] He was also found to have unguents and powders (presumably for use in magical ceremonies), as well as the tools of a cutpurse. He seems, in short, to have been a well-rounded "criminal type," a jack-of-all-unscrupulous-trades, and it is easy to see why conscientious secular authorities would do their best to protect their subjects from such persons by exposing their "miracles" as frauds. Ecclesiastical authorities, in contrast, like the bishop

[11] Dominici, *Cronaca*, pp. 164–165, 168–179, and 188.
[12] Toscani, *Le laude*, pp. 82–85.
[13] Archivio di Stato di Firenze, Consulte e pratiche, 34, fol. 15r.
[14] Archivio di Stato di Firenze, Consulte e pratiche, 34, fol. 15v.
[15] Dominici, *Cronaca*, pp. 204–206.
[16] Montemarte, *Cronaca*, pp. 267–268; and in the same volume (*RIS*², 15, part 5) Luca di Domenico Manenti, *Cronaca*, p. 407.

of Sutri, were more concerned to prove the truth of these miracles, and to that end they collected testimony from witnesses.

Far more important than the desire to protect their subjects from exploitation by religious charlatans was the secular authorities' concern for preserving their own positions. Faced with the sudden appearance of large crowds of hooded strangers, they worried about possible threats to the stability of their regime. In Savona in 1398, the authorities feared that the proto-Bianchi procession of flagellants was simply a cover for an attempt to seize Savona for the Adorno; they bolted the gates and let none of the *battuti* enter.[17] In Rome, Boniface IX, who as spiritual leader displayed the papal relics to the Bianchi and listened sympathetically to their songs, was as a temporal leader widely reported to be concerned about the potential for disturbance represented by these crowds. His control over the city of Rome and the surrounding territory was perennially shaky, and Francesco di Montemarte said that the pope was afraid the gathering of so many people might lead to rebellion against his authority, either in Rome itself or elsewhere in the papal state.[18] One businessman reported from Rome that the Roman *popolo* had indeed lived up to its reputation for unruliness, gathering in riotous crowds at any report of a dramatic miracle and making its presence felt through noise and numbers.[19] An employee of Francesco Datini passed on, with reservations, the reports from Rome that had reached him in Montpellier:

And so it seems that at Rome the pope was terribly afraid of these Bianchi and that he had eighteen of their leaders seized; and that the Romans, hearing that these men had been seized, immediately went to the prisons in an uproar and brought them out; and the pope, upon seeing this, apparently left Rome for fear of the Romans. This is the information which maestro Nadino, at Avignon, has, and there are letters to this effect. Giovanni Francieschi says that his letters report these things, but doesn't say that the pope has fled.[20]

[17] Archivio Datini di Prato, no. 660, lett. Genova-Firenze, comp. Datini; June 8, 1398.

[18] Montemarte, *Cronaca*, p. 268.

[19] Dominici, *Cronaca*, pp. 147–150, quoting a letter sent from Rome by "a factor of Gabriello di m. Bartolomeo Panciatichi."

[20] "E questo pare che a Roma il papa abia avutto gran paura di questi bianchi e che n'avea fatti prendere de' migliori da 18; e ch'e' romani, udendo chostoro erano pressi, subito a romore andarono a le prigioni e trasogli di fuori; e'l papa, vedendo

The information purveyed by maestro Nadino, the principal doctor at the papal court in Avignon, was more circumstantial but less accurate than that transmitted by Giovanni Francieschi: Boniface IX had mastered his fears and stayed in Rome, and even showed the Bianchi some favors, such as a special display of the Veronica. But his fears were not groundless. Less than four months later, Nicola Colonna, who had knelt before Boniface in the white robes of the Bianchi peacemakers, led an abortive uprising in Rome.[21]

The Elders of Lucca, as we have seen, were less worried about letting strangers into their city than about letting all of their people go out. In response to a planned Bianchi excursion, they issued an order that no citizen or resident, whether man or woman, should go forth from the city.[22] But those who had prepared to go on this procession left quickly, before the order could be put into effect. Although the Elders sought to satisfy those who remained behind by staging processions within the city, these internal processions evidently could not match the allure of parading piously abroad. In the end, the Elders yielded to popular pressure, though to preserve order they adopted the unusual expedient of letting their subjects go out in shifts.[23]

Such fears for the fundamental stability of the regime do not appear to have been particularly widespread, or justified. Control of several major cities did, in fact, change hands within a few months of

---

questo, pare si sia partitto di Roma per paura di romani. Queste novelle à detto maestro Nadino, a Vingnione, e che ci ène letere. Giovanni Francieschi dicie le sue letere chontano queste chose, ma no' dicie del papa sia fugita." Archivio Datini di Prato, no. 897, lett. Montpellier-Barcellona, comp. Datini a Baldo Villanuzzi; October 17, 1399.

[21] O. Raynaldi, *Annales ecclesiastici*, 17 (Rome, 1659), year 1400, par. 4. Nicola Colonna's rebellion is mentioned in letters in the Archivio Datini di Prato, no. 545, lett. Roma-Pisa, comp. Giovanni de' Medici a Manno d'Albizo degli Agli; January 17, 1400 (1399 Florentine style); and comp. di Tommaso Amidei e Niccolò Pellarcioni; January 17, 1400 (1399 Florentine style). The chilling effect of this abortive rebellion on the religious life of Rome, which by this date had shifted from the Bianchi devotions to the celebration of the jubilee year, can be gathered from Francesco di Montemarte, *Cronaca*, p. 268: "My son Ridolfo did not want to go with his brother Ranuccio or with any of the Orvietan Bianchi, even though messer Paolo Orsini begged him to go; but he was there many days later and found none of the Romans wearing those robes, and they were all very nervous because of the arrest of that priest named Giovanni and because of messer Nicola Colonna's rebellion."

[22] Sercambi, *Croniche*, p. 348; see also p. 349.

[23] Sercambi, *Croniche*, p. 367. For a fuller account of this episode, see Chapter 3, above.

the passage of the Bianchi. Siena and Perugia followed the lead of Pisa in submitting to the overlordship of Giangaleazzo Visconti, as a result of either diplomatic pressure or outright purchase. In Lucca, Paolo Guinigi assumed overt control of the tottering republic he had formerly dominated covertly.[24] In Bologna, the death of several key figures during the plague of 1399–1400 led to the collapse of the regime headed by Carlo Zambeccari, who himself perished in the epidemic.[25] But neither these changes in government nor Nicola Colonna's abortive attempt to raise rebellion in Rome can be ascribed in any plausible way to the destabilizing influence of the Bianchi.

The very orderliness of the movement was itself taken as proof that the Bianchi devotion was divinely inspired. Luca Dominici marveled that 2,000 Pisan Bianchi were received within the walls of San Miniato when there were only 500 Sanminiatesi there, and that 9,000 Perugian Bianchi were hosted by the barely 300 people who had stayed behind in Foligno.[26] In both cases, traditional enemies were allowed to enter towns which they then could easily have sacked, and rather than taking advantage of this singular opportunity, they behaved like the dearest of friends.

The authorities in a number of cities were bothered less by any fear of losing control of the *città dominante* than by worries about disorder in the myriad small towns of the subject territory. In Florence, Giovanni di Temperano Manni, speaking on behalf of the Standard-bearer of Justice, recommended that the Bianchi not be allowed to enter freely the fortified towns of the Florentine contado.[27] Florentine vicars followed this injunction. At Pescia, messer Fiorese Salviati of Florence would not let the Bianchi from Lucca enter; they had to stay outside the walls, at San Francesco and Sant'Antonio, where the people of Pescia and the surrounding area brought them supplies.[28] Similarly, at San Miniato, the Florentine vicar, Antonio da Uzzano, would not let the Bianchi from Lucca lodge inside; the populace, troubled by this order, insisted that the gates remain open much of the night so that they could take food to the Bianchi. In this case,

---

[24] Christine E. Meek, *Lucca 1369–1400: Politics and Society in an Early Renaissance City-State* (Oxford: Oxford University Press, 1978), pp. 335–338, 359–361.

[25] Sorbelli, *Corpus chronicorum Bononiensium*, p. 464.

[26] Dominici, *Cronaca*, p. 198.

[27] Archivio di Stato di Firenze, Consulte e pratiche, 34, fol. 10v (August 14, 1399).

[28] Sercambi, *Croniche*, p. 350.

personal grievances may have sharpened the vicar's sense of political duty: Giovanni Sercambi tells his readers not to be surprised at Antonio da Uzzano's attitude, for "this family never was a friend of the commune of Lucca."[29] But the Lucchese vicar at Pietrasanta, according to Sercambi, was simply doing his job when he ordered the guards to lock the Bianchi out, since he did this "not out of disrespect, but out of watchfulness."[30]

The same concern was evidently shared elsewhere. The viscount who represented the duke of Milan at Sarzana ordered his garrison to keep the Bianchi out of that town.[31] Dino di Giovanni dei Marzi, Sienese vicar in Lucignano, reported to his superiors on the turmoil stirred up by the Bianchi in this small town in his charge.[32] The residents of Lucignano had impetuously moved to recall home all banished men, but they suspended all efforts in that line when Dino made known to them the opinion of their Sienese lords. Dino believed that his actions would keep his superiors happy and his subjects safe, and he was not exaggerating when he said that the safety of this border town depended on preserving due order. Bands of mercenaries were traversing the area, and would have pounced quickly on any easy prey. That is precisely what happened to the south of Siena, in the territory of Orvieto, where so many people had joined the Bianchi processions that "few men [were] left in all the towns in this land." A small troop of infantry captured the town of Fichino "by finding the gate open, and inside there were just five women."[33] The Florentines, too, lost a castle in the Chianti, and had to levy troops from Pistoia to help recapture it.[34]

Aside from these military or police matters of public security, authorities had to confront the general problem of dealing with masses of transients. Lodging was not a great problem: the Bianchi, in princi-

---

[29] "Mai quella casa non fu amicha del comune di Luccha." Sercambi, Croniche, pp. 363–364.

[30] "Non per dispregio ma per buona guardia." Sercambi, Croniche, p. 316. Sercambi, of course, was Lucchese.

[31] Sercambi, Croniche, pp. 314–315.

[32] Archivio di Stato di Siena, Concistoro, Carteggio, 1845 (25 marzo 1399–25 ottobre 1399), fol. 72r (slightly damaged, upper right corner). The appointment of Dino di Giovanni di Marzi can be found in Archivio di Stato di Siena, Consiglio generale, 392, Elezione e cerne (23 maggio 1399–5 dicembre 1431), fol. 2v.

[33] "Per tutte le terre del paese pochi huomini ci rimaniano." "Per trovar la porta aperta, e dentro non erano se cinque donne." Montemarte, Cronaca, p. 268.

[34] Dominici, Cronaca, pp. 181, 187.

ple, were not supposed to sleep in beds or inside a walled town. Most of them undoubtedly slept in the open on these warm summer nights, though some were given shelter in religious institutions and a few wealthy Bianchi, like Francesco Datini, paid for their lodging in inns.[35] Food, however, was another matter. Datini, of course, brought food and drink for himself and his party, and they dined very well indeed; the single item on which Datini spent the most was wine. But most of the Bianchi expected to be fed by their hosts, and so food had to be provided by either private or public charity. The lord of Imola, Luigi Alidosi, set out food and invited the Bianchi to take whatever they needed.[36] The Concistoro of Siena ordered the officials in charge of provisions to bake bread and distribute it to the Bianchi at public expense.[37] The hospitality of the Sienese was repaid when they, in their turn, adopted the Bianchi devotion and went to Perugia. There the ten priors ordered the preparation of "bread, wax, wine, or other supplies needed by them," and decreed: "for their honor up to sixty bushels of grain from the town granary and forty barrels of wine could and should be given; and for the rest let them be allowed and empowered to give and disburse up to 16 2/3 gold florins for wax and other fitting things."[38] They further ordered the relevant officials to distribute up to 48 bushels of bread at communal expense to the Bianchi who were flocking to their city every day. The treasurers were to disburse 44 florins for the purchase of 40 barrels of wine and to contribute £40 for wax; another £35 were to come from the officials who managed communal property. The total sum disbursed "for the honor of the aforesaid commune of Perugia and love of God and divine inspiration" was impressive indeed.[39] The government of Pi-

---

[35] Mazzei, *Lettere di un notaro*, pp. xcix–cvi; Dominici, *Cronaca*, p. 58.

[36] *Cronaca Bolognetti*, in Sorbelli, *Corpus chronicorum Bononiensium*, p. 468.

[37] ". . . expensum nostri comunis senarum." Archivio di Stato di Siena, Concistoro, 210 (1 luglio 1399–31 agosto 1399), fol. 41r: meeting of August 23, 1399.

[38] "Panem, ceram, vinum vel alia necessaria victui ipsorum. . . ." "pro huiusmodi honore dari possit et debeat de grano comunis Perusie usque in quantitatem triginta corbium grani et quadriginta barilium vini, et pro reliquis pro cera et aliis opportunis usque ad quantitatem sexdecim florenorum auri et duorum tertiorum . . . possint et valeant dare et expendere." Archivio di Stato di Perugia, Consigli e riformanze, 44, fol. 130v: meeting of September 3, 1399.

[39] ". . . pro honore dicti communis Perusie et amore Dei et intuitu divino." Archivio di Stato di Perugia, Consigli e riformanze, 44, fol. 130v. However, the disbursement records do not mention any payments for food for the Bianchi (or for anything else) between August 24 and September 18, 1399. Archivio di Stato di

stoia, too, allocated a substantial sum to feed the Bianchi—£90 5s 9d
—on August 14, 1399.[40] The governing councils of Arezzo adopted
the expedient of reimbursing people after the fact for "expenses in-
curred in honoring the worthy and honorable citizens of Florence,
who in the present month of September and the month of August
just past were in the aforesaid city of Arezzo dressed in devout white
robes"—taking care, however, to cap their payments at the still considerable amount of £166.[41] Even without the prospect of being reim-
bursed, private individuals also pitched in to help feed the Bianchi:
"they were brought bread, wine, cheese, eggs, sugar, candies, ripe
grapes, fruit, and an infinity of things by citizens and by the commune, so that it seemed to rain upon them."[42] Many of the poorer
Bianchi may well have eaten better on the road than they did at
home, though it appears that they did adhere to the prohibition
against eating meat. And nearly everywhere, they dined at the expense of their hosts. Only in their progress along the Via Emilia,
through Modena, Bologna, Imola, and Faenza, were the Bianchi described as carrying with them all necessary provisions, and this was
because of local food shortages.[43]

All such problems of provisioning were dwarfed by the looming
threat of the plague. We have already seen how the spreading epidemic of bubonic plague evoked different responses to the north and
south of the Apennines, and how in the north the concern for public
health made the untrammeled propagation of the Bianchi devotions
impossible. Giangaleazzo Visconti, ruler of the largest congeries of
territories in the Po valley, was particularly conscientious and energetic in his public health measures, which included restrictions on
and suspension of Bianchi processions in many of the cities under his

---

Perugia, Conservatori della moneta, 34 (uscita a contanti dal febbraio 1399 al
marzo 1400), fol. 16r–v.

[40] Dominici, *Cronaca*, p. 65, note 3.

[41] ". . . expensas factas in honorando reverendos et honorabiles cives florentinos
qui de presente mense septembris et proxime passato mense augusti fuerunt in
dicta civitate Aretii sub devota veste alba induti." Archivio di Stato d'Arezzo, Deliberazioni del Magistrato dei Priori e del Consiglio Generale, 3, fol. 197 (meeting
of September 19, 1399). The cap on payments is found on fol. 198.

[42] "Fu loro portato pane, vino, cacio, uova, zucchero, confeti, uve mature,
frutta e roba infinita per li cittadini e per lo comune che pareva vi piovesse."
Dominici, *Cronaca*, p. 60.

[43] For the provisioning of Bianchi on the Via Emilia and its relation to local food
shortages, see above, Chapter 3.

lordship.[44] That he allowed the processions to take place at all is a testimony to two things: his awareness of the limited power of ducal decrees over distant possessions, which made it wise for him to avoid sapping his prestige by issuing commands he could not enforce; and his recognition that the Bianchi processions, despite their potential for unwittingly spreading a terrible contagion, were fundamentally laudable and worthy of official respect and approval.

The measure of official approval of the Bianchi devotion can be found in the willingness of authorities all over northern and central Italy to enact into law the program of social reform and pacification promoted by the Bianchi. The Bianchi demands for the release of prisoners, the repatriation of exiles, the abandonment of feuds and factionalism, and a new spirit of concord and purity in civic life were met by legislation and decrees. Galeotto Belfiore Malatesta wrote to his vicar at Borgo San Sepolcro, announcing a general amnesty for "each and every trial and sentence, both personal and pecuniary, which had been made and settled against any person in the city and district of the Borgo, up to the twenty-ninth day of the month of September just past, on which day I donned the most devout habit of the Bianchi."[45] He was also prepared to let exiles return home, but only if they were willing to make peace with their adversaries; he instructed his vicar to lead the recalcitrant to peace "through love or through force." At Montefiascone and Viterbo prisoners were released, and among the prisoners freed at Vetralla was a certain Marco di Ianne di messer Francesco di Viterbo who had been confined for thirty-nine years.[46] In Florence, after some hesitation, the priors decided to liberate their prisoners, with one notable exception: Jacopo da Montepulciano.[47] Jacopo, a member of the former ruling family of Montepulciano, had been imprisoned in Florence since 1390. He evidently hoped that the Bianchi devotions would lead to his release, and he wrote a lauda to encourage them. But the priors decided that

[44] See above, Chapter 3.

[45] "Ogni e ciaschuna condapnaxione e processo personali e pecuniarie, le quale avesse fatte e fermate contro qualunche persona de la terra e destretto del Borgo, per fine a dì XXVIIII del mese de septembre proximo passato, lo quale die presi el devotisimo abito de' Bianchi." Gino Franceschini, "Anna Montefeltro-Malatesta," in *Studi Riminesi e bibliografici in onore di Carlo Lucchesi* (Faenza: Fratelli Lega, 1952), p. 95.

[46] Montemarte, *Cronaca*, p. 267.

[47] Archivio di Stato di Firenze, Provvisioni, 88, fols. 147v–149v, 152v–155v. On Jacopo da Montepulciano, see above, Chapter 4.

in this case practical considerations outweighed pious mercy: Jacopo was a partisan of the duke of Milan, and if he were set loose the Florentine garrison in Montepulciano would have to be strengthened, at great expense. Jacopo vented his disappointment in the same way that he had worked to procure his release—in verse.

Even the cautious councillors of Lucca, meeting on August 22 in the midst of the Bianchi devotions, voted by better than three to one to accede to the Bianchi's cries for mercy and release eleven prisoners. The one condition they imposed was that those released make peace with the injured parties. Nuccio Grassini da Limano, who was imprisoned for complicity in an assault on a neighbor; Franceschino of Venice, who had wounded Marco di Giovanni; even Matteo di Biagio of Pescia, who had tried to bring twenty geldings to San Miniato without paying the tax on them: all were granted full pardons. Only Lorenzo di Jacopo, who had tried to cheat the grain office, was released conditionally: he was required to pay the money owed according to a set schedule and was barred from holding public office. But even he received his freedom.[48]

The full range of legislative response to the Bianchi program can be followed in the register of acts taken by the priors of Perugia. On September 15, as the local Bianchi processions came to an end, the priors issued new ordinances setting penalties for blasphemy, swearing, sodomy, murder, and harboring exiles or outlaws.[49] On September 20, with the cries of the crowd from more than a fortnight earlier still ringing in their ears, the priors responded to the Bianchi's calls for mercy.[50] "In consideration of the advent of the Bianchi of the city of Siena and their contrition and devotion," which the populace of Perugia had enthusiastically seconded, they decreed that prisoners should be liberated and "that their bans and sentences and trials should be cancelled, lifted, and annulled."[51] The day before, September 19, they had already set about repatriating exiles and appointed a commission of five citizens to restore the confiscated goods of those

[48] Archivio di Stato di Lucca, Consiglio generale, 13: Riformagioni pubbliche 1397–1400, pp. 256–257. This release of prisoners took the place of the one that would normally have come some three weeks later, on the feast of the Holy Cross.

[49] Archivio di Stato di Perugia, Consigli e riformanze, 44, fols. 132r–133r.

[50] On September 2, as the Priori recalled it, "almost the whole populace then present in the piazza, both men and women, clamored loudly that this grace be granted." Archivio di Stato di Perugia, Consigli e riformanze, 44, fol. 133v.

[51] "Quod eorum banna et condemnationes et processus debeant cassari, tolli, et anullari." Archivio di Stato di Perugia, Consigli e riformanze, 44, fol. 133v.

rebels who agreed to live peaceably and not attempt anything "against the Perugian republic or the present condition of the city of Perugia."[52] This action, too, was taken because of the movement of the Bianchi, which had made the republic of Perugia contrite of heart and disposed the community to virtuous living.[53]

However contrite of heart, and however willing to accede to the Bianchi's requests, the rulers of these cities nevertheless made it clear that they, and not the religious enthusiasts, remained in charge. In Florence, the statements of leading citizens in the *Consulte e pratiche*, the record of deliberative and consultative assemblies, repeatedly echo a common distrust of the Bianchi and concern for public order. The catchphrase was "super factis alborum provideatur," "with regard to this business of the Bianchi, let it be seen to": that they not enter the fortified towns of the contado, that they not congregate in the city, that eight citizens be elected to make sure that no "novelty" ensue, that "nothing detrimental come about."[54] In some cases, the speakers may well have been men who not only took part in the Bianchi devotions, but joined in such personal devotions as messer Rosso degli Orlandi's journey to Vallombrosa and La Verna. That party included several of the priors who had just finished their term in office, and Luca Dominici reported that both the priors who left office on September 1 and those who replaced them were dressed in white.[55] But in the discussions recorded in the *Consulte e pratiche* they were called upon to speak as public-minded citizens, not as private persons; and however much they may have been moved to acts of personal piety, in these debates public concerns carried the day.

Like other governing groups, the Concistoro of Siena took executive action to welcome the Bianchi: it ordered the communal treasurer to provide for bread for the visiting Bianchi, declared a holiday so that everyone could participate freely in the devotions, allowed debtors to participate without fear of being seized for their debts, and

---

[52] "Contra rem publicam Perusiam vel presentem statum civitatis Perusie." Archivio di Stato di Perugia, Consigli e riformanze, 44, fol. 135r–135v.

[53] Archivio di Stato di Perugia, Consigli e riformanze, 44, fol. 135r.

[54] "Aliquod sinistri non contingat." Archivio di Stato di Firenze, Consulte e pratiche, 34, fols. 10v, 12r–13v: meetings of August 14, 1399, and August 22, 1399.

[55] Archivio di Stato di Firenze, Corporazioni religiose soppresse, Badia di Firenze, 78, filza 315, lett. 212: Rosso di Andreozzo degli Orlandi to Piero di Bernardo Chiarini; Dominici, *Cronaca*, p. 115: "this morning in Florence the new priors took office dressed as Bianchi, and the old priors left office dressed likewise as Bianchi."

suspended criminal proceedings.[56] On August 30, the members of the Concistoro decided to investigate the possibility of releasing some prisoners, particularly those confined for debt; the following day, they named four citizens to look into the matter.[57] The Sienese were apparently ready to grab any opportunity to clear their prisons: they released a number of prisoners in celebration of the Assumption of the Virgin, following the "ancient custom" of the commune of Siena, and on September 12 the General Council proposed a further act of clemency in honor of God and Mary, on the occasion of accepting the overlordship of Giangaleazzo Visconti.[58] This made three pardons issued within thirty days. But in no case—change of government, customary devotion, or extraordinary religious excitement—did the governing councils allow enthusiasm to sweep away their concern for law and order. The General Council responded coolly to a proposal for a more general pardon of prisoners and repatriation of exiles, and the proposal was finally tabled.[59] The frequent support given the Bianchi by the Concistoro was at the same time a way of keeping careful track of their activities. It was the Concistoro, and not the ecclesiastical authorities, which granted the Bianchi permission to hear mass in the public square.[60] In thus licensing the Bianchi devotions, the Sienese councillors were demonstrating that even under these extraordinary circumstances, they retained the full extent of their power and authority.

In fact, by sponsoring the Bianchi devotions and embracing their social program, governing councils like the Concistoro of Siena, the priors of Florence, and the priors of Perugia reasserted the sacral character of civic life.[61] When the Florentine priors entered office

[56] Archivio di Stato di Siena, Concistoro, 210 (1 luglio 1399–31 agosto 1399), fols. 41r–42r: meetings of August 23, August 25, and August 28, 1399.

[57] Archivio di Stato di Siena, Concistoro, 210, fol. 43r.

[58] Archivio di Stato di Siena, Consiglio generale, 199, Deliberazioni (6 maggio 1399–22 marzo 1401), fols. 27v, 44v–45r: meetings of August 13 and September 12, 1399.

[59] Archivio di Stato di Siena, Consiglio generale, 259, Stracciafogli (1 maggio 1399–1 april 1401), fol. 21v: meeting of September 9, 1399. Siena had just passed under the rule of Giangaleazzo Visconti, and in this shifting political climate the governing councils were understandably cautious about welcoming home any potential dissidents.

[60] Archivio di Stato di Siena, Concistoro, 210, fol. 40v: meeting of August 20, 1399.

[61] For another aspect of the civic religion of fourteenth-century Italy, see André

robed in white or the Sienese Concistoro loaned the Bianchi the use of altar furnishings from the communal sacristy, these civic officials cloaked themselves in devout righteousness. In Perugia, the sweeping moral legislation enacted in the wake of the Bianchi devotions aimed to make of Perugia a godly state, as it transformed offenses against public morality into criminal infractions.[62] Ruling groups appeared as the guardians of moral order, the agents of God's will on earth, and thereby endowed their regimes with an aura of legitimacy. And as the fourteenth century came to an end amid political instability and religious divisions, legitimacy was a rare and lustrous commodity indeed.

Controlling the Sacred: Giovanni Dominici and Venice

This desire to demonstrate political legitimacy by exercising civic control over religious life provides a key for understanding an episode that, in its high drama of political confrontation, is unique in the history of the Bianchi devotions: the arrest of Giovanni Dominici and his expulsion from Venice. This notorious episode has always been interpreted as a clash of church and state: according to students of both the Bianchi movement and the history of Venice, Giovanni's pious attempt to introduce the Bianchi movement was summarily quashed by a Venetian government that had no sympathy for such devotions.[63] In fact, I would argue, Giovanni's procession was only

---

Vauchez, "Patronage des saints et religion civique," in *Patronage and Public in the Trecento*, ed. Vincent Moleta (Florence: Olschki, 1986), pp. 59–80.

[62] On the "godly state" and religious orthodoxy as a source of political legitimacy, see Christina Larner, *Enemies of God: The Witch-hunt in Scotland* (Baltimore: Johns Hopkins University Press, 1981), pp. 192–203, and Larner, *Witchcraft and Religion: The Politics of Popular Belief*, ed. Alan Macfarlane (Oxford: Basil Blackwell, 1984), pp. 122–126, 128–129, and 139.

[63] See, for instance, Giampaolo Tognetti, "Sul moto dei bianchi," pp. 313–324; Etienne Delaruelle, "Les grandes processions de pénitents de 1349 et 1399," in *Il Movimento dei Disciplinati*, pp. 135–137; Lia Sbriziolo, "Per la storia delle confraternite veneziane: Dalle Deliberazioni miste (1310–1476) del Consiglio dei Dieci: Le scuole dei Battuti," in *Miscellanea Gilles Gérard Meersseman* (Padua: Antenore, 1970), pp. 721–724; Sbriziolo, "Note su Giovanni Dominici, I: La 'spiritualità' del Dominici nelle lettere alle suore veneziane del Corpus Christi," *Rivista di storia della chiesa in Italia*, 24 (1970): 9–15 (with thorough references to earlier literature on the

obliquely related to the Bianchi movement. His decision to stage it was motivated by something other than simple piety. And his initiative disclosed deep and bitter disagreement within the Venetian patriciate over the proper role of the government in regulating religious activity.

While most cities received the Bianchi enthusiastically and some received them hesitantly, only Venice refused to receive them at all. On September 10, 1399, as the Bianchi were nearing Venetian territory, the Council of Ten voted to instruct the Venetian podestà at Chioggia to turn back the Bianchi and keep them from approaching Venice.[64] Contemporaries differed in their assessments of this decision. Those few who disapproved of the Bianchi deemed the Venetian action prudent and shrewd.[65] Those who looked unkindly on the Venetians murmured that they had banned the Bianchi for purely mercenary reasons, being unwilling to do what the Genoese had done and interrupt business for the nine days of the devotion.[66]

A more accurate assessment of the Ten's actions lies between these two extremes: in forbidding the Bianchi access to the city, the council was simply performing one of its regular duties. As part of its responsibility for state security, the Council of Ten maintained an unusually strict surveillance of public religious activity. It was the Ten, for instance, who in 1360 prohibited the formation of any new religious association without their permission, who issued the requisite licenses for the annual processions of the *scuole grandi*, and who even granted membership in the most fashionable confraternities (for

---

incident); Fernanda Sorelli, *La santità imitabile: "Leggenda di Maria da Venezia" di Tommaso da Siena*, Deputazione di storia patria per le Venezie, Miscellanea di Studi e Memorie, 23 (Venice: Deputazione, 1984), pp. 83–84; Giorgio Cracco, "Dai santi ai santuari: Un'ipotesi di evoluzione in ambito veneto," in Giorgio Cracco, Andrea Castagnetti, and Silvana Collodo, *Studi sul medioevo veneto* (Turin: Giappichelli, 1981), pp. 35–36 (and in French translation in Vauchez, *Faire Croire*, pp. 289–290). I develop my own interpretation in greater detail in "Giovanni Dominici, the Bianchi, and Venice: Symbolic Action and Interpretive Grids," *Journal of Medieval and Renaissance Studies*, 23 (1993): 143–171.

[64] Archivio di Stato di Venezia, Consiglio dei Dieci, Misti, 8 (1392–1407), fol. 53r. All subsequent references ASV, Consiglio dei Dieci are to this volume. This and most of the other measures concerning Giovanni's expulsion from Venice were published in Emmanuele Antonio Cicogna, *Delle inscrizioni veneziane* (Venice, 1853), vol. 6, pp. 142–145; two final deliberations of the Ten which were omitted by Cicogna can be found in Sbriziolo, "Note su Giovanni Dominici," pp. 10–11, n. 19.

[65] Girolamo da Forlì, *Chronicon*, pp. 4–5.

[66] Delayto, *Annales Estenses*, col. 957–958.

which there were long waiting lists) as a reward for service to the state.[67] In short, the Council of Ten strove to keep all public ritual under its control; if necessary, it forbade what it could not control, but more commonly it encouraged a broad range of pious observances. When the Bianchi appeared on the scene, the Ten proudly noted that Venice already had a surfeit of devotions and indulgences; accordingly, the council could see no need to introduce the Bianchi processions.[68] Nor was it necessary to call on the Bianchi as peacemakers, since the Ten were there to guard against faction and maintain public order.[69] And so the Council of Ten, while recognizing the properly religious character of the Bianchi and voicing no fears of political danger or disorder, closed to them the borders of the Venetian state. The Ten did their best to avoid any confrontation with the Bianchi, instructing the podestà at Chioggia to treat them courteously—and to give them the impression that he was acting on his own initiative ("quod hoc faciat a se").[70] This order was accepted docilely by the Bianchi: so far as we know, no effort was made to stage Bianchi processions at Chioggia, and a few calm words from the Venetian podestà at Treviso were all it took to disperse the group that wanted to bring the devotion to that subject city.[71] But in issuing this order, the Ten had unwittingly set the stage for their confrontation with the fiery preacher and fervent reformer Giovanni Dominici.

Giovanni enjoyed a peculiar ascendency in late trecento Venice.[72] He had arrived, or returned, there in 1388, sent by Raymond of

[67] Sbriziolo, "Per la storia delle confraternite veneziane," pp. 716–721, 736–742, 751–757.

[68] ASV, Consiglio dei Dieci, fol. 53r.

[69] On the role of the Council of Ten in maintaining security, see Guido Ruggiero, *Violence in Early Renaissance Venice* (New Brunswick: Rutgers University Press, 1980), pp. 6–17.

[70] ASV, Consiglio dei Dieci, fol. 53r.

[71] Luigi Pesce, *La chiesa di Treviso nel primo Quattrocento* (Rome: Herder, 1987), p. 48. The letter of the podestà in Treviso, Remigio Soranzo, clearly echoes ("quod vadant pro factis suis," that they should go about their business) the phrases of the Council of Ten's instructions to the Venetian podestà in Chioggia ("sed recendendo de Clugia vadant pro factis suis," turning back from Chioggia they should go about their business).

[72] This biographical sketch is based on Stefano Orlandi, *Necrologio di S. Maria Novella* (Florence: Olschki, 1955), vol. 2, pp. 77–126, and Giorgio Cracco, entry "Giovanni di Domenico Banchini," *Dizionario biografico degli italiani*, vol. 5 (Rome: Istituto della Enciclopedia Italiana, 1963), pp. 657–664.

Capua as lecturer in theology at San Zanipolo.[73] He quickly became one of the religious leaders of Venice and an important figure in the Dominican order. Acting as Raymond's vicar, he reformed the houses of San Domenico di Castello, San Domenico di Chioggia, and San Zanipolo to the strict observance and inspired a dozen Venetian noblemen to adopt the Dominican habit. He also founded the convent of Corpus Christi, which soon became one of the largest and most fashionable religious institutions in Venice. Members of the doge's family took part in its consecration in 1394, and within two years it housed more than seventy women, most of them drawn from leading families of the Venetian patriciate.[74] His energetic efforts on behalf of Dominican reform were recognized and rewarded by Raymond of Capua, who in 1393 named Giovanni vicar general of all the Observant houses in Italy.[75] Nor was his reforming zeal limited to the Dominican order: he strove to transform Venetian society by preaching regularly, engaging in pastoral care, acting as confessor and spiritual guide, and aiding those stricken by the plague in 1397. He was supported in this work not only by his fellow Dominicans, but by the Franciscans, by secular clergy of patrician stock such as Leonardo Pisani, by Bishop Angelo Correr (the future Pope Gregory XII), and by the Venetian government. He acted as spiritual adviser to the doge himself, Antonio Venier, and preached for the doge's wife on feast days.

[73] Giovanni had spent two years in Venice as a youth, learning commerce at his Venetian mother's instigation.

[74] The fundamental sources for the history of Corpus Christi are the *Cronaca del Corpus Domini* and the *Necrologio del Corpus Domini* written by Bartolomea Riccoboni, in Giovanni Dominici, *Lettere spirituali*, ed. Maria-Teresa Casella and Giovanni Pozzi (Freiburg: Edizioni Universitarie, 1969), pp. 257–330. Giovanni's epistolary description of the journey he undertook in order to obtain papal approval for the refoundation of Corpus Christi, commonly known as the *Iter perusinum*, has been published most recently in Dominici, *Lettere spirituali*, pp. 186–193. The convent of Corpus Christi has been the subject of a *tesi di laurea* prepared at the Università degli Studi di Padova under the direction of Antonio Rigon: Maria Ricci, "Il monastero del Corpus Christi di Venezia fra Tre-Quattrocento (con una silloge di trentadue documenti inediti)," anno academico 1982–1983. I am grateful to Elisabetta Bonato for bringing this work to my attention, and to Dottoressa Ricci for providing me with a copy of her meticulous *tesi*.

[75] The title is grander than the office truly was, since in all of Italy there were only four such houses—the three in or near Venice, and one in Città del Castello—all of them reformed by Giovanni. See in general Venturino Alce, "La riforma dell'ordine domenicano nel '400 e nel '500 veneto," in *Riforma della chiesa, cultura, e spiritualità nel Quattrocento veneto*, ed. Giovanni B. Francesco Trolese (Cesena: Badia di Santa Maria del Monte, 1984), pp. 333–343.

However, resentment of Giovanni Dominici flourished in the same patrician circles in which he was so respected. Giovanni's encouragement of chastity was seen to threaten the preservation and continuation of the patrician family, while his advocacy of the cloistered life called into question the traditional ordering of the patrician household, incidentally one of the key analogies for the well-ordered state.[76] "Many men and women left their relatives and their children to become friars and nuns," wrote Sister Bartolomea in her chronicle of Corpus Christi, "and for this reason their relatives grew angry with him [Giovanni], saying: 'This traitor is leading our children astray; let us remove him from the world.'" And so, she says, they mounted no fewer than seven attempts on his life.[77]

Within the Dominican order, too, attacks on Giovanni were mounting. In many ways, he brought these upon himself. Even an admiring biographer who supported the Observant movement noted that Giovanni was a harsh critic of those who failed to meet his exacting standards, and the inflexible fervor with which he pursued the reform of his order earned him the enmity of many fellow Dominicans.[78] Giovanni did his best to fortify himself against his enemies. In the spring of 1397, he obtained from Boniface IX a bull confirming that he would retain his office even after the death of Raymond of Capua, the master general of his order.[79] Raymond died in Nuremberg on October 5, 1399; the news of his mentor and protector's demise had undoubtedly reached Giovanni in Venice before the middle of November.

With his ascendency in Venice under increasing attack and his position in the Dominican order suddenly in doubt, Giovanni sought reaffirmation of his status in both Venice and the church. Formal support from the papacy came on November 26, when Boniface con-

[76] Margaret L. King, "Caldiera and the Barbaros on Marriage and the Family: Humanist Reflections of Venetian Realities," *Journal of Medieval and Renaissance Studies*, 6 (1976): 19–50; King, *Venetian Humanism in an Age of Patrician Dominance* (Princeton: Princeton University Press, 1986), pp. 92–98.

[77] "Molti e molte lassava li parenti e fiolli per farsi frati e muneghe e per questo li parenti se indegnava contra de lui dicendo: 'Questo traditor ne desvia li nostri fiolli, el desferemo del mondo'." Riccoboni, *Necrologio*, p. 317.

[78] "He was a rigid but honest reprover of vices." Biblioteca Riccardiana, Florence, ms. 1333, fol. 50r. Compare the comment of Riccoboni, *Necrologio*, p. 317: "He brought the friars of San Zanipolo back to proper observance [of the rule], so that those who did not want to observe it wanted to kill him."

[79] *Bullarium ordinis Fratrum Praedicatorum* (Rome, 1729), vol. 2, pp. 362–363.

firmed Giovanni as vicar with full authority over the reformed convents in Italy.[80] But by that time Giovanni's attempt to clarify his standing in Venice had already produced disastrous results. Since his preeminence in Venetian religious life was not institutional, Giovanni could not ask for formal confirmation of it. Instead, he put the Venetian government to the test by publicly and dramatically violating an edict of the Council of Ten: its ban on the Bianchi devotions.

On November 18, 1399, more than two months after the Council of Ten had closed the Venetian border to the Bianchi and a full month after the last major Bianchi procession elsewhere in Italy, Giovanni Dominici staged a "Bianchi" procession in Venice.[81] He assembled his followers at the church of San Geremia, where about 150 men and women gathered to hear mass before setting forth, singing hymns and crying "misericordia."[82] The group was small but distinguished: it included "gentlemen and ladies, both religious and secular," "with the friars of San Michele and many of the most spiritual people in Venice"—in short, a mixed group of men and women, lay and clerical, with a notable component of regular clergy and a marked patrician character. Giovanni himself, though born in Florence, was the son of a Venetian noblewoman. The other leaders of the procession, Leonardo Pisani and Antonio Soranzo, both long-term collaborators of Giovanni, were also well-born; Pisani, a priest and noted preacher, had helped to organize the procession, while Soranzo, a Dominican tertiary, carried the crucifix at its head. Although the procession was by all accounts orderly and well-planned, none of the organizers had obtained governmental permission to stage it. And so, on the *campo* in front of Giovanni's base in Venice, the Dominican church of San Zanipolo, the agents of the Ten halted and roughly dispersed the procession. They arrested the leaders—Antonio Soranzo, Leonardo Pisani, and Giovanni himself—and scattered their followers, handling with rude dispatch people who were accustomed to respect and deference. But despite the complaints of Giovanni's followers, the

---

[80] *Bullarium ordinis Fratrum Praedicatorum*, vol. 2, p. 388.

[81] The description of this procession is based on Archivio di Stato di Venezia, Corporazioni religiose soppresse, San Giorgio Maggiore, busta 174, processo 738 (letters to Giovanni Contarini), lett. 19 (December 22, 1399), Ruggero Contarini to Giovanni Contarini; Riccoboni, *Cronaca*, p. 273; and Dominici, *Lettere spirituali*, pp. 90–97.

[82] Note the difference between this cry and the Bianchi's usual one of "pace e misericordia": Giovanni's aim was confrontation, not peace.

police do not appear to have been particularly brutal. Their one startling act of violence—one which was almost certainly unintentional—injured not a person, but an object: in wrenching the crucifix from Antonio Soranzo, they broke one of its arms.

More than mere chronology set this procession apart from the mainstream of Bianchi devotions. Indeed, were it not for Giovanni's claim that his was a Bianchi procession, and the Ten's application to it of the ban on Bianchi processions, it would not be at all certain that the two were connected. The Bianchi processions typically included a large share of the local population, and so ranged from a few score participants in the case of small villages to several thousand in the major cities; Giovanni's procession included perhaps 150 persons, in a city of nearly 100,000. The Bianchi processions were composed principally of lay men and women, though secular and regular clergy also participated; Giovanni's procession, which included several priests and a large component of regular clergy, was markedly clerical. The Bianchi processions were sparked by direct contact with other groups of devotees, as people spontaneously elected to imitate the example of neighboring towns; Giovanni's procession was deliberately planned, in isolation from other processions.[83] The Bianchi processions expressed a moderate Marian piety and pressed this-worldly claims for peace and mercy; Giovanni's procession, which voiced no cry for peace, expressed a Christocentric piety and apocalyptic fears, for Giovanni interpreted the Bianchi in a way that was markedly different from the general tenor of the movement. He understood the Bianchi as the multitude robed in white of the Book of Revelations (7:9–14) and expected the opening of the seventh and last seal and the imminent end of the world.[84] This idiosyncratically radical interpretation of a most moderate popular devotion, like the timing of the procession, was in all likelihood shaped by Giovanni's personal crisis following the death of Raymond of Capua, and by his

---

[83] Tognetti, "Sul moto dei bianchi," p. 314, notes the same disparity between the way the Bianchi devotion spread elsewhere and the way it was introduced into Venice.

[84] Alfredo Galletti, "Una raccolta di prediche volgari inedita del Cardinale Giovanni Dominici," in Miscellanea di studi critici pubblicati in onore di Guido Mazzoni, ed. A. Della Torre and P. L. Rambaldi (Florence: Tipografia Galileiana, 1907), vol. 1, p. 266. This sermon dates from after Giovanni's expulsion from Venice, and it is quite possible that its apocalyptic tenor was due in part to his experience of arrest and exile.

need to get from the Venetian authorities an unambiguous indication of where he stood in Venice.

Giovanni's procession, in short, must be distinguished from the great public processions of the regular Bianchi devotions, and might more properly be grouped with the private devotions undertaken by select groups like the one formed by messer Rosso degli Orlandi and his Florentine friends. But whereas these other groups went in search of indulgences that would reward their manifest piety, Giovanni Dominici sought to demonstrate that his spiritual ascendency in Venetian ruling circles would enable him to violate with impunity a governmental edict regulating religious life. Despite the initial impression of defeat, he very nearly got what he wanted.

When the Ten convened on November 21 to decide what should be done with Giovanni and the other leaders of his procession, it was not immediately clear that they would do anything at all. A motion "to proceed against Fra Giovanni Dominici of the Order of Preachers on account of this assembly and procession of Bianchi which was done against the will of the government, since he was evidently one of the leaders of this gathering and assembly" carried by a very slim margin.[85] Once they had decided to proceed, the Ten had to consider a variety of proposed punishments. The penalties ranged from one month of confinement to San Zanipolo to the draconian suggestion of perpetual exile from Venetian territory, with a year in prison followed by renewed exile if the sentence should be violated and a fine of 1,000 ducats for anyone who tried to revoke this sentence.[86] Between these extremes lay proposals for two, three, or five years of exile. On the first ballot, the votes were broadly and fairly evenly distributed among all these proposals: five votes in favor of house arrest for a month, five for five years of exile, four for two years, two for three years, one for exile for life, and one abstention.[87] One might

---

[85] "Quod procedatur contra fratrem Johannem Dominici ordinis predicatorum propter istam congregationem et processionem alborum que facta fuit contra voluntatem dominii et cuius ordinationis et congregationis [cancelled: dicitur] apparet ipsum de principalibus extitisse." ASV, Consiglio dei Dieci, fol. 54v. The vote was nine to seven with one abstention.

[86] ASV, Consiglio dei Dieci, fols. 54v–55r.

[87] Rather than considering each proposal in turn, the Council of Ten voted on all the proposals at once; since a majority of the votes was required in order for a measure to pass, it might take more than one ballot for a proposal to win approval, especially if there were more than two or three alternative measures under

expect that on the second ballot, the measures that had attracted little support would be dropped entirely; and that is precisely what happened. One might also expect that in choosing among the three measures that had received substantial support on the first ballot—house arrest for a month, exile for two years, and exile for five years—the councillors would settle on the second, which offered itself as an attractive compromise midway between the two extremes. But quite the contrary happened, for on the second ballot, instead of reaching a consensus on the compromise measure, the Council of Ten split evenly between the two extremes: eight voted for house arrest and eight for five years of exile, with one abstention. And there the voting remained, evenly divided and bitterly polarized, for twenty-one more ballots.

This deadlock is absolutely extraordinary; there is nothing like it in the fifteen years covered by this register of the Council of Ten's activities. It was rare that a decision required more than two or three ballots, and no other decision took anything close to the twenty-four ballots needed in the case of Giovanni Dominici. Those cases that did require more than two ballots typically concerned ecclesiastical affairs. Evidently, there was considerable doubt within the Venetian patriciate over the propriety of proceeding against ecclesiastical figures, and so between a third and a half of the Council of Ten hobbled action by consistently abstaining from voting on such cases. Despite this sentiment, the Ten regularly exiled churchmen who posed a clear threat, in word or deed, to the Venetian state.[88] Giovanni Dominici, however, posed no such obvious threat. On the contrary, he was

---

consideration. Since the doge and the six ducal councillors took part in the deliberations of the Council of Ten, the Ten normally had seventeen voting members. (One of the *avogadori di commun*, the state attorneys, was present at the Ten's meetings, but did not vote.) This register of the Ten's activities records the measures proposed, the names of those who proposed them, and the number of votes each measure received; it does not record the names of those who voted for each measure. Guido Ruggiero very graciously answered a number of questions about the operating procedures of the Council of Ten; if I have misunderstood his lucid explanations, the fault is my own.

[88] In 1404, the Council of Ten (after considerable hesitation) exiled Antonio de Bellanzinis, bishop of Rethimnon in Crete, "for his foul and false words against the state and honor of our ducal dominion," and in 1406, it banished Francesco dei Bardi of Florence, bishop of Dragonara in southern Italy, "for the wicked words he spoke at the time of the past war, relishing the arrival of bad news concerning our dominion." ASV, Consiglio dei Dieci, fols. 94r–95r and 120r. For full particulars on these and other cases, see Bornstein, "Giovanni Dominici, the Bianchi, and Venice."

intimately linked with key elements of the ruling oligarchy, and his spiritual daughters in Corpus Christi devoutly prayed for the well-being of the Venetian state.[89] And so the Ten found themselves dead-locked. This was not a case in which there was a large bloc of absten-tions; hardly anyone was neutral. The question of how the govern-ment should respond to Giovanni's provocation was obviously of pressing importance to them, for they refused to break up the meet-ing until the issue was decided. Just as obviously, they were com-pletely polarized over what that decision should be. Half of them were convinced that Giovanni must be exiled for an extended period of time for his infraction; the other half were equally convinced that he deserved no more than a token punishment, a symbolic slap on the wrist. Both sides must have had some reason to hope that the deciding vote, the lone abstention, would eventually swing in their favor, and so they kept putting the same two proposals to the vote. Finally, on the twenty-fourth ballot, the abstaining councillor threw up his hands and voted for exile.

By this narrowest of margins, Giovanni Dominici lost his gamble and was forced to leave Venice. The closeness of the decision testifies eloquently to his standing in that city, and to the reluctance of many Venetian patricians to interfere in ecclesiastical affairs. But despite the misgivings of a substantial minority, in this case as in so many others, the Council of Ten reaffirmed its prerogatives in the sphere of religious life. Ecclesiastical institutions controlled too much wealth, and ecclesiastical persons constituted too large and important a body, for them to be ignored by the Venetian government, or by any gov-ernment interested in asserting its fiscal and jurisdictional authority. Nor could the Council of Ten allow an individual interloper to en-croach on its responsibility for preserving civic order and promoting sacred harmony. In this respect, the oligarchy of Venice was no dif-ferent from its counterparts in Florence, or Siena, or Perugia: all shared a common desire to maintain social order and encourage rev-

[89] The Venetian government had rewarded the sisters of Corpus Christi for their fidelity by aiding them in very practical ways. On June 2, 1395, the Council of Ten granted the sisters' request to sponsor a confraternity for both men and women, which would meet in their convent church (ASV, Consiglio dei Dieci, fol. 27v); and in November 1398 Doge Antonio Venier himself interceded on their behalf with Niccolò d'Este, winning for them permission to transfer some funds from Ferrarese territory to Venice: *I libri commemoriali della Repubblica di Venezia: Regesti*, ed. R. Predelli and P. Bosmin, R. Deputazione veneta di storia patria, Monumenti storici, ser. 1: Documenti, vol. 3 (Venice: La Società editrice, 1883), no. 145, p. 267.

erence for the regime. Nearly everywhere, governing councils sought to achieve these goals by sponsoring and regulating the Bianchi devotions. They could hardly do otherwise, since the evident piety and orderliness of the Bianchi who appeared before their gates made it difficult to refuse them admittance. Only in Venice, where the lagoon kept the Bianchi at a distance, could the government effectively bar the introduction of this unlicensed devotion and maintain, in the face of Giovanni Dominici's challenge, its exclusive control over public displays of piety.

CHAPTER SIX

THE LEGACY OF THE BIANCHI

In those days there arose a company known as the Bianchi, which went all over the world crying "mercy," so that many religious men and women and all sorts of people were moved to follow them, and they all dressed themselves in white cloth like the others and went in procession through all lands with the crucifix at their head, crying and singing "mercy" with great devotion and tears, and many enemies made peace, for which reason those processions were held to perform great miracles.
> —Bartolomea Riccoboni, a Venetian nun, describing the movement
> that had been barred from entering her city

Bʏ ᴛʜᴇ ᴇɴᴅ ᴏꜰ 1399, the Bianchi processions were over. In Lombardy, they were halted by Giangaleazzo Visconti, who feared that interurban processions would obstruct efforts to control the epidemic of plague. In the Veneto, they ran into the barrier imposed by the Council of Ten. In the Romagna, where they had progressed so regularly down the Via Emilia, they simply petered out or turned inland when that road came to an end. And in central Italy, where they had converged on the great pilgrimage center of Rome, there was no comparable goal capable of drawing them beyond Rome to the south.

Some small parties of Bianchi continued to circulate. According to the seventeenth-century historian Cesare Clementini, the inhabitants

Epigraph: Bartolomea Riccoboni, *Cronaca del Corpus Domini*, in Giovanni Dominici, *Lettere spirituali*, ed. Maria-Teresa Casella and Giovanni Pozzi, Spicilegium Friburgense, 13 (Freiburg: Edizioni Universitarie, 1969), p. 273.

of a cluster of fortified towns in the contado of Rimini—Verucchio, Monte Scutolo, and Castel Sant'Angelo—went in procession toward Cesena on October 14; they had not been able to go earlier, when the main procession passed through, because they were busy with the vintage.[1] Luca Dominici reported the passage of similar small groups of Bianchi through Pistoia throughout the closing months of the year: 60 from Monte Spertoli on November 11, 18 from San Miniato and 120 from Fucecchio on November 12, 30 from Pescia on December 3, and so on. But these scattered little processions gradually ceased to have a separate identity as Bianchi processions, and were increasingly swept up in the more general movement of pilgrims toward Rome for the jubilee of 1400. Luca Dominici mentioned a very distinguished party of 60 Paduan Bianchi—the group included members of Padua's ruling family, the Carraresi—who passed through Florence on November 15 on their way to Rome. And on December 3 he noted a continual passage of people, journeying to Rome from distant lands.[2]

In fact, it was probably the unexpected press of the Bianchi toward Rome that had stimulated Boniface IX to proclaim the jubilee of 1400. At this time the celebration of jubilee years was not yet established on a regular schedule.[3] The first jubilee began to take shape when a crowd of pilgrims descended on Rome at the end of 1299, moved by rumors of a plenary indulgence to be granted on Christmas Day, as it had supposedly been granted a century before.[4] Boniface VIII had the records of the papal chancellery searched for any memory of such an event, but no evidence could be found—which is hardly surprising, since the event had never taken place. Nonetheless, Boniface decided to reward this spontaneous demonstration of reverence for the relics

[1] Cesare Clementini, *Raccolto istorico della fondazione di Rimino e dell'origine e vite de' Malatesti* (Rimini, 1617–1627; rpt. Bologna: Forni, 1969), vol. 2, p. 251.

[2] Dominici, *Cronaca*, pp. 210 (November 11–12), 211 (November 15), 214 (December 3).

[3] A survey of the development of the jubilee celebrations can be found in Herbert Thurston, *The Holy Year of the Jubilee: An Account of the History and Ceremonial of the Roman Jubilee* (St. Louis: B. Herder, 1900; rpt. New York: AMS Press, 1980), and, more briefly, in Jonathan Sumption, *Pilgrimage: An Image of Medieval Religion* (London: Faber and Faber, 1975).

[4] Arsenio Frugoni, "Il Giubileo di Bonifacio VIII," *Bullettino dell'Istituto Storico Italiano per il Medio Evo e archivio muratoriano*, 62 (1950): 1–121, now reprinted in his *Incontri nel Medio Evo* (Bologna: Il Mulino, 1979), pp. 73–177; Raffaello Morghen, "Il giubileo del 1300," in his *Medioevo cristiano* (Bari: Laterza, 1974), pp. 265–282.

of the apostles by declaring 1300 a jubilee year, and he displayed the fullness of papal power by actually granting the rumored plenary indulgence to those who took part in the jubilee celebration.[5] The grand success of the jubilee of 1300 ensured that this experiment forced on Boniface VIII by popular enthusiasm would be repeated as a deliberately ordained celebration. It was first conceived as a centennial event, but in 1342 the time between jubilees was shortened to fifty years at the request of a delegation of Roman citizens, who hoped that an influx of pilgrims would help reverse the economic decline which had followed the removal of the papacy from Rome to Avignon. The first regularly proclaimed jubilee thus took place in 1350, and it brought hordes of pilgrims to Rome despite the ravages of the Black Death, the hazards of war-troubled roads, and an earthquake that rendered housing even more scarce than it would have been in any case.[6] Further jubilees followed at irregular intervals, and with indifferent success, throughout the Great Schism and conciliar period, in 1390, 1400, and 1423. Finally, in 1450, with the schism healed and the conciliar threat quelled, Nicholas V celebrated the restoration of the monarchical papacy with a jubilee that turned out to be tremendously successful.[7] The recurrence of the jubilee year was thereupon shortened even more, to every twenty-five years; and that pattern has been maintained ever since.

The jubilee of 1400 has a peculiar place in this development. Boniface IX was not eager to proclaim another jubilee so soon after the one of 1390. Indeed, there is some doubt that he actually *did* proclaim it: the official bull of proclamation, if one was issued, has been lost. But if the absence of this official document has led some historians to wonder whether the jubilee of 1400 actually took place, people at the time had no such doubts.[8] All the trappings of a jubilee celebration were there. Boniface displayed the greatest of the papal relics, including the Veronica, which since 1350 had surpassed the remains of the apostles as an object of devotion, and he opened the

[5] The bull "Antiquiorem habet," dated February 22, 1300, granted a plenary indulgence retroactive to Christmas 1299.

[6] Guillaume Mollat, "Le Jubilé de 1350," *Journal des Savants* (juillet–septembre, 1963): 191–195; Emmanuel Rodocanachi, "Le premier jubilé: 1350," in his *Etudes et fantaisies historiques* (Paris: Hachette, 1912), pp. 153–164.

[7] Giovanni Rucellai, "Il Giubileo dell'anno 1450," *Archivio della R. Società romana di storia patria*, 55 (1881): 563–580.

[8] Federigo Melis, "Movimento di popoli e motivi economici nel giubileo del 1400," in *Miscellanea Gilles Gérard Meersseman*, pp. 343–367.

Porta Santa to the pilgrims. Luca Dominici himself went to Rome and proudly recorded his devotions: "I note that on April 4 [1400] we went to Rome. We left early on Sunday morning, the Sunday of San Lazzaro; there were more than thirty of us, and we stayed there from Palm Sunday until Good Friday. We received the pope's benediction three times, and we saw the Veronica three times and the heads of St. Peter and St. Paul twice, as well as all the other sights of Rome; and I entered by the Holy Door sixteen times."[9]

Peasants from the estates of Monte Oliveto Maggiore also made the pilgrimage to Rome at various slack moments in the agricultural year, taking out small loans to meet the expenses of the journey and requesting permission from their monastic masters to leave temporarily the lands they worked southeast of Siena.[10] One of them, Tome di Gilio, who went to Rome early in 1400, was also moved a few months later to give the monastery nine denari in memory of the nine days he had gone about with the Bianchi.[11] This connection between the jubilee celebrations and the memory of the Bianchi was neither fortuitous nor peculiar to Tome. Indeed, the jubilee pilgrimages to Rome by individuals as diverse as the notary Luca Dominici and the peasant Tome di Gilio were made possible by the concourse there of Bianchi the preceding autumn, and the subsequent flux of smaller groups of white-robed pilgrims. Like Boniface VIII in 1300, Boniface IX in 1399 was moved to transform an unexpected surge of pilgrims into something more official, to recognize and regularize a spontaneous eruption of devotion. In so doing, he happened to fulfill the original plan of a centenary celebration of the jubilee, and set that festival on its way to the regular twenty-five-year recurrence it has followed ever since 1450.

---

[9] "Memoria che a dì 4 di aprile [1400] andiamo a Roma: movemoci in domenica mattina per tempo, era la domenica di S. Lazzero: fumo più di 30, stamovi dentro la domenica dell'Ulivo infine al Venerdì Santo. Avemo tre volte la benedizione dal papa e vedemo tre volte il Sudario e due volte le teste di S. Piero e di S. Pavolo e tutte le belle cose di Roma, e 16 volte entrai per la Porta Santa." Dominici, *Cronaca*, p. 223.

[10] Gabriella Piccinni, *"Seminare, fruttare, raccogliere": Mezzadri e salariati sulle terre di Monte Oliveto Maggiore (1374–1430)* (Milan: Feltrinelli, 1982), pp. 152, 166.

[11] "Item donò Tome al monastero nove d. quando andaro atorno i bianchi." Piccinni, *Seminare, fruttare, raccogliere*, p. 166, n. 142. The entry is recorded between May and June, 1400. Tome seems to have been notably pious: he helped out another peasant who wanted to make the pilgrimage to Rome, and he himself later became an oblate, or lay associate, of the monastery.

More direct attempts to institutionalize the Bianchi devotions met little success. Some local cults grew up around crosses that had worked miracles when they were carried at the head of the Bianchi processions. On April 20, 1400, the tiny Tuscan town of Borgo a Buggiano voted to declare August 18 a holiday, in perpetual memory of the occasion on which their crucifix had shed blood and inspired them to make peace.[12] In Lucca, the cross that the Bianchi had carried in procession was deposited on their return in the oratory of the flagellant confraternity of San Paolo della Misericordia, where it continued to perform miracles.[13] A formal deposition was taken from more than twenty witnesses, including some of the leading citizens of Lucca, who described the miracles performed by this crucifix during the Bianchi procession; another record was kept of the miracles that followed its return. The cult of this miracle-working crucifix was promoted with indulgences and festivals, and the cross was regularly paraded forth in times of trouble or celebration. The crypt of the church of San Bartolomeo in Prato houses a crucifix traditionally associated with the Bianchi movement; like the crucifixes carried by the Bianchi in the watercolors that adorn Giovanni Sercambi's chronicle, this one has a cross of rough-hewn logs.[14] In Florence, crosses purportedly carried by the Florentine Bianchi were to be found in Sant'Orsola, San Michele Visdomini (moved there from San Pier Murrone in 1552), Santa Trinità, and the convent of Regina Coeli, also known as that of the Blessed Chiarito.[15] The one in Santa Trinità can still be seen in the first chapel on the right of the entrance, where

[12] Carlo Natali, "Il 18 agosto a Borgo a Buggiano," *Bullettino storico pistoiese*, ser. 3, 10 (1975): 98–99. The miracle performed by this crucifix was mentioned by Giovanni Sercambi, *Croniche*, pp. 351–352, and Luca Dominici, *Cronaca*, p. 58.

[13] Telesforo Bini, *Storia della Sacra Effigie, Chiesa, e Compagnia del SS. Crocifisso de' Bianchi* (Lucca: Giuseppe Giusti, 1855).

[14] See Giovanni Sercambi, *Le illustrazioni delle Croniche nel codice Lucchese*, with commentary by Ottaviano Banti and M. L. Testi Cristiani (Genoa: Silvio Basile, 1978), vol. 2, pp. 190–191 and 195–202. Giuseppe Richa, *Notizie istoriche delle chiese fiorentine*, 10 vols. (Florence: Pietro Gaetano Viviani, 1754–1762; rpt. Rome: Multigrafica, 1972), depicts one such crucifix (vol. 7, p. 25) and describes another (vol. 5, p. 208) as "a trunk with some knots."

[15] Ferdinando Leopoldo Del Migliore, *Firenze città nobilissima illustrata* (Florence, 1684; rpt. Bologna: Forni, 1968), pp. 359–360, 367 (San Pier Murrone/San Michele Visdomini); Richa, *Notizie istoriche delle chiese fiorentine*, vol. 3, p. 162 (Santa Trinità); vol. 5, pp. 206–210 (monastero del Chiarito); vol. 7, pp. 24 (San Michele Visdomini) and 51 (Sant'Orsola); and Walter Paatz and Elisabeth Paatz, *Die Kirchen von Florenz*, 6 vols. (Frankfurt am Main: Vittorio Klostermann, 1952–1955), vol. 4, pp. 198–199, 206–207 (San Michele Visdomini) and 561 (Sant'Orsola); vol. 5, pp. 290 and 355 (Santa Trinità).

it still receives ex-voto offerings in recognition of its succoring powers.[16] But in this case, as in that of the crucifix of the Bianchi in Lucca, the continuing cult of the cross is prompted by its still-active thaumaturgical qualities, and not by any living memory of its past connection with the Bianchi.

According to some chroniclers, confraternities were founded to perpetuate the devotion of the Bianchi; and modern historians have enthusiastically and uncritically identified many such Bianchi confraternities. Gennaro Maria Monti names a score of confraternities as either founded or reformed by the Bianchi, but he generally fails to give an exact date.[17] Many of the confraternities associated with the Bianchi clearly existed well before that movement, though they may well have been reinvigorated by the mass devotions of 1399; examples include the "Devozioni" in the market towns of Cento and Pieve, between Bologna and Ferrara, and the flagellant confraternity of San Paolo della Misericordia in Lucca, which provided the crucifix for one of the Bianchi processions and received it back on its return.[18] Others were founded well after the passage of the Bianchi, and only at this later date claimed an association with them. The Genoese Compagnia della Misericordia, which Giovanna Balbi connects with the Bianchi, was not founded until 1455; two other Ligurian confraternities "dei Bianchi" are not documented before 1461 and 1467.[19] Another, the Confraternita di Santa Chiara at Bogliasco, just to the east of Genoa, continues to trace its origins to 1403 and the aftermath

---

[16] Touring Club Italiano, *Firenze e dintorni* (Milan: Aldo Garzanti, 1974), p. 286. This crucifix, on smooth planks, has presumably been remounted.

[17] Gennaro Maria Monti, *Le confraternite medievali dell'alta e media Italia* (Venice: La Nuova Italia, 1927). Monti's lack of precision is not limited to the Bianchi confraternities. Gilles Gérard Meersseman remarked of Monti's survey: "There one generally finds a great mass of detailed information, but missing three essential things: the exact origins of each confraternity, the particular spirit that inspired it, and the date and origins of its eventual reform before the Council of Trent." "La riforma delle confraternite laicali in Italia prima del Concilio di Trento," in *Problemi di vita religiosa in Italia nel Cinquecento: Atti del Convegno di storia della chiesa in Italia* (Padua: Antenore, 1960), pp. 29–30.

[18] Antonio Samaritani, "Mentalità religiosa specie nell'ora del testamento in un castello bolognese: Cento nel sec. XIV," *Analecta Pomposiana*, 12 (1987): 32–33, and Samaritani, "La 'societas devotorum' di Cento e il suo ospedale nei sec. XIII–XVI," in *L'Ospedale di Cento nei secoli* (Cento, 1975), pp. 20–26; Bini, *Storia della Sacra Effigie*, pp. 28–29.

[19] Giovanni Balbi, "La Compagnia della Misericordia di Genova nella storia della spiritualità laica," in *Momenti di storia e arte religiosa in Liguria* (Genoa: n.p., 1963), p. 147; Domenico Cambiaso, "Casacce e confraternite medievali in Genova e Liguria," *Atti della società ligure di storia patria*, 71 (1948): 85, n. 8.

of the Bianchi processions, even though the oldest documentation in the confraternity's archives dates from 1591.[20]

Only in rare instances can we document a direct causal connection between the Bianchi movement and the founding or reform of a lay confraternity. In Bologna, the Bianchi inspired the transformation of a *laudesi* confraternity dedicated to the Virgin Mary, which had run a hospital in the *borgo* of San Felice since the 1320s.[21] With the passage of the Bianchi in 1399, the confraternity adopted the use of white robes, withdrew from the operation of its hospital, and assumed the title of Santa Maria della Misericordia. The confraternity treated this as a new foundation: it redacted new statutes to reflect these changes, and drew up a full list of its members. The thirty-one men who formed the original nucleus of Santa Maria della Misericordia at the time of its refounding sprang from the artisan class, a reflection both of the typical social composition of *laudesi* confraternities and the appeal that the Bianchi movement had exercised in those circles.

Another Bianchi confraternity dedicated to Santa Maria della Misericordia was the "fraternitas alborum," or "confraternity of whites" founded in Montagnana, a small city in the diocese of Padua, on October 13, 1399—only eight days after the end of the Bianchi processions in Padua and explicitly inspired by those processions.[22] In its statutes the confraternity institutionalized certain external characteristics of the Bianchi, such as the devotion to the white robes of the brethren. The Bianchi's thrice-repeated call for "misericordia" was adopted as part of the public confession of confraternity members. While no mention was made of the cry for "pace," members were enjoined to make peace "with others," though this may not actually mean "with those outside the confraternity": the general practice was to insist on peace only among fellow confraternity members. If the intent of this statute was really to promote general pacification, then it aimed to capture not simply the ritual trappings but the essential spirit of the Bianchi. The statutes were also faithful to the spirit of the

[20] Pier Luigi Gardella, *La Confraternita di S. Chiara di Bogliasco* (Genoa: Scuola Tip. Sorriso Francescano, 1990), pp. 19–20.

[21] Mario Fanti, "La compagnia e l'ospedale delle Laudi del borgo di S. Felice e il moto dei Bianchi," in *S. Maria della Carità in Bologna: Storia e arte* (Bologna: n.p., 1981), pp. 25–42. I am grateful to Nicholas Terpstra for providing me with a photocopy of the statutes of this confraternity, which are found in the Archivio di Stato di Bologna, fondo Demaniale, 4/7673, no. 1.

[22] Giuseppina De Sandre Gasparini, "Un'immediata ripercussione del movimento dei Bianchi del 1399: La regola di una 'fraternitas alborum' in diocesi di Padova (13 ottobre 1399)," *Rivista di storia della chiesa in Italia*, 26 (1972): 354–368.

Bianchi in directing confraternal devotions toward the very heart of ecclesiastical life: they called for processions on major universal festivals such as Easter and Christmas, rather than on those particular festivals more commonly celebrated by confraternities, such as the feast day of the patron saint. These statutes were approved by Stefano da Carrara, the apostolic administrator who exercised locally the functions of the bishop; at the same time, he encouraged the fledgling confraternity by granting it an indulgence. But despite this encouragement, this is the last we hear of the "fraternitas alborum" of Montagnana; there is no further record of this confraternity after the approval of its statutes. Similarly, a *laudesi* confraternity founded in Genoa to sing the praises of the Virgin Mary on the first Saturday of each month is known only through the brief mention of its creation, at the end of Giorgio Stella's description of the Bianchi devotions in Genoa.[23] Given the increasing amount of documentation on confraternities throughout the fifteenth century, the reasonable presumption is that these confraternities of which there is no continuing record soon ceased to exist.

A similar fate befell the confraternity "del crocifisso" or "dei Bianchi" that was founded in Pistoia to venerate a Bianchi crucifix.[24] This confraternity dedicated its chapel in Santa Maria a Ripalta on May 2, 1400. Its members, who were the cream of the citizenry, "il fiore e capo de' cittadini," participated that spring in a piously civic-minded procession to ward off the plague. They also played a leading part in the celebration of the anniversary of the Bianchi devotion in Pistoia, on August 17, 1400. But the following year, just before his death, Bishop Andrea Franchi, who had been the prime mover behind this Compagnia dei Bianchi, charged the confraternity with celebrating the feast of the Crown of Thorns, which it duly did on May 2, 1401. Thus, in less than two years, this confraternity had metamorphosed from a Bianchi confraternity into one dedicated to the Passion.

Assessment and Reassessment

Not only did these efforts to institutionalize the Bianchi devotion meet with little success; soon after it ended, the movement itself was

---

[23] Stella, *Annales Genuenses*, p. 241.
[24] Dominici, *Cronaca*, pp. 216, 223–228, and 286–289.

judged to be a dismal failure. As the peace agreements inspired by the Bianchi turned out to be fleeting, hopes were dashed and delight turned into derision. Coluccio Salutati's letters trace a curve from the enthusiasm of that summer to disenchantment the following winter. In August, when he wrote to Zaccaria Trevisan, the Venetian patrician who was then the senator of Rome, Salutati was carried away by the religious excitement that then gripped Florence: "the reputation of this movement is great, its appearance even greater, but its effect is greatest."[25] By March, Salutati's mood was markedly different. No longer dazzled by the movement's reputation and appearance, he was outspokenly skeptical about its effect, which now seemed ambiguous and ephemeral. He thought the stories about the origins of the Bianchi were nothing but foolishness; he hesitated to say that the conversion of sinners had been the work of God; he suspended all judgment on whether this had been a good thing or not until its lasting effects could be determined.[26]

Salutati's understanding of the Bianchi devotion as an extraordinary yet inconsequential moment of blessed peace in the midst of the protracted war between Florence and Milan shaped the interpretation of a long series of humanist historians and their followers. Leonardo Bruni, Matteo Palmieri, Poggio Bracciolini, Sozomeno da Pistoia, Gianozzo Manetti, and Antonino Pierozzi all adopted Salutati's interpretation.[27] Bruni gave this line of thought its definitive formulation in his *History of the Florentine People*, where he set the appearance of the Bianchi "in the midst of wars," and concluded his account by noting bluntly: "While religion occupied men's minds, no thought was given to the perils of war; but after the fervor of the Bianchi had ended, their thoughts returned to their former concerns."[28] All too often,

---

[25] "Magna quidem horum fama, maior aspectus, sed maximus est effectus." Coluccio Salutati, *Epistolario*, vol. 3, pp. 355–359. See also his letter to Thomas Fitz-Alain, archbishop of Canterbury, on pp. 360–363.

[26] Salutati, *Epistolario*, pp. 381–382.

[27] Leonardo Bruni, *Historiarum Florentini populi Libri XII*, ed. Emilio Santini and Carmine di Pierro, in *RIS²*, 19, part 3, p. 278; Poggio Bracciolini, *Historiae Florentini populi*, in his *Opera omnia*, ed. Riccardo Fubini (Turin: Bottega d'Erasmo, 1964), vol. 2, pp. 232–233; Matteo Palmieri, *Liber de temporibus*, ed. Gino Scaramella, in *RIS²*, 26, part 1, p. 120; Sozomeno da Pistoia, *Specimen historiae*, in *RIS*, 16, col. 1168; Gianozzo Manetti, *Historiae Pistoriensem*, in *RIS*, 19, cols. 1068–1069; Antonino Pierozzi (Sant'Antonino), *Historiarum Domini Antonini Archipraesulis Florentini* (Lyon, 1543), Pars 3, Titulus 22, Capitulum 3, par. 32.

[28] "Dum religio tenuit animos, de periculis belli nihil cogibatur; sed postquam

those concerns involved bloodshed and vengeance. Piero di Niccola Baronti, who had led the procession of Bianchi from Lucca as it entered his native Pistoia and abandoned his wife for the religious life, was struck down by an assassin on Corpus Christi of 1401—another victim of the interminable feud between the Cancellieri and the Panciatichi that divided even the clergy of Pistoia, and that the Bianchi had momentarily hoped to heal.[29]

The rancor that fed such feuds was too ingrained, too habitual, to be swept aside by a flamboyant gesture of reconciliation; and when the emotion that had inspired the reconciliation passed, old enemies returned, unsurprisingly, to familiar ways. Salutati's disappointment was widely shared, and Bruni's concise formulation nicely captured the less well defined feelings of larger groups of Florentines. It was plain for all to see that the pacification achieved by the Bianchi had proven hardly more enduring than the movement itself, and the general disenchantment made it that much more difficult to sustain any effort to institutionalize and preserve the Bianchi devotion. But the memory of the Bianchi remained alive; preaching in his native city in 1427, Bernardino of Siena referred to the Bianchi as a means of dating the performance of his first miracle.[30]

Later in the fifteenth century, when the bitterness of recent disillusionment had faded, people could begin to look back on the passage of the Bianchi as a rare and precious moment of devout concord and evoke that memory as the basis for pious foundations that, it was hoped, would restore a part of the community to the Edenic state it had once enjoyed. Such was the nostalgic rationale behind the creation of Bianchi confraternities in Liguria in the mid-quattrocento.[31] And during the troubled years of the late fifteenth and early sixteenth centuries, when Italy served as the battlefield on which Spain and France contended for European hegemony and the government of Florence stumbled from one crisis to another, Florentines could look

---

finis fuit dealbatorum fervori ad primas rursus curas animi redierunt." Bruni, *Historiarum*, p. 278.

[29] Dominici, *Cronaca seconda*, ed. Giovan Carlo Gigliotti, Pubblicazioni della Società pistoiese di storia patria, Rerum Pistoriensium Scriptores, 3 (Pistoia: Alberto Pacinotti, 1939), p. 31.

[30] "I want to tell you about the first miracle I ever did, and that was before I became a friar, which was after the Bianchi." Bernardino da Siena, *Prediche volgari sul Campo di Siena, 1427*, ed. Carlo Delcorno (Milan: Rusconi, 1989), vol. 2, p. 788.

[31] Balbi, "La Compagnia della Misericordia di Genova," p. 147; Cambiaso, "Casacce e confraternite medievali," p. 85, n. 8.

back on the time of the Bianchi as a marvelous interlude of peace and piety. Several confraternities dedicated to perpetuating the Bianchi devotion appeared at this time; the prologue to the statutes of one of them, that of the Crucifix of Santa Maria Maddalena dei Bianchi, mentions four such confraternities.[32] But despite their claim to have been founded in 1399, springing directly from the Bianchi, none of these confraternities is documented before the second half of the fifteenth century.[33] Their founders evidently saw the Bianchi devotion as a moment when all troubles vanished in an efflorescence of holiness, as the hand of God transformed Florentine society: "It was the work of God that in those days all the wars were suspended. And an infinite number of peace agreements were made between factions, and there was general forgiveness of old enmities, of injuries of many sorts, even murders and wounds, and within many cities and towns friendships were formed that would have been impossible to make by any other means."[34] They hoped to reproduce the sacred harmony of the Bianchi in their own strife-torn time, just as they reproduced

----

[32] The other three are the Compagnia del Crocefisso dei Bianchi, in Santo Spirito; the Compagnia di Santa Lucia, near Santa Lucia sul Prato; and the Compagnia di San Lorenzino. Ronald F. E. Weissman, *Ritual Brotherhood in Renaissance Florence* (New York: Academic Press, 1982), pp. 51–52.

[33] The statutes of the Compagnia del Crocefisso di Santa Maria Maddalena dei Bianchi date from 1531; those of the Compagnia del Crocefisso dei Bianchi in Santo Spirito from 1513; those of the Compagnia di Santa Lucia, near Santa Lucia sul Prato, from 1582. See Weissman, *Ritual Brotherhood*, pp. 238–240. John Henderson lists seven additional confraternities as having a possible link to the Bianchi; see the appendix to "Piety and Charity in Late Medieval Florence: Religious Confraternities from the Middle of the Thirteenth Century to the Late Fifteenth Century," Ph.D. diss., University of London, 1983. In these cases, however, the connection with the Bianchi appears even more tenuous and the documentation even more exiguous. The Compagnia di San Domenico, which Meersseman says "was linked in some fashion with the Bianchi devotions," gives its date of foundation as June 16, 1398, more than a year before the Bianchi appeared in Florence: Meersseman, *Ordo fraternitatis*, pp. 698–699. The Compagnia di San Francesco, which claims to have been founded in 1400, had its statutes approved only in 1427. The Compagnia di Santa Maria del Suffragio in Sant'Egidio, known as the confraternity "of the Bianchi," is linked with the Bianchi movement in a seventeenth-century work of erudition, though the basis for this connection is not clear; the confraternity did wear white robes, but white was the most common color for confraternal garb both before and after 1399. Del Migliore, *Firenze città nobilisima*, p. 359; Luigi Santoni, *Raccolta di notizie storiche riguardanti le chiese dell'arci-diogesi di Firenze* (Florence, 1847), p. 17. The other cases involve crucifixes linked by local tradition with the "compagnia dei Bianchi"— that is, the Bianchi movement itself—and do not indicate the existence of otherwise unknown confraternities. See above, note 15.

[34] Prologue to the *Statuti della Compagnia del Crocefisso di Santa Maria Maddalena dei Bianchi*, cited by Weissman, *Ritual Brotherhood*, p. 51.

the old chronicle descriptions of the Bianchi in the introductions to their statutes.[35] The nostalgic idealization of a now-distant past had gradually superseded the bitter disenchantment of those who actually witnessed the passage of the Bianchi.

Social Concord and Popular Orthodoxy

The movement of the Bianchi thus left no major legacy of new institutions or new ideas; except for a few minor cults of purely local interest and a few feebly rooted confraternities, it vanished as quickly as it had appeared. Its importance lies not in any imagined role as the fountainhead of novel developments, but rather in the way it throws into relief the traditional institutions and practices of the religious culture of late medieval Italy. The wealth of documentation generated by the movement of the Bianchi enables us to recover the beliefs and practices that defined Christian devotion in this era of popular orthodoxy and fundamental religious concord.

It may seem odd to characterize thus a period that was, after all, in the very middle of the Great Schism. That, however, is precisely how it appears through the optic of the Bianchi movement. True, prelates and theologians were profoundly shaken by the schism, and some, like Guillaume de Salvarville, tried to explain to a wider audience the significance of the rift:

> Se le scisme plus dure, dont Jhesu Christ nous guart,
> Celi qui est faulz pape, par son faulz art,
> Faulses promotions, faulz prelas de sa part.
> Foy, loy et sacremens seront mis à essart.
>
> Les falz prelas feront falses promocions
> D'abbés et de curés, qui absolutions
> Falses ministreront, et dissipations
> Seront faites en lieu de dispensations.

---

[35] Weissman notes that "this description dates from the sixteenth century but conforms to contemporary descriptions" (*Ritual Brotherhood*, p. 51, n. 30), which he takes to be proof of its authenticity. I think it is far more plausible that this passage was deliberately modeled on the earlier accounts as part of the effort to lay claim to the Bianchi heritage.

Quant l'en dispensera sur fait de mariage
En degré deffendu pour prochain cousinage,
En lieu de sacrement sera concubinage,
Et les enfans bastars pourserront l'heritage.³⁶

If the schism lasts, from which may Jesus Christ protect us,
he who is false pope, through his false art,
false promotions, [will make] false prelates on his part.
Faith, law, and sacraments will be laid waste.

The false prelates will make false promotions
of priests and curates, who will administer
false absolutions, and dissipations
will be made in place of dispensations.

When one receives a dispensation
for marriage forbidden by near relation,
this sacrament will become mere concubinage
and bastard offspring will take over the inheritance.

But such concerns hardly surfaced in the Bianchi movement. There
are hints of a vague yearning for restored harmony in the church,
and a glancing reference to the man who was to be the new pope,
since the schism would soon be healed by God's grace, but in general
the Bianchi appear to have been untroubled by the schism.³⁷ Other
sources confirm the impression that for most of the faithful, the
schism was merely an affair of the ecclesiastical hierarchy. There
were many, according to Franco Sacchetti, who said: "I believe in
God, but not in pope or antipope," and who asked, "Tell me, ought I
to do what I am told by the French, who side with the antipope? I tell
you that you can live without changing God's faith, and with virtue
as you should, and without sinning."³⁸ Indifferent to hierarchical dif-

---

³⁶ Guillaume de Salvarville, *Apologia super generali concilio*, quoted in Zenon Ka-
luza, "Note sur Guillaume de Salvarville auteur de deux poèmes sur le grand
schisme," *Mediaevalia Philosophica Polonorum*, 19 (1974): 162.

³⁷ "E dicesi esservi tra loro chi de' esser nuovo papa; perchè si dice qui tosto
questo scisma si leverà via con la grazia di Dio." Dominici, *Cronaca*, p. 56.

³⁸ "Sono molti che dicono: 'Io credo in Dio, ma non credo né a Papa, né a Antipapa.'" Franco Sacchetti, *Opere*, ed. Aldo Borlenghi (Milan: Rizzoli, 1957), pp.

ferences, great numbers of pilgrims from Aragon and Castile, Paris, Provence, and other lands subject to Benedict XIII flowed through Barcelona and Marseille, where they took ship for Rome to celebrate Boniface IX's jubilee of 1400.[39]

Religious belief, like religious practice, remained unshaken by the disputes at the summit of the ecclesiastical hierarchy. People thronged to see the Bianchi, to rally around their crucifixes and join in their processions, as they thronged to no heresiarch. They joined orthodox confraternities rather than heretical conventicles, flocked to hear the friars rather than their foes, expressed in word and deed their reverence for the saints and ceremonies of the church. Excess of devotion was more of a problem than was the lack of it. Heresy was largely confined to the fringes of Europe—the Lollards in England, the Hussites in Bohemia—and only in Bohemia did heretical teachings attract much of a popular following, largely as a vehicle of Czech nationalism. In Italy, as elsewhere in Western Europe, popular heresy had ceased to exist by 1400. The few remaining heretics were largely lone individuals, bereft of any institutional structure or even a coherent body of belief. One typical example is Giacomo di Ristolassio, who went to the stake in Chieri on March 10, 1395, for refusing to renounce a confused ragbag of doctrines whose origins might be traced to Fra Dolcino and the Apostolici, the Fraticelli, the Brethren of the Free Spirit, or the Waldensians.[40] Even aside from the blending of their doctrines by a syncretistic individual like Giacomo di Ristolassio, these groups had themselves lost any secure identity, their doctrines so smeared by the pressure of long persecution that it becomes impossible to speak of them as distinct entities.[41] The "increasing doctrinal incoherence of sectarian heresy" hardly offered a per-

---

816–817. "Dimmi: Deb'io fare quello che mi dicono quelli di Francia che tengono con l'Antipapa? Dico che ti puo' vivere non mutando la fede di Dio, e con virtù come tu déi, e non pecchi." Sacchetti, *Opere*, p. 862.

[39] Melis, "Movimento di popoli," pp. 355–365.

[40] The charges against Giacomo di Ristolassio are summarized in Grado G. Merlo, *Eretici e inquisitori nella società piemontese del Trecento* (Turin: Claudiana, 1977), p. 40; the record of the case is edited by Giuseppe Boffito, *Eretici in Piemonte al tempo del gran scisma (1378–1417)*, extract from *Studi e documenti di storia e diritto*, 18 (1897) (Rome: Tipografia Poliglotta, 1897), pp. 13–24.

[41] The plurality of beliefs gathered under the rubric "Waldensian" is emphasized by Grado G. Merlo, *Valdesi e valdismi medievali: Itinerari e proposte di ricerca* (Turin: Claudiana, 1984).

suasive alternative to orthodox theology.[42] It did, however, give scope to some strikingly idiosyncratic expressions of belief, though none juxtaposes heretical conviction with pragmatic realism more bizarrely than Giacomo di Ristolassio's final request: that his executioners take good care of his clothes, because on the third day he would be resurrected.[43] He could expect to need heavy clothing in Piedmont in midMarch, once the warming embers of his pyre were extinguished.

Even the last diehard Fraticelli, unbending in their adherence to absolute poverty and unforgiving in their denunciation of the worldly church, were increasingly isolated. The execution of Fra Michele da Calci in 1389 was movingly described by a sympathizer, who tells us that a few people shouted words of encouragement to Michele as he was paraded through Florence and that some murmuring against the authorities followed his death; and there was public opposition to the condemnation of Giovanni Cani da Montecatini in 1450.[44] But this opposition had less to do with any broad sympathy for heretical teachings than with a sense that the authorities were reacting too harshly to solitary cranks who posed no real threat. In any case, whatever lingering admiration there might be for the Fraticelli's cult of poverty was rapidly being redirected into support for the Observant movements, those institutionalized efforts at moral reform that touched all of the religious orders around 1400.[45]

In the absence of any cogent challenge, orthodoxy could be left loosely defined. The guardians of orthodoxy tolerated a range of beliefs and encouraged a profusion of devotional practices. The single movement of the Bianchi, in its brief four months of life, displayed regional, local, and even individual variations. The *laudesi* and flagellant confraternities emphasized very different devotional practices and appealed to different sorts of people.[46] Even on the level of formal theology, there was a variety of opinions on such crucial issues as the doctrine of the eucharist, the plan of salvation, and the com-

[42] John N. Stephens, "Heresy in Medieval and Renaissance Florence," *Past and Present*, 54 (February 1972): 48.

[43] Boffito, *Eretici in Piemonte*, p. 21.

[44] "Il supplizio di fra Michele di Calci," in *Scrittori di religione del Trecento: Testi originali*, ed. Giuseppe De Luca (Turin: Einaudi, 1977), pp. 209–232; Stephens, "Heresy in Medieval and Renaissance Florence," pp. 47–48.

[45] Mario Fois, "L''Osservanza' come espressione della 'Ecclesia sempre renovanda'," in *Problemi di storia della chiesa nei secoli XV–XVII* (Naples: Edizioni Dehoniane, 1979), pp. 13–107.

[46] Weissman, *Ritual Brotherhood*, pp. 68–76.

munication of grace.[47] But this variety did not entail fundamental rupture. Indeed, the doctrinal pluralism of the later Middle Ages was possible precisely because it was not held to pose a threat to the basic unity of the faith, and the latitude in devotional practice and religious outlook was accepted because there was perceived to be an underlying concord between the religious elite and the mass of believers.

Social concord was another matter. If the Bianchi indicated by their actions which devotional practices were most meaningful to them and which ecclesiastical institutions were most congenial, they also indicated which social problems they found most troubling and most in need of a religious solution. And on this subject there is no room for doubt: wherever the Bianchi went, their thoughts and actions were turned to pacification.

One might have thought that in northern and central Italy, home to both St. Francis of Assisi and the most highly developed commercial economy of the late Middle Ages, feelings of religious tension would coalesce around the problem of wealth. Commercial need for credit, like the requirements of public finance, ran up against the usury prohibition. Notions of the just wage and just price were strained by the abrupt rise in commodity prices and labor costs that followed the Black Death. And the social and political consequences were terrifyingly apparent in the great wave of rebellions that washed over Europe in the late fourteenth century: insurrections in Perugia and Siena in 1371, the revolt of the Ciompi in Florence in 1378, and then, in the revolutionary years 1378–1382, the risings of the French peasantry, the Flemish cloth workers, and the English peasants and artisans.[48] In such a setting, one might expect that wealth—its acquisition, its distribution, its use, its very existence—would be identified as the central moral problem of society and avarice deemed the chief social vice, religious conversion would be expressed by the renuncia-

---

[47] Jaroslav Pelikan, *The Christian Tradition: A History of the Development of Doctrine*, vol. 4: *Reformation of Church and Dogma (1300–1700)* (Chicago: University of Chicago Press, 1984), pp. 10–68.

[48] Victor Rutenberg, *Popolo e movimenti popolari nell'Italia del '300 e '400*, trans. Gianpiero Borghini (Bologna: Il Mulino, 1971); Michel Mollat and Philippe Wolff, *Ongles bleus, Jacques, et Ciompi: Les révolutions populaires en Europe aux XIVe et XVe siècles* (Paris: Calmann-Lévy, 1970); Rodney Hilton, *Bond Men Made Free: Medieval Peasant Movements and the English Rising of 1381* (New York: Viking, 1973); *The English Rising of 1381*, ed. Rodney H. Hilton and Trevor H. Aston (Cambridge: Cambridge University Press, 1984); *Il tumulto dei Ciompi: Un momento di storia fiorentina ed europea* (Florence: Olschki, 1981).

tion of wealth, and movements of religious reform would be devoted above all to attacks on luxury.[49]

This may indeed have been true of the twelfth and thirteenth centuries, when avarice supplanted pride as the greatest of sins, and heretics and saints alike embraced religious poverty.[50] But something changed in the course of the fourteenth century. Wealth came to seem less dangerous, less defiling. Early in the fourteenth century, the *Mirror of Perfection* showed St. Francis graphically equating coins with excrement, the long-running quarrel over the use of property pitted the Franciscan Spirituals against the leadership of their order, and Michele da Cesena's clash with John XXII over evangelical poverty (after the two of them had cooperated in suppressing the Spirituals) briefly threatened to drag the entire Franciscan order into opposition to the papacy.[51] But support for Michele within his order quickly eroded, and even in Italy, where he had a certain following among the Fraticelli, the adepts of absolute poverty were soon reduced to a tiny remnant. Fraticelli rigor gradually gave way to Observant moderation. And at the very end of the century, the crowds who swelled the ranks of the Bianchi showed themselves to be as indifferent to the ostentatious display of morally tainted wealth as they were to the subtler issues of economic justice. Since wealth was no longer shunned as perilous and polluting by the general populace, the Florentine civic humanists had no reason to fear touching a live nerve when they articulated their celebration of wealth and acquisitiveness in the early quattrocento. Far from representing a "sudden and radical rejection of medieval attitudes towards the world and worldly goods," their writings followed rather than led public opinion, advancing arguments just bold enough to be interesting and amusing.[52] The defense of wealth had lost its power to shock, for the desire for wealth was no longer seen as a pressing danger to society.

[49] Lester K. Little, *Religious Poverty and the Profit Economy in Medieval Europe* (Ithaca: Cornell University Press, 1978).

[50] Lester K. Little, "Pride Goes before Avarice: Social Change and the Vices in Latin Christendom," *American Historical Review*, 76 (1971): 16–49.

[51] *The Mirror of Perfection*, in *St. Francis of Assisi, Writings and Early Biographies: English Omnibus of the Sources for the Life of St. Francis*, ed. Marion A. Habig (Chicago: Franciscan Herald Press, 1983), p. 1140; David Burr, *Olivi and Franciscan Poverty: The Origins of the Usus Pauper Controversy* (Philadelphia: University of Pennsylvania Press, 1989); Decima L. Douie, *The Nature and the Effect of the Heresy of the Fraticelli* (Manchester: University of Manchester Press, 1932).

[52] For the argument that the humanist justification of wealth was part of a

That danger came rather from violence. In small communities, where frequent, close contact in an intensely competitive society gave innumerable occasions for friction, the impulse to violence could be nearly irresistible. When failure to exact personal vengeance for a personal affront was commonly scorned as the vilest weakness, deliberate refusal to exact it was a heroic act of will. Forgiveness was the rarest of virtues, friendship the most precious commodity. Peace was a social miracle, and much of religious life, from the formal friendship of the confraternities to the kiss of peace during the mass, aimed at invoking this miracle.[53] Peace was so desirable that the very word left a sweet taste on the lips, said Bernardino da Siena to his fellow citizens in 1427.[54] "Do you know why I left this sermon on peace until nearly the end?" he asked, as his sermon cycle drew to its close.

Only so that once you had first seen the sins that you commit and known the punishment that God has prepared for the obstinate, this sermon would be able to move your hearts and make them soften towards those who have done you harm and restore peace with them. . . . Let whoever can help in the slightest way set about creating peace and concord with one another. And if you thus reestablish peace among yourselves, you will have peace here on earth and peace once again in heavenly glory.[55]

Nothing this important could be left to chance—or to the searing words of a saintly friar and the quicksilver enthusiasm of a devotional movement. It was not just pliancy before popular pressure, or even shared conviction, that made town governments so ready to enact

---

sweeping revolt against earlier attitudes, see Hans Baron, *In Search of Florentine Civic Humanism: Essays on the Transition from Medieval to Modern Thought* (Princeton: Princeton University Press, 1988), vol. 1, pp. 158–257; the passage quoted is from p. 186.

[53] John Bossy, *Christianity in the West, 1400–1700* (Oxford: Oxford University Press, 1985), pp. 57–75.

[54] Bernardino da Siena, *Prediche volgari sul Campo di Siena*, vol. 2, p. 1254.

[55] "Sapete voi perché io indugio quasi dietro dietro questa predicha de la pace? Solo perché avendo voi veduto da prima i peccati che voi fate, e dimostrato la pena che Idio darà a chi sta in ostinazione, questa poi suole commuovare i cuori e condùciagli a piegarsi inverso coloro che hanno fatte le ingiurie, e fannoli rapacificare. . . . Chi può aitare a nulla, mettisi a far fare ogni pace e concordia l'uno coll'altro. Che se così sarete rapacificati insieme, voi arete la pace qui in terra, e di là l'arete poi in gloria." Bernardino da Siena, *Prediche volgari sul Campo di Siena*, vol. 2, pp. 1258–1259 and 1270.

the social program urged by a Bernardino of Siena or by the Bianchi. Governing groups recognized that a legal order that seemed self-evidently just and righteous would inspire a willing compliance that no amount of policing could compel. The Bianchi movememt swept a flood of vivifying holiness through dessicated political institutions; but the peace, harmony, and righteousness of the Bianchi would swiftly evaporate, as it did before Coluccio Salutati's jaded eyes, if it were not carefully husbanded.

And so town governments fed the emotions stirred by the Bianchi into juridical reservoirs, thereby providing a legal, enforceable form that could conserve this impulse and help it to last. In the wake of the Bianchi, during the same meeting in which they approved reimbursement for sums spent on receiving them, the governing councils of Arezzo named ambassadors to act as mediators in arranging peace between Città di Castello and a clan of rural nobility.[56] Six weeks later, in early November, they named another set of representatives to perform the same service, this time negotiating a binding peace between the Ubaldini clan and Città di Castello.[57] Nor did they neglect their own affairs while promoting peace abroad: eight prominent Aretines were named official *pacieri*, charged with making peace and concord in city and countryside, and vested with the full authority of the commune and people of Arezzo. Like the ambassadors, who were endowed with plenary power to act in the name of Arezzo, these domestic peacemakers were empowered to punish with condemnations, penalties, and fines anyone who impeded their work.[58] The urge to peace and reconciliation stirred by the Bianchi was thus given legal form and institutional structure. And as the fifteenth century wore on, official peacemakers, acting on behalf of town governments or semipublic organizations like the Fraternita dei Laici in Arezzo, came to perform regularly the peacemaking role that had been played so spontaneously, and fleetingly, by the Bianchi.

The other side of the proliferation of communal peacemakers was the increase in policing. Throughout Italy, police forces grew, while courts multiplied and extended their jurisdictions. In Florence, the

---

[56] Archivio di Stato d'Arezzo, Deliberazioni del Magistrato dei Priori e del Consiglio Generale, 3, fol. 197v (meeting of September 19, 1399).

[57] Archivio di Stato d'Arezzo, Deliberazioni del Magistrato dei Priori e del Consiglio Generale, 3, fol. 199v (meeting of November 6, 1399).

[58] Archivio di Stato d'Arezzo, Deliberazioni del Magistrato dei Priori e del Consiglio Generale, 3, fol. 197v (meeting of September 19, 1399).

police force doubled in size in the second half of the fourteenth century; in Venice, even after the reductions caused by the budget cuts of 1382, there was one police patroller for every 350 Venetians.[59] But the purpose of these newly numerous and resolute agents of order was rather different from the social discipline of the sixteenth and seventeenth centuries.[60] To be sure, those deemed to be enduring threats to society or, worse, not truly a part of society at all were ruthlessly eliminated, by execution or, more often, by exile or forced flight. But whenever possible, the courts sought social reconciliation, not social discipline: the goal was to encourage forgiveness, provide restitution, and reincorporate the offender into society.[61] In Lucca, where prisoners were released from their bonds at Christmas, Easter, and the feast of the Holy Cross, a standard formula excluded from this civic act of Christian mercy all those who had blasphemed against God and his saints, who had served less than a month in prison, or who "had not made peace with the injured party, where peace is required and where it is possible to obtain it."[62] And in Arezzo, the councils received the appeal of Luca del fu Andrea, who in a quarrel had seized a rock and laid open the head of his neighbor, Paolo Tani. Luca, who had fled rather than face judgment and condemnation, was captured and remanded to the Stinche in Florence, where he had languished for several months. But since "this Luca has received peace from the aforesaid injured Paolo," the governing councils of Arezzo saw no reason to reject his petition.[63]

Fundamentally, for all its tensions and disturbances, Christian society was held to be an organic whole. Lapses from the ideal were ascribed to personal and individual causes, to moral failure and ingrained wickedness, rather than to structural opposition between

[59] Marvin B. Becker, "Changing Patterns of Violence and Justice in Fourteenth- and Fifteenth-Century Florence," *Comparative Studies in Society and History*, 18 (1976): 287; Guido Ruggiero, *Violence in Early Renaissance Venice* (New Brunswick: Rutgers University Press, 1980), p. 15.

[60] On the concept of social discipline, see R. Po-chia Hsia, *Social Discipline in the Reformation: Central Europe 1550–1750* (London: Routledge, 1989), and the essays in *Annali dell'Istituto storico italo-germanico in Trento*, 8 (1982); for its application in northern Italy during the Counter-Reformation, see Daniele Montanari, *Disciplinamento in terra veneta* (Bologna: Il Mulino, 1987).

[61] Becker, "Changing Patterns," p. 282.

[62] Archivio di Stato di Lucca, Consiglio generale, 13: Riformagioni pubbliche 1397–1400, pp. 29, 55–56, 85, 118–119, 139, 177, 235, 277, 318, and 338.

[63] Archivio di Stato d'Arezzo, Deliberazioni del Magistrato dei Priori e del Consiglio Generale, 3, fol. 211r–211v (meeting of July 12, 1401).

social groupings. All elements of Christian society were integral members of a single community, just as they shared the universal condition of sinfulness and the lone possibility of redemption. When those who strayed beyond the wide bounds of this community were excised, the sense of human solidarity was strengthened. For if those who did not form an integral part of Christian society—the habitual criminals, vagabonds, and other "deviants" who did not abide by social norms; the heretics and Jews who did not accept Christian truth—were treated in an inhuman way, it was because they were held to be less than human, even bestial. This appears in the Franciscan rhetoric that urged the careful use of distinguishing signs to mark Jews off from Christian society, a rhetoric enshrined in the statutes of the Monti di Pietà which were created to ease social tensions by providing credit to established and potentially productive members of the community.[64] The Jews, according to one typical statute, were "those rabid and thirsty dogs which have sucked and continue to suck our blood, and take, seize, and destroy the wealth and substance of our people."[65]

But by the time this statute was drafted, at the end of the fifteenth century, the confident vision of a single Christian people united by a common set of beliefs was beginning to waver. Even in this statute, the phrase "our people" hints at the existence of a "we" that is different from "our people," a religious and political elite that had to look after the welfare of ordinary folks. And as humanism spread among that elite, it encouraged a widening sense of cultural difference between the few who were trained in classical Latin literature and familiar with the ideas it expressed, and the many who knew only the vernacular and, perhaps, the workaday Latin of the business world. In the course of the fifteenth century, educational institutions confirmed and solidified this cultural difference by elaborating distinct curricular tracks: for the elite, a Latin curriculum that rejected the medieval inheritance and turned instead to the classical *studia humanitatis*; for boys interested in business careers, a vernacular curriculum

---

[64] Diane Owen Hughes, "Distinguishing Signs: Ear-Rings, Jews, and Franciscan Rhetoric in the Italian Renaissance City," *Past and Present*, 112 (August 1986): 3–59.

[65] "Questi sonno quelli veri rabbiosi e setibundi cani che el nostro sangue hanno succhiato e succhiano e le substantie e ricchecçe del nostro populo tolgano guastano e rapiscano e con gravissima iactura di quello mandano ali alieni e loro si venghono aricchire." Archivio Storico del Comune di Cortona, I'.3: Capitoli del Monte Pio, 1494–1632, fol. 3.

that stressed practical mathematics and continued the literary and religious traditions of the Middle Ages.[66] Humanists, eager to establish their intellectual credentials and challenge the traditional scholarship of the universities, encouraged scorn of all that was not properly classical; and humanistically trained elites grew increasingly disdainful of anything that bore the taint of "popular" origins.[67] The sense of a unified culture, in which religious ideas and cultural models circulated freely among different social groups, began to erode.

Between 1494 and 1530, the political upheavals of the Italian wars shook the confidence of the leaders of church and state, and for a few decades the ruling elite, desperate for guidance in an uncertain world and eager for sacred props to its authority, was again open to the most varied models, regardless of their source. Female visionaries and prophets gravitated to the princely courts of the Po valley, where they swayed rulers with their advice and impressed their confessors with vatic pronouncements on the state of the church and the world.[68] Supernatural visions, prophecies, and signs were eagerly awaited and anxiously examined at all levels of society.[69] In some ways, humanism could even feed this interest: as Ottavia Niccoli points out, interest in the world of classical antiquity brought with it a renewed fascination with monsters, prodigies, and portents. But with the restoration of peace and political order after 1530, visionary insight into future events and thaumaturgical validation of present regimes were less urgently needed. At the same time, the spread of the Lutheran Reformation made independent religious initiatives far more suspect. As the elites increasingly cut themselves off from popular culture, they also lost touch with all forms of folkloric religious beliefs and practices.[70] The free circulation of religious ideas and cultural models

---

[66] Paul F. Grendler, *Schooling in Renaissance Italy: Literacy and Learning, 1300–1600* (Baltimore: Johns Hopkins University Press, 1989), esp. p. 289.

[67] Anthony Grafton and Lisa Jardine, *From Humanism to the Humanities: Education and the Liberal Arts in Fifteenth- and Sixteenth-Century Europe* (Cambridge: Harvard University Press, 1986), pp. xiii–xiv.

[68] Gabriella Zarri, *Le sante vive: Profezie di corte e devozione femminile tra '400 e '500* (Turin: Rosenberg & Sellier, 1990).

[69] Ottavia Niccoli, "Visioni e racconti di visioni nell'Italia del primo Cinquecento," *Società e storia*, 28 (1985): 253–279.

[70] Ottavia Niccoli has written persuasively on this point: *Prophecy and People in Renaissance Italy*, trans. Lydia G. Cochrane (Princeton: Princeton University Press, 1990), p. 193.

was replaced by a carefully controlled one-way traffic, in which the only acceptable movement was from the top down.

In that direction, at least, religious ideas flowed with increasing force and urgency, for the humanistically trained elites had made a curious discovery: the beliefs and practices of the lower classes, and particularly the rural populace, deserved the label of "superstitions"—literally, leftovers or survivals—because they bore a striking resemblance to many of the beliefs found in non-Christian, classical texts. The term "pagan" had referred originally to dwellers in rural districts and only later acquired the meaning of "non-Christian" when the countryside clung to polytheism well after the cities of the late Roman Empire had converted to Christianity. Now the classically educated elites of Renaissance Italy could resurrect that ancient sense, as to their eyes the peasants on their country estates came to seem ever less like proper Christians.[71]

It would be utterly wrong to accept that disparaging judgment and believe that around 1500 the rural populace of Europe was pagan.[72] They were, as we have seen, good Christians—but in a fourteenth-century sense, one that no longer satisfied the religious leaders of the sixteenth century. And so, on all sides of the widening confessional divides that split Europe after 1520, determined proselytizers strove to bridge the recently discovered gulf between their fresh understandings of what it meant to be Christian and the traditional beliefs of the mass of the populace. While Protestant reformers spread their teachings through pamphlets and sermons, catechisms and iconoclasm, the Catholic reformers remade the old confraternities and established new ones, founded new religious orders, devised new sorts of religious orders, redefined the nature and role of the secular clergy and created seminaries to train them, wrote catechisms to educate the faithful in the tenets of their faith, and sent missions to bring this faith to the rural masses of Europe, just as they sent them to the New

[71] Grendler, *Schooling in Renaissance Italy*, pp. 356–359; Adriano Prosperi, "*Otras Indias*: Missionari della Controriforma tra contadini e selvaggi," in *Scienze, credenze occulte, livelli di cultura* (Florence: Olschki, 1982), pp. 205–234.

[72] Though this is in fact argued by the scholar who has propounded the model of a sixteenth-century Christianization of Europe, Jean Delumeau. See Delumeau's *Le Catholicisme entre Luther et Voltaire* (Paris: P.U.F., 1971), pp. 237–258; "Christianisation et déchristianisation, XVe–XVIIIe siècles," in *Etudes Européenes: Mélanges offerts à Victor-Lucien Tapié* (Paris: Publications de la Sorbonne, 1973), pp. 111–131; and Delumeau's inaugural lecture on assuming his chair at the Collège de France, February 13, 1975 (Paris: Collège de France, 1975).

World. Catholics, Calvinists, Lutherans, Anglicans, and any number
of other eager proselytizers all participated in a great effort to Chris-
tianize Europe anew.

By the end of the seventeenth century, this movement of Christianization had run its course, brought to an end by its very success.
The strenuously achieved religious consensus of the late seventeenth
and the eighteenth centuries may look like "a point of repose" or an
era of "apparent moribundity"—though the similarity of these terms
to the negative judgments scholars have often passed on the religious
culture of the fourteenth and fifteenth centuries should warn us
against too facile a condemnation of the religiosity of this epoch, too.[73]
And this period of popular orthodoxy, like that of the time of
the Bianchi, was followed by yet another wave of Christianization, as
the challenge of the secularized world of industrial society provoked
the foundation of new orders, the drafting of new catechisms, and
the establishment of new shrines as beacons of the faith.[74]

Perhaps it is best to see European religious history as one in which
periods of Christianization alternate with periods, like the fourteenth
and fifteenth centuries, in which the work of Christianization is
thought to have been finished. In the periods of active Christianization, distinctions and disparities are strongly felt. People are sensitive
to the gap between the standards demanded by religious ideals and
those tolerated by religious practice, and they call for changes to
make practice conform more closely to the ideals. They are sensitive
to the implications of different beliefs, and they demand both more
coherent formulations of doctrine and stricter adherence to them.
They note the insufficiency of current institutions, and they create
new ones to meet their needs. And the leaders in this work of reform
are conscious of a terrible gulf between their understanding of the
faith and that accepted by the bulk of the faithful, as they strive to
bring their elite understanding of Christianity to the masses.

In the periods of popular orthodoxy, distinctions and disparities
are weakly felt and so are tolerated. When people note the gap between religious ideals and religious practice, they ridicule the short-
comings without believing that they entail a fundamental failure.
They tolerate a range of beliefs, for they are convinced that this diver-

---

[73] H. Outram Evennett, *The Spirit of the Counter-Reformation*, ed. John Bossy (Notre Dame: Notre Dame University Press, 1970), pp. 19–20.

[74] See, for instance, Jonathan Sperber, *Popular Catholicism in Nineteenth-Century
Germany* (Princeton: Princeton University Press, 1984).

sity poses no threat to basic agreement on the essentials of the faith. They find current institutions sufficient to meet their needs, and so do not make the effort to found new ones. And both the religious elite and the masses of the faithful believe, perhaps a trifle complacently, that they share a common understanding of what it means to be properly Christian.

BIBLIOGRAPHY

Editions of anonymous works are listed under the editor's name. Edited works by a known author are listed under the author's name. Publications for which neither an author nor an editor is given are listed under the title.

Alphabetizing names with particles, such as Alessandro de Ritiis or Bernardino da Siena, presents problems, since the period covered by this book falls within the time of transition from medieval names to something approaching modern surnames. In general, those whose second name is a family name are alphabetized by that surname. Those whose second name is a geographical identifier (Bernardino da Siena, Dietrich von Niem) or a patronym (Pietro di Mattiolo = Pietro, son of Mattiolo) are alphabetized by their first name. Because some names can plausibly be construed either way, readers who do not find someone under one name are encouraged to look under the alternative name.

Manuscript Sources

Arezzo. Archivio di Stato. Compagnie religiose, II: Compagnia di S. Antonio.
——. Archivio di Stato. Deliberazione del Magistrato dei Priori e del Consiglio Generale.
Assisi. Archivio capitolare di San Rufino. Mss. 20 and 21.
Bologna. Archivio di Stato. Provvisioni in Capreto.
Cortona. Archivio Storico del Comune di Cortona. Catasto vecchio.
——. Archivio Storico del Comune di Cortona. Monte Pio.

——. Biblioteca del Comune e dell'Accademia Etrusca di Cortona. Ms. 411: Capitoli della Compagnia della Croce Santa posta in San Francesco di Cortona.

——. Biblioteca del Comune e dell'Accademia Etrusca di Cortona. Ms. 532: Compendio delle cose di Cortona.

Florence. Archivio di Stato. Carte Strozziane.

——. Archivio di Stato. Consulte e pratiche.

——. Archivio di Stato. Corporazioni religiose soppresse. Badia di Firenze.

——. Archivio di Stato. Manoscritti.

——. Archivio di Stato. Provvisioni.

——. Biblioteca Riccardiana. Ms. 1333: Baldovino Baldovini, "Del Sacramento dell'altare."

——. Biblioteca Riccardiana. Ms. 1808: Priorista Fiorentina.

Lucca. Archivio di Stato. Consiglio generale.

Milan. Biblioteca Ambrosiana. Fondo Trotti, 245: Registrum litterarum 1397–1400.

Perugia. Archivio di Stato. Conservatori della moneta.

——. Archivio di Stato. Consigli e riformanze.

Prato. Archivio Datini.

Rimini. Biblioteca Civica Gambalunga. SC-MS. 1161: Broglio di Tartaglia da Lavello. "Cronaca universale."

Siena. Archivio di Stato. Concistoro.

——. Archivio di Stato. Consiglio generale.

Venice. Archivio di Stato. Consiglio dei Dieci.

——. Archivio di Stato. Corporazioni religiose soppresse. San Giorgio Maggiore.

——. Biblioteca del Museo Correr. Mss. Cicogna.

Published Sources

The abbreviation *RIS* refers to the *Rerum Italicarum Scriptores*, ed. Lodovico Antonio Muratori, 28 vols. (Milan, 1723–1751). RIS^2 refers to the new edition of the *Rerum Italicarum Scriptores*.

Agazzari, Giovanni. *Cronica civitatis placentiae.* In *Monumenta historica ad provincias parmensem et placentinam pertinentia.* Parma: Pietro Fiaccadori, 1862.

Agnoletti, Anna Maria, ed. *Statuto dell'Arte della Lana di Firenze, 1313–1319.* Florence: Le Monnier, 1940.

Alberigo, Giuseppe, et al., eds. *Conciliorum oecumenicorum decreta.* Bologna: Istituto per le Scienze Religiose, 1973.

Alighieri, Dante. *La divina commedia.* Ed. C. H. Grandgent. Revised by Charles S. Singleton. Cambridge: Harvard University Press, 1972.

Aliprandi, Bonamente. *Cronica di Mantova*. In Ludovico Antonio Muratori, *Antiquitates Italicae Medii Aevi*, 5: cols. 1065–1242. Milan, 1741.

Annales Forolivienses. *RIS*, 22.

Anselm of Canterbury. *Opera omnia*. Ed. F. S. Schmitt. Stuttgart: Friedrich Fromman Verlag, 1968.

Bellondi, Elina, ed. *Cronica volgare di Anonimo Fiorentino dall'anno 1385 al 1409, già attribuita a Piero di Giovanni Minerbetti*. *RIS²*, 27, part 2.

Bernardino da Siena. *Prediche volgari sul Campo di Siena, 1427*. Ed. Carlo Delcorno. 2 vols. Milan: Rusconi, 1989.

Bonardi, A., ed. *Liber regiminum Padua*. *RIS²*, 8, part 1.

Borbona, Niccolò di. *Cronaca delle cose dell'Aquila, dall'anno 1363 all'anno 1424*. In Ludovico Antonio Muratori, *Antiquitates Italicae Medii Aevi*, 6. Milan, 1743.

Borselli, Girolamo. *Cronica gestorum civitatis Bononie*. Ed. Albano Sorbelli. *RIS²*, 23, part 2.

Bracciolini, Poggio. *Opera omnia*. Ed. Riccardo Fubini. 4 vols. Turin: Bottega d'Erasmo, 1964.

Branchi, Baldo. *Cronaca Malatestiana*. Ed. A. F. Massèra. *RIS²*, 15, part 2.

Broglio di Tartaglia da Lavello. *Cronaca universale*. Ed. A. F. Massèra. *RIS²*, 15, part 2.

Bruni, Leonardo. *Historiarum Florentini populi Libri XII*. Ed. Emilio Santini and Carmine di Pierro. *RIS²*, 19, part 3.

Bullarium ordinis Fratrum Praedicatorum. 8 vols. Rome, 1729.

Caesarius of Heisterbach. *The Dialogue on Miracles*. Trans. H. Von E. Scott and C. C. Swinton Bland. London: George Routledge & Sons, 1929.

Capasso, Carlo, ed. *Chronicon Bergomense guelpho-ghibellinum*. *RIS²*, 16, part 2.

Cappelletti, Ermanno, ed. *Laude di Borgo San Sepolcro*. Florence: Olschki, 1986.

Caterina da Siena. *The Dialogue*. Trans. Suzanne Noffke. New York: Paulist Press, 1980.

——. *Le lettere di S. Caterina da Siena, ridotte a miglior lezione, e in ordine nuovo disposte con note di Niccolò Tommaseo*. Ed. Piero Misciattelli. 6 vols. Siena: Giuntini & Bentivoglio, 1913–1921.

Cicogna, Emmanuele Antonio. *Delle inscrizioni veneziane*. 6 vols. Venice: G. Orlandelli, 1824–1853.

Clementini, Cesare. *Raccolto istorico della fondazione di Rimino e dell'origine e vite de' Malatesti*. 2 vols. Rimini, 1617–1627; reprint Bologna: Forni, 1969.

Compagni, Dino. *Cronica*. Turin: Einaudi, 1968.

Conversini, Giovanni. *La processione dei Bianchi nella città di Padova (1399)*. Ed. and trans. Libia Cortese and Dino Cortese. Padua: Centro Studi Antoniani, 1978.

Corio, Bernardino. *L'Historia di Milano*. Padua: Paolo Frambotto, 1646.

Cornazani, Giovanni de'. *Istoria di Parma*. *RIS*, 12.

Cronaca di Cremona. In *Biblioteca Historica Italica*, 1. Milan, 1876.

Delaito, Jacopo. *Annales Estenses*. *RIS*, 18.

Delcorno, Carlo, ed. *La predicazione nell'eta comunale*. Florence: Sansoni, 1974.

De Luca, Giuseppe, ed. *Scrittori di religione del Trecento: Testi originali*. Turin: Einaudi, 1977.

De Minicis, Gaetano, and Marco Tabarrini, eds. *Cronache della città di Fermo*. *Documenti di storia italiana*, 4. Florence, 1870.

De Sandre Gasparini, Giuseppina, ed. *Statuti di confraternite religiose di Padova nel Medio Evo*. Fonti e ricerche di storia ecclesiastica padovana, 6. Padua: Istituto per la Storia Ecclesiastica Padovana, 1974.

Dietrich von Niem. *De Scismate libri tres*. Ed. G. Erler. Leipzig: Veit, 1890.

Domenico da Peccioli. *Chronica antiqua conventus Sanctae Catharinae de Pisis*. Ed. Francesco Bonaini. *Archivio storico italiano*, 6, part 2 (1845): 399–593.

Dominici, Giovanni. *Lettere spirituali*. Ed. Maria-Teresa Casella and Giovanni Pozzi. Spicilegium Friburgense, 13. Freiburg: Edizioni Universitarie, 1969.

Dominici, Luca. *Cronaca della venuta dei Bianchi e della moria, 1399–1400*. Ed. Giovan Carlo Gigliotti. Pubblicazioni della Società pistoiese di storia patria, 1. Pistoia: Alberto Pacinotti, 1933.

——. *Cronaca seconda*. Ed. Giovan Carlo Gigliotti. Pubblicazioni della Società pistoiese di storia patria, 3. Pistoia: Alberto Pacinotti, 1939.

Fabretti, Ariodante, ed. *Cronache della città di Perugia*. 4 vols. Turin: Tipi privati dell'editore, 1887–1892.

Faloci Pulignani, D. M., ed. "Le cronache di Spello degli Olorini." *Bollettino della R. Deputazione di storia patria per l'Umbria*, 23 (1918): 239–298.

Francesco da Fiano. "Poesie religiose di Francesco da Fiano." Ed. Roberto Weiss. *Archivio italiano per la storia della pietà*, 2 (1959): 201–206.

Francesco di Castiglione. *Vita S. Antonini*. In *Acta Sanctorum*, Maii, 1. Antwerp, 1680.

Gabotto, Ferdinando, ed. *Chronicon Parvum Ripaltae*. *RIS²*, 17, part 3.

Galletti, Alfredo. "Una raccolta di prediche volgari inedita del Cardinale Giovanni Dominici." In *Miscellanea di studi critici pubblicati in onore di Guido Mazzoni*, ed. A. Della Torre and P. L. Rambaldi, vol. 1, pp. 253–278. Florence: Tipografia Galileiana, 1907.

Gatari, Bartolomeo. *Cronaca Carrarese*. Ed. Antonio Medin and Guido Tolomei. *RIS²*, 17, part 1.

Giovio, Benedetto. *Historiae patriae sive Novocomensis libri duo*. In *Thesaurus antiquitatem et historiarum Italiae*, ed. Georgius Graevius and Petrus Burmannus, 4, part 2. Leiden: Petrus Vander Aa, 1722.

Girolamo da Forlì. *Chronicon*. Ed. Adamo Pasini. *RIS²*, 19, part 5.

Guerriero da Gubbio. *Cronaca*. Ed. Giuseppe Mazzatinti. *RIS²*, 21, part 4.

Habig, Marion A., ed. *St. Francis of Assisi, Writings and Early Biographies: English Omnibus of the Sources for the Life of St. Francis.* Chicago: Franciscan Herald Press, 1983.

John of Salisbury. *Policraticus: Of the Frivolities of Courtiers and the Footprints of Philosophers.* Ed. and trans. Cary J. Nederman. Cambridge: Cambridge University Press, 1990.

Licitra, Vincenzo. "Gerardo Anechini cantore dei Bianchi." *Studi medievali,* ser. 3, 10 (1969): 399–459.

Machiavelli, Niccolò. *Lettere.* Ed. Franco Gaeta. Milan: Feltrinelli, 1961.

——. *Il teatro e tutti gli scritti letterari.* Ed. Franco Gaeta. Milan: Feltrinelli, 1965.

Manenti, Luca di Domenico. *Cronaca.* Ed. Luigi Fumi. *RIS²,* 15, part 5.

Manetti, Gianozzo. *Historiae Pistoriensem. RIS²,* 19.

Marcovaldi, Sandro. "La Cronaca di Sandro Marcovaldi." Ed. Ruggero Nuti. *Archivio storico pratese,* 18 (1940): 49–69.

Mazzei, Lapo. *Lettere di un notaro a un mercante del secolo XIV.* Ed. Cesare Guasti. 2 vols. Florence: Le Monnier, 1880.

Meoni, Noemi. "Visite pastorali a Cortona nel Quattrocento." *Annuario dell'Accademia Etrusca di Cortona,* 22 (1985–1986): 111–200.

——. "Visite pastorali a Cortona nel Trecento." *Archivio storico italiano,* 129 (1971): 181–256.

Montemarte, Francesco di. *Cronaca.* Ed. Luigi Fumi. *RIS²,* 15, part 5.

Monti, Gennaro Maria. *Un laudario umbro quattrocentista dei Bianchi.* Todi: Atanòr, 1920.

Mussi, Giovanni de'. *Chronicon Placentinum. RIS,* 16.

Nerli, Antonio. *Breve chronicon monasterii Mantuani.* Ed. Orsini Begami. *RIS²,* 24, part 13.

Nicolini, Ugolini, Enrico Menestò, and Francesco Santucci, eds. *Le fraternite medievali di Assisi: Linee storiche e testi statutari.* Perugia: Centro di Ricerca e di Studio sul Movimento dei Disciplinati, 1989.

Palmieri, Matteo. *Liber de temporibus.* Ed. Gino Scaramella. *RIS²,* 26, part 1.

Pellini, Pompeo. *Dell'historia de Perugia.* Venice, 1664; reprint Bologna: Forni, 1968.

Peruzzi, Agostino. *Storia d'Ancona dalla sua fondazione all'anno MDXXXII.* 2 vols. Pesaro: Tipografia Nobili, 1835.

Pierozzi, Antonino. *Historiarum Domini Antonini Archipraesulis Florentini.* Lyons, 1543.

Pietro di Mattiolo. *Cronaca Bolognese.* Ed. Corrado Ricci. Bologna, 1885; reprint Bologna: Forni, 1969.

Pitti, Buonaccorso. *Cronica.* Bologna: Romagnoli dall'Acqua, 1905.

Platina. *Historia urbis Mantuae Gonziacaesque familiae. RIS,* 20.

——. *Liber de vita Christi ac omnium pontificum.* Ed. Giacinto Gaida. *RIS²,* 3, part 1.

Pontano, Giovanni Gioviano. *I Dialoghi.* Ed. Carmelo Previtera. Florence: Sansoni, 1943.

Predelli, R., and P. Bosmin, eds. *I libri commemoriali della Repubblica di Venezia: Regesti*. R. Deputazione veneta di storia patria, Monumenti storici, ser. 1: Documenti, vol. 3. Venice: La Società editrice, 1883.

Promus, Domenico, ed. *Chronicorum Cunei libri tres*. In *Miscellanea di storia italiana*, 12. Turin, 1871.

Riccoboni, Bartolomea. *Cronaca del Corpus Domini*. In Giovanni Dominici, *Lettere spirituali*, pp. 257–294.

———. *Necrologio del Corpus Domini*. In Giovanni Dominici, *Lettere spirituali*, pp. 295–330.

Ritiis, Alessandro de. *Chronica civitatis Aquilae*. Ed. Leopoldo Cassese. *Archivio storico per le provincie napoletane*, n.s., 27 (1941): 151–216.

Rucellai, Giovanni. "Il Giubileo dell'anno 1450." *Archivio della R. Società romana di storia patria*, 55 (1881): 563–580.

Rusconi, Roberto, ed. *Predicazione e vita religiosa nella società italiana da Carlo Magno alla Controriforma*. Turin: Loescher, 1981.

Sacchetti, Franco. *La Battaglia delle belle donne; Le Lettere; Le Sposizioni di Vangeli*. Ed. Alberto Chiari. Bari: Laterza, 1938.

———. *Il libro delle rime*. Ed. Alberto Chiari. Bari: Laterza, 1936.

———. *Opere*. Ed. Aldo Borlenghi. Milan: Rizzoli, 1957.

———. *Il Trecentonovelle*. Ed. Emilio Faccioli. Turin: Einaudi, 1970.

Salutati, Coluccio. *Epistolario*. Ed. Francesco Novati. Fonti per la storia d'Italia, 15–18. 4 vols. Rome: Istituto Storico Italiano, 1891–1911.

Santoro, Caterina. *I registri dell'ufficio di provvisione e dell'ufficio dei sindaci sotto la dominazione viscontea*. Milan: Castello Sforzesco, 1929.

Sardo, Ranieri. *Cronaca di Pisa*. Ed. Ottavio Banti. Fonti per la storia d'Italia, 99. Rome: Istituto Storico Italiano, 1963.

Scalvanti, Oscar, ed. "Cronaca perugina inedita di Pietro Angelo di Giovanni (già detta del Graziani) Parte II—(Anni 1461–1494)." *Bollettino della R. Deputazione di storia patria per l'Umbria*, 9 (1903).

Schroeder, H. J., ed. and trans. *Canons and Decrees of the Council of Trent*. Rockford, Illinois: TAN Books, 1978.

Sercambi, Giovanni. *Croniche*. Ed. Salvatore Bongi. Fonti per la storia d'Italia, 19–21. 3 vols. Rome: Istituto Storico Italiano, 1892.

———. *Le illustrazioni delle Croniche nel codice Lucchese*. Commentary by Ottaviano Banti and M. L. Testi Cristiani. Accademia Lucchese di scienze, lettere, arti, Studi e testi, 10. 2 vols. Genoa: Silvio Basile Editore, 1978.

Sorbelli, Albano, ed. *Corpus chronicorum Bononiensium* RIS^2, 18, vol. 3, part 1.

Sozomeno da Pistoia. *Speculum historiae*. *RIS*, 16.

Stella, Giorgio. *Annales Genuenses*. Ed. Giovanna Petti Balbi. RIS^2, 17, part 2.

Tassoni, Alessandro. *Cronaca modenese*. Ed. L. Vischi, T. Sandonnini, and O. Raselli. *Monumenti di storia patria delle provincie modenesi*, 15. Modena: Società tipografica, 1888.

Thomas of Spalato. *Historia pontificum Salonitanorum et Spalatinorum*. Ed. L. de Heinemann. *Monumenta Germaniae Historica, Scriptorum*, 29. Hanover, 1892.

Toscani, Bernard, ed. *Le laude dei Bianchi.* Florence: Libreria Editrice Fiorentina, 1979.

Trexler, Richard C., ed. *The Libro Cerimoniale of the Florentine Republic by Francesco Filarete and Angelo Manfidi: Introduction and Text.* Geneva: Droz, 1978.

Varanini, Giorgio, Luigi Banfi, Anna Ceruti Burgio, and Giulio Cattin, eds. *Laude cortonesi dal secolo XIII al XV.* 4 vols. Florence: Olschki, 1981–1985.

Vedriani, Lodovico. *Historia dell'antichissima città di Modona.* Modena, 1667.

Villani, Giovanni. *Croniche.* Trieste: Lloyd Austriaco, 1857.

Villani, Matteo. *Cronica.* Ed. Francesco Gherardi Dragomanni. Florence: S. Coen, 1846.

William of Canterbury. *Vita et passio S. Thomae.* In *Materials for the History of Thomas Becket, Archbishop of Canterbury,* ed. James Craigie Robertson. Rolls Series, 67, vol. 1. London: Longman & Co., 1875.

Zampolini, Parruccio. *Frammenti degli annali di Spoleto dal 1304 al 1424.* In *Documenti storici inediti in sussidio delle memorie umbre,* ed. Achille Sansi. Foligno: P. Sgariglia, 1879.

Secondary Works

This selected bibliography of secondary works includes only those which have been most useful in understanding the broader religious culture of medieval and Renaissance Italy. Full citations to works of social, economic, and political history, as well as to more circumscribed studies of religious history, can be found in the footnotes.

Adam, Paul. *La vie paroissiale en France au XIVe siècle.* Paris: Sirey, 1964.

Banker, James R. *Death in the Community: Memorialization and Confraternities in an Italian Commune in the Late Middle Ages.* Athens: University of Georgia Press, 1988.

Benvenuti Papi, Anna. *"In castro poenitentiae": Santità e società femminile nell'Italia medievale.* Rome: Herder, 1990.

Bizzocchi, Roberto. *Chiesa e potere nella Toscana del Quattrocento.* Annali dell'Istituto storico italo-germanico, Monografia 6. Bologna: Il Mulino, 1987.

——. "Clero e Chiesa nella società italiana alla fine del Medio Evo." In *Clero e società nell'Italia moderna,* ed. Mario Rosa, pp. 3–44. Rome and Bari: Laterza, 1992.

Black, Christopher F. *Italian Confraternities in the Sixteenth Century.* Cambridge: Cambridge University Press, 1989.

Boesch Gajano, Sofia, and Lucia Sebatiani, eds. *Culto dei santi, istituzioni, e classi sociali in età preindustriale.* L'Aquila and Rome: Japadre, 1984.

Bornstein, Daniel. "Giovanni Dominici, the Bianchi, and Venice: Symbolic Action and Interpretive Grids." *Journal of Medieval and Renaissance Studies*, 23 (1993): 143–171.

———. "The Shrine of Santa Maria a Cigoli: Female Visionaries and Clerical Promoters." *Mélanges de l'Ecole Française de Rome, Moyen Age–Temps Modernes*, 98 (1986): 219–228.

Bossy, John. "Blood and Baptism: Kinship, Community and Christianity in Western Europe from the Fourteenth to the Seventeenth Centuries." In *Sanctity and Secularity: The Church and the World*, ed. Derek Baker, pp. 129–143. Studies in Church History, 10. Oxford: Basil Blackwell, 1973.

———. *Christianity in the West, 1400–1700*. Oxford: Oxford University Press, 1985.

———. "The Counter-Reformation and the People of Catholic Europe." *Past and Present*, 47 (May 1970): 51–70.

———. "The Social History of Confession in the Age of the Reformation." *Transactions of the Royal Historical Society*, ser. 5, 25 (1975): 21–38.

Bynum, Caroline Walker. *Holy Feast and Holy Fast: The Religious Significance of Food to Medieval Women*. Berkeley and Los Angeles: University of California Press, 1987.

———. *Jesus as Mother: Studies in the Spirituality of the High Middle Ages*. Berkeley and Los Angeles: University of California Press, 1982.

Cantimori, Delio. *Eretici italiani del Cinquecento*. Florence: Sansoni, 1939.

Chittolini, Giorgio, ed. *Gli Sforza, la Chiesa lombarda, la corte di Roma: Strutture e pratiche beneficiarie nel ducato di Milano (1450–1535)*. Europa Mediterranea, Quaderni 4. Naples: Liguori, 1989.

Chittolini, Giorgio, and Giovanni Miccoli, eds. *La Chiesa e il potere politico dal Medioevo all'età contemporanea*. Storia d'Italia, Annali 9. Turin: Einaudi, 1986.

Cohn, Norman. *The Pursuit of the Millennium*. Revised edition. New York: Oxford University Press, 1970.

Cracco, Giorgio. "La spiritualità italiana del Tre-Quattrocento: Linee interpretative." *Studia Patavina*, 18 (1971): 74–116.

De La Roncière, Charles M. "Les confréries en Toscane aux XIV et XV siècles d'après les travaux récents." *Ricerche per la storia religiosa di Roma*, 5 (1984): 50–64.

———. "Dans la campagne florentine au XIVe siècle: Les communautés chrétiennes et leurs curés." In *Histoire vécue du peuple chrétien*, ed. Jean Delumeau, vol. 1, pp. 281–314. Toulouse: Privat, 1979.

———. "La place des confréries dans l'encadrement religieux du contado florentin: L'example de la Val d'Elsa." *Mélanges de l'Ecole Française de Rome, Moyen Age–Temps Modernes*, 85 (1973): 31–77, 633–671.

Delaruelle, Etienne. *La piété populaire au moyen age*. Turin: Bottega d'Erasmo, 1975.

Delaruelle, Etienne, E.-R. Labande, and Paul Ourliac. *L'Eglise au temps du Grand Schisme et de la crise conciliaire (1378–1449)*. Vol. 14 of *Histoire de l'Eglise depuis les origines jusqu'à nos jours*, ed. Augustin Fliche and Victor Martin. Paris: Bloud & Gay, 1964.

Delcorno, Carlo. *Giordano da Pisa e l'antica predicazione volgare.* Florence: Olschki, 1975.

De Luca, Giuseppe. *Introduzione alla storia della pietà.* Rome: Edizioni di storia e letteratura, 1962.

Delumeau, Jean. *Le Catholicisme entre Luther et Voltaire.* Paris: P.U.F., 1971.

——. "Christianisation et déchristianisation, XVe–XVIIIe siècles." In *Etudes Européenes: Mélanges offerts à Victor-Lucien Tapié*, pp. 111–131. Paris: Publications de la Sorbonne, 1973.

De Sandre Gasparini, Giuseppina. *Contadini, chiesa, confraternita in un paese veneto di bonifica: Villa del Bosco nel Quattrocento.* Fonti e ricerche di storia ecclesiastica padovana, 10. Padua: Istituto per la Storia Ecclesiastica Padovana, 1979.

——. "Un'immediata ripercussione del movimento dei Bianchi del 1399: La regola di una 'fraternitas alborum' in diocesi di Padova (13 ottobre 1399)." *Rivista di storia della chiesa in Italia*, 26 (1972): 354–368.

De Sandre Gasparini, Giuseppina, Antonio Rigon, Francesco Trolese, and Gian Maria Varanini, eds. *Vescovi e diocesi in Italia dal XIV alla metà del XVI secolo*, Atti del VII Convegno di storia della Chiesa in Italia (Brescia, 21–25 sett. 1987). Rome: Herder, 1990.

Fois, Mario. "L''Osservanza' come espressione della 'Ecclesia sempre renovanda'." In *Problemi di storia della chiesa nei secoli XV–XVII*, pp. 13–107. Naples: Edizioni Dehoniane, 1979.

Frugoni, Arsenio. "La devozione dei Bianchi del 1399." In *L'attesa dell'età nuova nella spiritualità della fine del medioevo*, pp. 232–248. Convegni del Centro di studi sulla spiritualità medievale, 3. Todi: Accademia Tudertina, 1962.

——. *Incontri nel Medio Evo.* Bologna: Il Mulino, 1979.

Gennaro, Clara. "Movimenti religiosi e pace nel XIV secolo." In *La pace nel pensiero, nella politica, negli ideali del Trecento*, pp. 93–112. Convegni del Centro di studi sulla spiritualità medievale, 15. Todi: Accademia Tudertina, 1975.

——. "Venturino da Bergamo e la 'peregrinatio' romana del 1335." In *Studi sul Medioevo cristiano offerti a Raffaello Morghen*, pp. 375–406. Rome: Istituto Storico Italiano per il Medio Evo, 1974.

Ginzburg, Carlo. *The Cheese and the Worms: The Cosmos of a Sixteenth-Century Miller.* Trans. John Tedeschi and Anne Tedeschi. New York: Penguin Books, 1982.

——. "Folklore, magia, religione." In *Storia d'Italia*, vol. 1: *I caratteri originali*, pp. 603–676. Turin: Einaudi, 1972.

Grundmann, Herbert. *Movimenti religiosi nel Medioevo.* Bologna: Il Mulino, 1970.

Hay, Denys. *The Church in Italy in the Fifteenth Century.* Cambridge: Cambridge University Press, 1977.

Klapisch-Zuber, Christiane. *Women, Family, and Ritual in Renaissance Italy.* Trans. Lydia G. Cochrane. Chicago: University of Chicago Press, 1985.

Landi, Aldo. *Il papa deposto (Pisa 1409): L'idea conciliare nel Grande Scisma.* Turin: Claudiana, 1985.

Larner, Christina. *Witchcraft and Religion: The Politics of Popular Belief.* Ed. Alan Macfarlane. Oxford: Basil Blackwell, 1984.

Le Bras, Gabriel. *Etudes de sociologie religieuse.* 2 vols. Paris: P.U.F., 1955–1956.

——. *Institutions ecclésiastiques de la Chrétienté médiévale.* Vol. 12 of *Histoire de l'Eglise depuis les origines jusqu'à nos jours,* ed. Augustin Fliche and Victor Martin. Paris: Bloud & Gay, 1959–1964.

Little, Lester K. *Religious Poverty and the Profit Economy in Medieval Europe.* Ithaca: Cornell University Press, 1981.

Longo, Pier Giorgio. *Letteratura e pietà a Novara tra XV e XVI secolo.* Novara: Associazione di Storia della Chiesa Novarese, 1986.

Magli, Ida. *Gli uomini della penitenza.* Milan: Garzanti, 1977.

Marcianò, Ada Francesca. *Padova 1399: Le processioni dei Bianchi nella testimonianza di Giovanni di Conversino.* I centri storici del Veneto. Fonti e testi, 1. Padua: Centro Grafico editoriale, 1980.

Marcianò, Ada Francesca, and Maria Spina. "La processione dei Bianchi a Padova, 1399: Una fonte per lo studio della città tra Medioevo e Rinascimento." *Storia della città,* 4 (1977): 3–30.

Meersseman, Gilles Gérard. *Ordo fraternitatis: Confraternite e pietà dei laici nel medioevo.* Rome: Herder, 1977.

Melis, Federigo. "Movimento di popoli e motivi economici nel giubileo del 1400." In *Miscellanea Gilles Gérard Meersseman,* pp. 343–367. Padua: Antenore, 1970.

Merlo, Grado G. *Eretici e inquisitori nella società piemontese del Trecento.* Turin: Claudiana, 1977.

——. *Valdesi e valdismi medievali. Itinerari e proposte di ricerca.* Turin: Claudiana, 1984.

——. *Valdesi e valdismi medievali, II: Identità valdesi nella storia e nella storiografia: Studi e discussioni.* Turin: Claudiana, 1991.

——. "Vita di chierici nel Trecento: Inchieste nella diocesi di Torino." *Bollettino storico-bibliografico subalpino,* 73 (1975): 181–210.

Miccoli, Giovanni. "La storia religiosa." In *Storia d'Italia,* vol 2: *Dalla Caduta dell'Impero romano al secolo XVIII,* pp. 431–1079. Turin: Einaudi, 1974.

Moeller, Bernd. "Piety in Germany around 1500." In *The Reformation in Medieval Perspective,* ed. Steven E. Ozment. Chicago: Quadrangle Books, 1971.

Molho, Anthony. "*Tamquam vere mortua:* Le professioni religiose femminili nella Firenze del tardo Medioevo." *Società e storia,* 12 (1989): 1–44.

Montanari, Daniele. *Disciplinamento in terra veneta.* Bologna: Il Mulino, 1987.

Monti, Gennaro Maria. *Le confraternite medievali dell'alta e media Italia*. 2 vols. Venice: La Nuova Italia, 1927.

Morghen, Raffaello. *Medioevo cristiano*. Bari: Laterza, 1974.

Le mouvement confraternel au Moyen Age: France, Italie, Suisse. Collection de l'Ecole Française de Rome, 97. Rome: Ecole Française de Rome, 1987.

Il movimento dei Disciplinati nel settimo centenario dal suo inizio. Perugia: Deputazione di Storia Patria per l'Umbria, 1962.

Muir, Edward. *Civic Ritual in Renaissance Venice*. Princeton: Princeton University Press, 1981.

Niccoli, Ottavia. *Prophecy and People in Renaissance Italy*. Trans. Lydia G. Cochrane. Princeton: Princeton University Press, 1990.

Oakley, Francis. *The Western Church in the Later Middle Ages*. Ithaca: Cornell University Press, 1979.

"Les ordres mendiants et la ville en Italie centrale (v. 1220-v. 1350)." *Mélanges de l'Ecole Française de Rome, Moyen Age–Temps Modernes*, 89 (1977): 557–773.

Ozment, Steven. *The Age of Reform, 1250–1550*. New Haven: Yale University Press, 1980.

Pazzelli, Raffaele, and Lino Temperini, eds. *Prime manifestazioni di vita communitaria maschile e femminile nel movimento francescano della penitenza (1215–1447)*. Atti del Convengno di studi francescani, Assisi, 30 giugno-2 luglio 1981. Rome: Commissione Storica Internazionale T.O.R., 1982.

Pelikan, Jaroslav. *The Growth of Medieval Theology (600–1300)*. Vol. 3 of *The Christian Tradition: A History of the Development of Doctrine*. Chicago: University of Chicago Press, 1978.

——. *The Reformation of Church and Dogma (1300–1700)*. Vol. 4 of *The Christian Tradition: A History of the Development of Doctrine*. Chicago: University of Chicago Press, 1984.

Pesce, Luigi. *La Chiesa di Treviso nel primo Quattrocento*. 3 vols. Rome: Herder, 1987.

Pievi e parrocchie in Italia nel basso Medioevo (sec. XIII–XV), Atti del VI Convegno di storia della Chiesa in Italia (Firenze, 21–25 settembre 1981). Rome: Herder, 1984.

"Predicazione francescana e società veneta nel Quattrocento: Committenza, ascolto, ricezione." *Le Venezie francescane*, 6 (1989): 7–270.

Problemi di vita religiosa in Italia nel Cinquecento: Atti del Convegno di storia della chiesa in Italia. Padua: Antenore, 1960.

Prodi, Paolo, and Peter Johanek, eds. *Strutture ecclesiastiche in Italia e in Germania prima della Riforma*. Annali dell'Istituto storico italo-germanico, Quaderno 16. Bologna: Il Mulino, 1984.

Pullan, Brian. *Rich and Poor in Renaissance Venice: The Social Institutions of a Catholic State, to 1620*. Cambridge: Harvard University Press, 1971.

Raitt, Jill, ed., with Bernard McGinn and John Meyendorff. *High Middle Ages and Reformation*. Vol. 2 of *Christian Spirituality*. New York: Crossroad, 1987.

Rando, Daniela. "Laicus religiosus: Tra strutture civili ed ecclesiastiche: l'Ospedale di Ogni Santi in Treviso (sec. XIII)." *Studi medievali*, ser. 3, 24 (1983): 617–656.

Rapp, Francis. *L'Eglise et la vie religieuse en Occident à la fin du Moyen Age*. 2d ed. Paris: P.U.F., 1980.

Risultati e prospettive della ricerca sul movimento dei Disciplinati. Perugia: Deputazione di Storia Patria per l'Umbria, 1972.

Rubin, Miri. *Corpus Christi: The Eucharist in Late Medieval Culture*. Cambridge: Cambridge University Press, 1991.

Rusconi, Roberto. *L'attesa della fine: Crisi della società, profezia, ed Apocalisse in Italia al tempo del grande scisma d'Occidente (1378–1417)*. Rome: Istituto Storico Italiano per il Medio Evo, 1979.

——. "Fonti e documenti su Manfredi da Vercelli ed il suo movimento penitenziale." *Archivum Fratrum Praedicatorum*, 47 (1977): 51–107.

——. "Note sulla predicazione di Manfredi da Vercelli e il movimento penitenziale dei terziari manfredini." *Archivum Fratrum Praedicatorum*, 48 (1978): 93–135.

Rusconi, Roberto, ed. *Il movimento religioso femminile in Umbria nei secoli XIII–XIV*. Florence: La Nuova Italia, 1984.

Sambin, Paolo. *Ricerche di storia monastica medievale*. Padua: Antenore, 1959.

Sambin, Paolo, ed. *Pievi, parrocchie, e clero nel Veneto dal X al XV secolo*. Venice: Deputazione di Storia Patria per le Venezie, 1987.

Sbriziolo, Lia. "Note su Giovanni Dominici, I: La 'spiritualità' del Dominici nelle lettere alle suore veneziane del Corpus Christi." *Rivista di storia della chiesa in Italia*, 24 (1970): 4–30.

——. "Per la storia delle confraternite veneziane: Dalle deliberazioni miste (1310–1476) del Consiglio dei Dieci: Scolae communes, artigiane e nazionale." *Atti dell'Istituto veneto di scienze lettere ed arti*, 126 (1967–1968): 405–442.

——. "Per la storia delle confraternite veneziane: Dalle deliberazioni miste (1310–1476) del Consiglio dei Dieci: Le scuole dei Battuti." In *Miscellanea Gilles Gérard Meersseman*. Padua: Antenore, 1970. Pp. 715–763.

Sensi, Mario. "Predicazione itinerante a Foligno nel secolo XV." *Picenum Seraphicum*, 10 (1973): 139–195.

Sorelli, Fernanda. "Per la storia religiosa di Venezia nella prima metà del Quattrocento: Inizi e sviluppi del terz'ordine domenicano." In *Viridarium Floridum: Studi di storia veneta offerti dagli allievi a Paolo Sambin*, ed. Maria Chiara Billanovich, Giorgio Cracco, and Antonio Rigon, pp. 89–114. Padua: Antenore, 1984.

——. *La santità imitabile: "Leggenda di Maria da Venezia" di Tommaso da Siena*. Deputazione di storia patria per le Venezie, Miscellanea di Studi e Memorie, 23. Venice: Deputazione Editrice, 1984.

"La spiritualità medievale: Metodi, bilanci, prospettive." *Studi Medievali*, ser. 3, 28 (1987): 1–65.

Stephens, John N. "Heresy in Medieval and Renaissance Florence." *Past and Present*, 54 (February 1972): 25–60.

Temi e problemi nella mistica femminile trecentesca. Convegni del Centro di Studi sulla Spiritualità Medievale, 20. Todi: Accademia Tudertina, 1983.

Tentler, Thomas N. *Sin and Confession on the Eve of the Reformation*. Princeton: Princeton University Press, 1977.

Tognetti, Giampaolo. "Sul moto dei bianchi nel 1399." *Bullettino dell'Istituto Storico Italiano per il Medio Evo e archivio muratoriano*, 78 (1967): 205–343.

Trexler, Richard C. "Charity and the Defense of Urban Elites in the Italian Communes." In *The Rich, the Well Born and the Powerful*, ed. Frederic Cople Jaher, pp. 64–109. Urbana: University of Illinois Press, 1973.

——. "Florentine Religious Experience: The Sacred Image." *Studies in the Renaissance*, 19 (1972): 7–41.

——. *Public Life in Renaissance Florence*. New York: Academic Press, 1980.

Trinkhaus, Charles, ed., with Heiko A. Oberman. *The Pursuit of Holiness in Late Medieval and Renaissance Religion*. Leiden: E. J. Brill, 1974.

Trolese, Giovanni B. Francesco, ed., *Riforma della chiesa, cultura, e spiritualità nel Quattrocento veneto*. Cesena: Badia di Santa Maria del Monte, 1984.

Van Engen, John. "The Christian Middle Ages as an Historiographical Problem." *American Historical Review*, 91 (1986): 519–552.

Vauchez, André. "Une campagne de pacification en Lombardie autour de 1233." *Ecole Française de Rome, Mélanges d'archéologie et d'histoire*, 78 (1966): 503–549.

——. *Les laïcs au Moyen Age: Pratiques et expériences religieuses*. Paris: Cerf, 1987.

——. *La Sainteté en occident aux derniers siècles du Moyen Age d'après les procès de canonisation et les documents hagiographiques*. Rome: Ecole Française de Rome, 1981.

——. *La spiritualité du Moyen Age occidental, VIIIe–XIIe siècles*. Paris: P.U.F., 1975.

Vauchez, André, ed. *Faire croire: Modalités de la diffusion et de la réception des messages religieux du XIIe au XVe siècle*. Collection de l'Ecole Française de Rome, 51. Rome: Ecole Française de Rome, 1981.

Verdon, Timothy, and John Henderson, eds. *Christianity and the Renaissance: Image and Religious Imagination in the Quattrocento*. Syracuse: Syracuse University Press, 1990.

Vescovi e diocesi in Italia nel Medioevo (sec. XI–XIII), Atti del II Convegno di storia della Chiesa in Italia (Roma, 5–9 settembre 1961). Rome: Herder, 1964.

Violante, Cinzio. *Studi sulla Cristianità medioevale: Società, istituzioni, spiritualità*. Milan: Vita e pensiero, 1972.

Volpe, Gioacchino. *Movimenti religiosi e sette ereticali nella società medievale italiana, secoli XI–XIV*. 1922; reprint Florence: Sansoni, 1977.

Ward, Benedicta. *Miracles and the Medieval Mind: Theory, Record and Event, 1000–1215*. Philadephia: University of Pennsylvania Press, 1982.

Webb, Diana M. "Penitence and Peace-Making in City and Contado: The Bianchi of 1399." In *The Church in Town and Countryside*, ed. Derek Baker, pp. 243–256. Studies in Church History, 16. Oxford: Basil Blackwell, 1979.

Weissman, Ronald F. E. *Ritual Brotherhood in Renaissance Florence*. New York: Academic Press, 1982.

Wilson, Blake. *Music and Merchants: The Laudesi Companies of Republican Florence*. New York: Oxford University Press, 1992.

Zafarana, Zelina. *Da Gregorio VII a Bernardino da Siena: Saggi di storia medievale*. Ed. Ovidio Capitani, Claudio Leonardi, Enrico Menestò, and Roberto Rusconi. Florence: La Nuova Italia, 1987.

Zarri, Gabriella. *Le sante vive: Profezie di corte e devozione femminile tra '400 e '500*. Turin: Rosenberg & Sellier, 1990.

INDEX

Library of Congress Cataloging-in-Publication Data

Bornstein, Daniel Ethan, 1950–
   The Bianchi of 1399 : popular devotion in late medieval Italy /
Daniel E. Bornstein.
      p.   cm.
   Includes bibliographical references and index.
   ISBN 0-8014-2910-2 (alk. paper)
      1. Bianchi (Italian religious movement)—History.   2. Italy—
Church history—476–1400.   3. Spirituality—Catholic Church—
History.   4. Spirituality—Italy—History.   5. Catholic Church—
Italy—History.   I. Title.
BR874.B67   1993
267'.18245'09023—dc20   93-2311